'Alí-Murád Dávúdí

Revelation, Reality, and Reason

'Alí-Murád Dávúdí's
Philosophical Discourses
on the Foundations of Bahá'í Belief

Edited by Vargha Bolodo-Taefi

Revelation, Reality, and Reason: 'Alí-Murád Dávúdí's Philosophical Discourses on the Foundations of Bahá'í Belief/ 'Alí-Murád Dávúdí, author; Vargha Bolodo-Taefi, editor

© 2025 'Alí-Murád Dávúdí
c/o Association for Bahá'í Studies
34 Copernicus Street
Ottawa, ON
K1N 7K4 Canada
https://www.bahaistudies.ca

First edition, first printing 2025

Includes bibliographical references
Softcover: ISBN 978-0-920904-46-6
Ebook: ISBN 978-0-920904-47-3

Every effort has been made to acquire permission for copyright material used in this text, and to acknowledge all such indebtedness accurately. Any errors and omissions called to the publisher's attention will be corrected in future printings.

All rights reserved. No part of this publication may be reproduced, stored in a retrieval system, or transmitted, in any form or by any means, without the prior written consent of the publisher.

Copy editing: Michael Sabet
Cover image: Sean Pierce
Cover design and book design: Nilufar Gordon

Revelation, Reality, and Reason

'Alí-Murád Dávúdí's
Philosophical Discourses
on the Foundations of Baháʼí Belief

Edited by Vargha Bolodo-Taefi

Contents

INTRODUCTION	vii
1. Introduction to the tenets of Bahá'í belief	1
2. Denying and proving the existence of God	7
3.1 Confessing the sanctity of the Divine Essence – Part one	23
3.2 Confessing the sanctity of the Divine Essence – Part two	43
3.3 Confessing the sanctity of the Divine Essence – Part three	59
4. Breathings of the Holy Spirit	77
5. Prayer and meditation	89
6. Life in the next world	101
7. Religion is the truth and the truth is one	113
8. The oneness of religion	123
9. Unity in diversity	143
10. Countering the forces in our environment	159
11. Liberty	177
12. Liberty in the Bahá'í Faith	189
13. Conceptions of liberty	195
BIBLIOGRAPHY	211
BIOGRAPHICAL INFORMATION	215
INDEX	217

Introduction

Vargha Bolodo-Taefi and Omid Ghaemmaghami

The emergence of the Bahá'í Faith in the intellectual and cultural milieu of Iran fostered a tradition of scholarship that sought to build on the heritage of Islamic thought and serve the evolving needs of a new religion. As the Bahá'í Faith has no clergy, this scholarship has flourished through the voluntary efforts of individuals. From the earliest days of the Bahá'í Faith, Iran has been home to a number of eminent Bahá'í scholars including Áqá Muḥammad-i-Qá'iní (surnamed Nabíl-i-Akbar), Mírzá Abu'l-Faḍl-i-Gulpáygání (surnamed Abu'l-Faḍá'il), Mírzá Asadu'lláh Fáḍil-i-Mázindarání, and 'Abdu'l-Ḥamíd Ishráq-Khávarí. These and other individuals, trained primarily in the traditional seminaries of Islamic learning, studied such disciplines as Quranic studies; Islamic theology, philosophy, law, and mysticism; and Arabic grammar. Their intellectual pursuits were shaped by the prevailing educational paradigms of their time, which remained largely insulated from the currents of modern Western philosophy, non-classical logic, and the broader humanities. While their scholarly endeavors bore fruit and contributed to the development of a foundational corpus, their educational background, the prevailing intellectual climate, and the pressing needs of promoting and defending the Bahá'í teachings shaped the nature of their scholarly contributions.

It is against this backdrop that the trailblazing scholarship of 'Alí-Murád Dávúdí is situated. Dávúdí's unswerving commitment to Bahá'í teachings and institutions, encyclopaedic knowledge of the writings of the Bahá'í Faith, academic rigor, contributions to the intellectual development of the Iranian population, and nobility of character earn him a unique place in the history of Bahá'í scholarship in Persian. Dávúdí engaged both classical and contemporary intellectual currents. His scholarly pursuits encompassed the academic study of Islamic, Eastern, and

Western philosophies, alongside disciplines like logic, theology, and mysticism. He possessed a remarkable command of Persian and Arabic literature, mastered French, and was well-versed in different branches of knowledge and approaches to intellectual inquiry. These achievements, combined with a rigorous and methodical approach to the study of the Bahá'í writings, enabled him to elevate Bahá'í scholarship beyond the traditional domains of apologia, commentaries, compilations, annotated dictionaries, and historical studies and advance it to new heights of conceptual and philosophical analysis. His intellectual legacy endures in his skillful examination of the philosophical, theological, and ethical tenets of the Bahá'í Faith within broader frameworks of both Eastern and Western philosophical traditions. In short, he pioneered a new frontier in Bahá'í studies.

The Life and Character of Dávúdí: A Biographical Overview

'Alí-Murád Dávúdí was born in 1922 in the village of Shamsábád in northwest Iran. His paternal great-grandfather had been the governor of Georgia before being exiled to Russia. Dávúdí's grandfather, Dávúd Khán, was later appointed governor of a region that was eventually ceded to Russia. Dávúd Khán and his family settled in Khalkhál, in Iran's Ádhirbáyján region. As a result of his service to Fatḥ-'Alí Sháh, Dávúd Khán and his family were granted extensive lands. His descendants took the family name "Dávúdí" after him. They treated the local farmers with kindness and generosity, earned people's respect, and attained governmental and military positions. Over time, they investigated the Bahá'í Faith and eventually Dávúdí's uncle, 'Abdu'lláh Khán, surnamed Mas'údu'l-Mamálik, and then Dávúdí's father, Asadu'lláh Khán, surnamed Sá'idu's-Sulṭán, embraced the Faith. Dávúdí's mother, Bilqays Khánum, was a granddaughter of Fatḥ-'Alí Sháh and embraced the Bahá'í Faith herself. The Dávúdí family was highly regarded in their village, where they owned land and received a portion of the crops from tenant farmers.

At the age of ten, Dávúdí left Shamsábád for Tabríz to further his education. He studied the Qur'án and read voraciously from the Persian literary canon. During this period, the public disclosure of his father's belief in the Bahá'í Faith had significant social and economic repercussions for the family, including the loss of support and respect from their fellow villagers. The passing of Dávúdí's father a few years later inflicted a material and emotional toll on the family. At eighteen, Dávúdí moved to the country's capital and enrolled at Ṭihrán University to study philosophy and education. His bachelor's thesis on the philosophy of the Qur'án earned acclaim from his professors. After completing his degree, he embarked on a career in education, teaching in various cities including Sanandaj and Zanján.

In 1951, Dávúdí married Malakih-Áfáq Íránpúr. They had three daughters and two sons. While supporting his family on a modest government salary and some income from his inherited land, Dávúdí remained dedicated to education. During summers, he returned to Shamsábád to contribute to the villagers' healthcare and education. In 1955, he enrolled in the newly founded doctoral program in philosophy at Ṭihrán University. With a dissertation on the philosophy of Aristotle and Descartes, he became the first individual in Iran to earn a doctorate in philosophy—an achievement that underscored his pioneering spirit and academic distinction.

During the land reforms of the Pahlavi era, agricultural land was redistributed among farmers, which significantly reduced the Dávúdí family's income. Consequently, they permanently relocated to Ṭihrán. Despite these financial setbacks, Dávúdí remained committed to his academic and teaching career. In 1964, he secured an academic appointment at Ṭihrán University, where he taught courses on elementary philosophy, the history of medieval philosophy, and metaphysics. His tenure as a university professor was one of the most intellectually productive periods of his life. It provided him the opportunity to devote significant time to the study and research of philosophical questions, with a particular focus on Islamic mysticism and intellectual history, French literature, and, of course, the Bahá'í writings. He later served as the head of the Department of Philosophy, a role in which he furthered intellectual discourse and inspired generations of students.

Beyond his knowledge and achievements, Dávúdí is remembered for his eloquence. His writings, translations, and lectures attest to the graceful flow of his thought and logic, the clarity of his utterance, and the conciseness, rigor, and dignity of his expression. He elucidated concepts, adduced proofs, and unveiled meanings free from superfluity, exaggeration, ambiguity, and prejudice. Remarkably, many of his lectures were delivered extemporaneously, often without prior knowledge of the subject matter, yet were characterized by an exceptional quality of exposition, eloquence, flow of thought, and choice of words. When recording lectures for the audio-visual committee of the National Spiritual Assembly, for instance, he was often only informed of the topic of his lecture once he arrived at the session. On other occasions, he would arrive at the recording studio expecting to speak on a previously agreed-upon topic, only to be informed that the subject had been changed. Húshang Maḥmúdí recalled a specific occasion when Dávúdí was invited to speak on the theme of love, but upon arriving at the studio was instead asked to speak on the topic of materialism. He readily accepted the change. Then, just as the recording was about to begin, he was requested to speak on an entirely different subject: the immortality of the human soul. Without hesitation, he complied and delivered a masterful exposition.

Dávúdí's personal qualities were no less distinguished than his intellectual attainments. Those who knew him have attested to his humility, dignity, and fairness. He was gentle, elegant, benevolent, responsible, and courteous. He modelled the ideals described in Bahá'u'lláh's Tablet of Wisdom:

> Human utterance is an essence which aspireth to exert its influence and needeth moderation. As to its influence, this is conditional upon refinement which in turn is dependent upon hearts which are detached and pure. As to its moderation, this hath to be combined with tact and wisdom as prescribed in the Holy Scriptures and Tablets. (*Tablets* 143)

His nobility of character and immense erudition made him not only a scholar of distinction but also a source of solace and inspiration for the Iranian Bahá'í community.

Sadly, the beleaguered and oppressed community of the Bahá'ís of Iran was robbed of its stalwart and erudite defender during one of the most challenging periods in its history. The opponents of the Bahá'í Faith, who saw in his elimination a victory for themselves and a defeat for the Bahá'í community, abducted him on 11 November 1979. Dávúdí had a daily habit of going for walks. On that day, he left his home in the Amírábád district of Ṭihrán for his usual stroll in Lálih Park. He never returned home. In the days leading up to his disappearance, he had received numerous threatening phone calls. When friends attempted to trace his whereabouts that same day, the signs of an abduction became clear. Despite efforts to uncover the truth, his fate remains unknown. He has been presumed a victim of state execution. The silencing of Dávúdí's voice and pen at the age of fifty-seven was a deplorable injustice and grievous cruelty, committed not only against the Iranian Bahá'í community but against the field of philosophy and the world of scholarship.

Despite his tragic fate, Dávúdí's legacy endures. In a poignant tribute to his unwavering dedication, five months after his abduction, the Bahá'í community of Iran elected him to the National Spiritual Assembly in absentia, a gesture of profound love and appreciation. This act stands as a testament to the lasting impact left on the hearts and minds of those he served by a hero whose light continues to illuminate.

Dávúdí's Contributions to Iranian Intellectual and Academic Development

Since the time of the Báb and Bahá'u'lláh, the prevailing climate of prejudice against Their followers in Iran has led—with rare exceptions—to the systematic exclusion of their contributions, and even their mention, from mainstream historical and intellectual discourse. The caliber and breadth of knowledge demonstrated by the followers of the Báb and Bahá'u'lláh have been consistently neglected, erased, or omitted from historical accounts in the cradle of the Bábí and Bahá'í Faiths. A striking example of this erasure is Ṭáhirih, whose intellectual distinction and contributions to social transformation and women's rights remain largely unacknowledged. This selective amnesia also extends to the field of philosophy, where luminaries such as Dávúdí, despite their rigorous scholarship and penetrating insights, have been largely disregarded within academic circles. The omission of Bahá'í contributions to Iranian intellectual history underscores the challenging circumstances under which Dávúdí produced his works and renders his extensive intellectual legacy all the more remarkable.

Dávúdí's contributions to Iranian intellectual life are of enduring significance and marked by a rare synthesis of erudition, precision, and scholarly breadth. His tenure as a professor at Ṭihrán University provided the setting for some of his most influential works, including the Persian translations of Aristotle's *On the Soul* (published under the title *Darbáriy-i-Nafs*), the first two volumes of Émile Bréhier's *Histoire de la Philosophie* (*Táríkh-i-Falsafih*), and Léon Meynard's *La Connaissance* (*Shinásá'í va Hastí*). These works not only introduced pivotal philosophical texts to a Persian-speaking audience but also demonstrated Dávúdí's ability to translate complex philosophical ideas with clarity and rigour. Complementing these efforts, his original contributions to the study of Peripatetic philosophy—as exemplified in his seminal volume on the philosophical explorations of soul and reason from Aristotle to Avicenna titled *'Aql dar Ḥikmat-i-Mashshá': Az Arasṭú tá Ibn-i-Síná*—further cemented his reputation as a leading scholar in both classical and Islamic thought.

Among his major contributions is an anthology of essays that delve into an impressive array of philosophical subjects, published posthumously in Iran under the title *Maqálát-i-Dávúdí*. This collection encompasses treatises on such themes as the concept of the soul in al-Fárábí's thought, a comparative study of the philosophies of Aristotle and Avicenna, ancient Greek theories of spirit and psyche, and the intellectual legacy of the Sophists. His treatment of topics such as knowledge of self, metaphysical anxiety, and the critique of infinite regress arguments reflects a deep engagement with both the historical and contemporary dimensions of philosophical inquiry. By addressing these subjects with analytical rigour and philosophical depth, Dávúdí provided scholars and students alike with a comprehensive resource that continues to inform contemporary Iranian philosophical discourse.

A crowning achievement of Dávúdí's scholarly career was his Persian translation of Étienne Gilson's *L'Esprit de la Philosophie Médiévale* (*Rúḥ-i-Falsafiy-i-Qurún-i-Vusṭá*), completed prior to his abduction in 1979. This work, published posthumously after a delay of eight years, received the highest national accolade for excellence in book publication, a recognition that testifies to its scholarly merit and literary elegance. The conferral of such an honour in a socio-political climate where Bahá'ís faced systemic discrimination underscores the calibre of his intellectual contributions and the impact of his work. Despite the challenges imposed by religious prejudice, his translation remains a significant milestone in the study of medieval philosophy in Iran.

Dávúdí's intellectual legacy has been acknowledged by scholars outside the Bahá'í community. In his acclaimed exploration of Iran's evolution over the past five centuries, historian Abbas Amanat recognized Dávúdí's expertise in the philosophy of René Descartes (Amanat, *Iran: A Modern History* 854). The prominent philosopher Seyyed Hossein Nasr—despite his long history of statements misrepresenting the Bahá'í Faith—proudly claimed that Dávúdí (who was eleven years Nasr's senior) was among Nasr's most outstanding students (Nasr and Jahanbegloo, *In Search of the Sacred* 69). Nasr added that Dávúdí was "most likely killed at the beginning of the Revolution," without indicating that his death was due to his belief in the Bahá'í Faith. In a survey of Islamic philosophy in Iran in the 1950s and 1960s, Nasr numbered Dávúdí among a small and select group of the country's scholars proficient in both traditional and modern philosophical disciplines (Nasr, *The Islamic Intellectual Tradition in Persia* 325). And the influential Iranian writer and thinker Abdolkarim Soroush—a former member of the anti-Bahá'í Hujjatiyyih society and author of an anti-Bahá'í polemical work—remarked that Dávúdí's intellectual stature and philosophical knowledge surpassed that of many of those among his contemporaries who are today hailed for their philosophical expertise (Soroush, "Khaláf va Vifáq-i-'Ilm va Dín" 1:19:12).

Dávúdí's Legacy: The Iranian Bahá'í Community and Bahá'í Scholarship in Persian

Late twentieth century Iran was fraught with political instability and ideological conflict, culminating in the 1979 Islamic revolution. It was within this turbulent milieu—marked by social unrest, ideological polarization, and the increasing persecution of Bahá'ís—that Dávúdí dedicated himself to the advancement of Bahá'í scholarship. By situating his scholarship within this broader historical and intellectual context, we gain a deeper appreciation for the enduring relevance of his contributions and the unique challenges he navigated in advancing Bahá'í scholarship. Despite his pressing responsibilities and the urgent demands of a rapidly changing socio-political landscape, he persevered in his intellectual pursuits and scholarly exploration of Bahá'í teachings, produced an array of works that addressed the exigencies of his time, and laid the foundation for future Bahá'í philosophy. Philosophical inquiry usually flourishes at times of peace and tranquillity. That Dávúdí achieved so much without these conditions makes his accomplishments all the more notable and attests to his resilience and dedication.

One of Dávúdí's most important contributions to the Iranian Bahá'í community was his service for a number of years on the National Spiritual Assembly, which oversaw the affairs of a Bahá'í community numbering nearly half a million. Membership on the National Spiritual Assembly—including for a period of time as its principal executive officer—called for extensive correspondence, lengthy consultations, and frequent travel across the country. In 1978, Dávúdí travelled to the Holy Land with his fellow elected National Spiritual Assembly members to participate in the Fourth International Bahá'í Convention. His work with the national committee for literature review, the national publication board, and the national committee for research and publication was instrumental in the publication of several foundational series of volumes, such as *Áthár-i-Qalam-i-A'lá* and *Makátíb-i-'Abdu'l-Bahá*—collections of the Writings of Bahá'u'lláh and 'Abdu'l-Bahá—which marked an essential step in preserving and disseminating the Bahá'í Writings, as well as the scholarly series *Muṭáli'iy-i-Ma'árif-i-Bahá'í*, dedicated to the introduction of the tenets of the Bahá'í Faith.

Perhaps Dávúdí's most enduring service to Iran's Bahá'í community was his scholarly lectures on the Bahá'í teachings and writings, delivered in deepening seminars and summer schools. These fruits of his scholarly pursuits uplifted and enriched the community and cultivated intellectual engagement, especially among Bahá'í youth. His contributions to fostering a culture of scholarship reached their peak with the establishment of the

Institute for Advanced Bahá'í Studies in 1976. The National Spiritual Assembly of Iran created the Institute in fulfilment of a goal of the Five Year Plan (1974–1979) to train a number of capable Bahá'í youth in the research and study of the Bahá'í teachings, as well as traditional religious and philosophical themes. The National Assembly entrusted the Institute's formation, planning, supervision, and administration to Dávúdí and Badí'u'lláh Faríd. In the Institute, besides his other responsibilities, Dávúdí taught various subjects and works of philosophy and mysticism. The Institute provided a new model for the study of the Bahá'í Faith in an intellectually sophisticated context. Thanks to Dávúdí's scholarship and academic standing, as well as his tireless and systematic efforts, both within the Institute and without, Bahá'í studies and scholarship was elevated to new heights of academic rigour. Through his leadership at the Institute and his extensive body of lectures and essays, Dávúdí made an unparalleled contribution to the development of Bahá'í scholarship, thought, and culture in Iran and fostered the growth of a new generation of Bahá'í scholars.

A defining feature of Dávúdí's work is its interdisciplinary nature. His writings and talks seamlessly integrate such fields as theology, metaphysics, psychology, history, education, philosophy, sociology, ethics, political science, and literature to advance a holistic understanding of the Bahá'í Faith. Dávúdí's scholarship is distinguished by his methodical approach to addressing Bahá'í themes in which he masterfully blends rigorous philosophical reasoning with spiritual principles. His careful analysis and synthesis of both Western and Eastern intellectual traditions allowed him to present Bahá'í teachings in a manner that resonated with a broad audience and bridged cultural and intellectual divides. His contributions continue to serve as invaluable resources for those seeking a deeper understanding of the Bahá'í Faith, and his work remains a cornerstone of Bahá'í scholarship in Persian.

Dávúdí's contributions can be categorized into several key areas. In theology and metaphysics, he delved into questions surrounding the existence of God, revelation, the Manifestations of God, and the station of Bahá'u'lláh. His talks and essays on "Proofs of the Existence of God," "God and Revelation," and "Manifestation" demonstrate his engagement with profound theological questions and offer insights that remain relevant for contemporary scholars. He explores moral philosophy, ethics, and the nature of ethical decision-making in such works as "Determinism and Free Will," "Liberty in the Bahá'í Faith," and "Criteria of Good and Evil." In relation to human nature and psychology, Dávúdí's scholarship examines human ontology and the spiritual dimensions of human existence through works such as "A Discourse on the Soul," "Human Station," and "The Eternal Life of the Soul." His reflections on the history and historiography of the Bahá'í Faith in "Philosophy of History," "The Importance of Studying History," and "The Bahá'í Method of Writing History in the Present and Future," foster a Bahá'í understanding of historical interpretation, religious progress, and the role of history in shaping human civilization. Through his talks and essays on education and social philosophy, such as "Education in the Bahá'í Faith," "Progressive Education," "Unity in Diversity," "The Oneness of Religion," and "Countering the Forces in our Environment," Dávúdí explores the unique spiritual and intellectual aspects of humanity, the evolution of religion, and human development.

Following the 1979 Islamic Revolution, the Bahá'í community in Iran faced systematic and intensifying persecution at the hands of the new regime. Bahá'ís were subjected to arbitrary arrests, torture, and execution; they were expelled from their jobs and educational institutions; and their properties were confiscated. Members of their elected administrative bodies, as well as prominent individuals within the community, were deliberately targeted. The material and intellectual foundations of Bahá'í life were subjected to coordinated and sustained attacks.

Amid this climate of repression, Dávúdí's knowledge, scholarship, experience, and insight coalesced in a resolute defense of the Bahá'í Faith and in efforts to console and uplift the Iranian Bahá'í community during one of the most perilous and trying periods of its history. He arose to articulate, protect, and deepen understanding of the Bahá'í teachings in the face of criticism, misrepresentation, and ideological hostility. His intellectual defense of the Faith manifested itself in apologetics (including retorts to anti-Bahá'í polemical attacks, bearing his name and published in newspapers), theological clarification, philosophical engagement, historical contextualization, scriptural exegesis, and sociocultural analysis.

Among the subjects he addressed were the transcendence and sanctity of God in light of Bahá'u'lláh's claims to divine authority—a theme explored in a series of talks published in this volume; the existence of injustice and tyranny in the world and how such realities might be reconciled with belief in a just and omnipotent Creator; the station of Muḥammad in Bahá'í scripture; the Bahá'í Faith as a distinct and independent religion; 'Abdu'l-Bahá's knighthood; the moral and existential implications of being a Bahá'í in Iran; the principle of refraining from contentious debate in response to attacks and accusations; the injustice of state-led persecution and the testimony of history to such injustice; the policies of the Iranian government against the Bahá'ís and their broader implications; the Bahá'í principle of non-interference in politics; the moral imperative of fairness in judgment; the meaning of martyrdom and steadfastness in the face of persecution; and the abiding love that Bahá'ís around the world feel for Iran.

Dávúdí's scholarship has also made invaluable contributions to Bahá'í scriptural and doctrinal studies and provided extensive expositions and commentaries on several of the Báb's and Bahá'u'lláh's best-known Writings. His analysis of the Bahá'í teachings in response to contemporary issues, including his works on the impact of our surroundings, the imperative for a fruitful Bahá'í life, beauty and dignity, and the requisites of the path of sacrifice, further underscores the breadth of his intellectual contributions. Through his scholarship, Dávúdí not only enriched the intellectual fabric of the Iranian Bahá'í community but also laid the foundation for the future of Bahá'í studies.

A prime example is his extended essay "Amr-i-Bahá'í va Falsafiy-i-Sharq" ("The Bahá'í Faith and Eastern Philosophy"). In this tour de force, Dávúdí explores the historical and conceptual connections of the Bahá'í Faith to Islamic philosophy and Persian intellectual history, and their integration of earlier philosophical traditions, notably Hellenistic philosophy. Using Aristotelian concepts, Dávúdí posits that all religions possess a "form" (divine revelation) and a "matter" (the cultural and intellectual readiness of humanity at a given time). Using this framework, he explains how religions adapt and integrate elements from the context in which they emerge. He proceeds to highlight how the Bahá'í Writings refer or allude to the works of eminent figures from the Islamic philosophical tradition—including Avicenna, Suhravardí, and Mullá Ṣadrá—while forging a distinctive doctrinal identity that at once renews and reinterprets earlier traditions. He addresses historical tensions between religious orthodoxy and philosophical reasoning, noting that Bahá'í teachings bridge these divides through explicit textual affirmations of philosophical truths, including the unity of existence, the concept of emanation, and the metaphysical hierarchy of creation. Rather than merely adopting earlier ideas, the Bahá'í teachings recast or reframe them, elevating concepts like divine unity, justice, and human purpose into universal principles for individual and collective progress. The integration of philosophical inquiry and spiritual principles offers a model for resolving conflicts between faith and reason and synthesizing metaphysical and ethical dimensions into practical teachings that address contemporary challenges.

Some of Dávúdí's works were published in periodicals such as *Áhang-i-Badí'* and *'Andalíb*, and in the form of essays and transcripts of talks compiled by Vahid Rafati in the volumes *Insán dar Á'ín-i-Bahá'í* (1987), *Maqálát va Rasá'il dar Mabáḥith-i-Mutanavvi'ih* (1993), *Ulúhíyyat va Maẓharíyyat* (1996), *Malakút-i-Vujúd* (1998), and *Rahá'í* (2010). Among these works, the text of thirteen of the nineteen talks from *Insán dar Á'ín-i-Bahá'í*, along with an additional talk about the Bahá'í principle of non-involvement in political affairs, have been translated into English under the title *Human Station in the Bahá'í Faith* (Juxta Publishing, 2013). The entirety of *Malakút-i-Vujúd* has been translated as *The Kingdom of Existence* (Nehal Foundation, 2022). And a treatise in *Ulúhíyyat va Maẓharíyyat* on the foundations of Bahá'í theology has been translated and annotated as "A Discourse on Bahá'í Theology: A Treatise by Dr. 'Alí-Murád Dávúdí on God and Revelation" in *The Journal of Bahá'í Studies* (Vol. 30, no. 4, 2020).

The Continuing Impact of Dávúdí's Scholarship

The translation of more of Dávúdí's extensive body of work into English allows readers to witness and benefit from a model of Bahá'í scholarship that is measured, thorough, and precise;

anchored in the Covenant; and centred in the authoritative Texts of the Faith. In doing so, readers will not only gain knowledge and inspiration from the depth and breadth of his work but will also draw upon it to generate new knowledge and develop fresh perspectives, methodologies, and interpretations across a range of scholarly fields.

Central to Dávúdí's body of work is of course the oneness of humankind, the pivotal principle of the Bahá'í Faith. His writings and talks explore this principle not merely as an ideal but as a practical necessity for advancing civilization. He emphasizes the importance of overcoming divisions of race, religion, and nationality to foster a unified global society. By articulating the principle of unity in diversity with philosophical rigour and depth, his work serves as a valuable resource for exploring the implications of the Bahá'í Faith's foundational teaching in fields such as philosophy, sociology, political science, history, and religious studies.

The theme of spiritual liberation—encapsulated in the title given to the most recent collection of his talks (*Rahá'í*, mentioned above)—pervades much of Dávúdí's work. He conceptualizes freedom not merely as the absence of external constraints but as the transcendence of self-centeredness and materialistic worldviews. His philosophical reflections delve deeply into humanity's potential and its relationship with the Divine. This idea is closely tied to his views on education, which he defines as the means for cultivating virtue and aligning the self with divine purpose. By emphasizing the interplay between intellectual development and spiritual growth, Dávúdí's scholarship offers valuable insights for Bahá'í educators and policymakers seeking to integrate ethical dimensions into modern education systems.

Dávúdí's reflections on the harmony of science and religion, as well as his reflections on the challenges of modernity, provide guidance for Bahá'ís researching social justice, environmental ethics, and the deep implications of technological advancements for our essential relationships as children, parents, community members, citizens, and stewards. Engaging with his ideas encourages Bahá'ís to contribute to the growing body of literature addressing the moral dimensions of global challenges. His writings on topics such as the nature of the soul, the interplay of reason and faith, and the ethical dimensions of human behaviour offer insights for Bahá'ís contributing to discourses in philosophy, psychology, and the natural sciences.

Dávúdí's writings and talks frequently underscore, sometimes implicitly, that the Bahá'í Faith did not emerge in a vacuum. It is rather part of a rich tapestry that constitutes the shared religious, mystical, and philosophical heritage of the human race. Through his works, readers gain a deeper understanding of how the Bahá'í Faith has historically engaged with prevailing intellectual currents, critically reinterpreted familiar concepts, and charted new pathways of thought and discovery. His insights provide contemporary readers with fresh perspectives for interreligious dialogue, comparative theology, and the study of religion's role in public life.

That the scholarship of 'Alí-Murád Dávúdí constitutes a landmark in the intellectual and scholarly development of the Bahá'í Faith is undeniable. His writings and talks—characterized by an uncommon combination of spiritual insight, academic rigor, and sweeping eloquence—address a vast range of complex subjects and questions with remarkable clarity and cogency. These works not only illuminate the theological, philosophical, and social foundations and dimensions of the Bahá'í Faith, but also set a high standard for future research, encouraging a more nuanced and contextually aware approach to understanding both its intellectual background and the potential of its teachings to transform the individual, rebuild a broken world, and carry forward a divine civilization.

Iranian Bahá'ís are indebted to Dávúdí for his profound elucidations of Bahá'í theology and philosophy, through which they have attained a richer comprehension of the Bahá'í writings. The fortunate few who attended his lectures in the 1970s directly absorbed his knowledge and insights. After his abduction and disappearance, countless more benefited from his writings, recordings and transcriptions of his talks. His work has provided three generations of Iranians a depth and breadth of understanding that surpasses what they would have otherwise gleaned from reading the Bahá'í writings on their own. As many Iranian Bahá'ís relocated to the global West in the 1980s and 1990s, they encountered a stark absence of comparable resources in English—a situation that has fortunately improved since that time, in large measure thanks to English-language scholarship influenced by Dávúdí. The publication of this collection realizes a long-held aspiration among many Persian-speaking Bahá'ís to share the intellectual and spiritual wealth of Dávúdí's talks and writings, previously inaccessible to those who do not read Persian.

The talks and essays in this volume have been selected to offer a comprehensive perspective on the philosophical underpinnings of Bahá'í belief. The volume opens with an introduction to the basic tenets of the Bahá'í Faith and proceeds to examine core theological themes such as the nature of God, the nature of revelation, and the station of Bahá'u'lláh. It then turns to the personal and social implications of these teachings, addressing topics such as the oneness of religion, the immortality of the soul, and the dynamic interplay between unity and diversity. The volume concludes by considering the application of Bahá'í principles to social issues, with particular emphasis on the concept of liberty.

The translations presented here provide a window into Dávúdí's reflections on the theological, spiritual, and social dimensions of the Bahá'í Faith. They lay a scholarly foundation for more nuanced and rigorous academic engagement with Bahá'í thought. It is hoped that this volume will enrich English-language discourse on the Bahá'í Faith by inspiring new lines of inquiry, encouraging the application of interdisciplinary approaches, supporting the development of new theoretical frameworks, and expanding the range of topics addressed in scholarly research.

Chapter 1

Introduction to the Tenets of Bahá'í Belief

Translated by Azita Vahdat Mottahedeh

Founded one hundred and thirty-five[1] years ago in the sacred land of Iran, the Bahá'í Faith gradually spread far and wide throughout the globe, with its increasingly numerous followers representing all races, nations, and tribes. In the land of its birth, however, it is not yet recognized as it should be. Its principal teachings and ordinances have remained unknown to a great many Iranians, giving rise to all kinds of misrepresentations, and obscuring the verities on which the Faith is established. The Bahá'ís, therefore, feel compelled to briefly describe the principal tenets of their beliefs and, by removing the misunderstandings and suspicion about the Cause of God, to familiarize their fellow citizens with their aspirations and ideals, aiming to demonstrate the truth that Bahá'ís profess belief in the incomparable Creator; worship the Source of divinity; set forth arguments in proof of the existence of God; and regard Him Who is the Absolute Truth to have no peer or partner, and His divine Essence to be sanctified above all things. They believe in the existence and the immortality of the human soul; fully acknowledge the concept of future reward and punishment in the eternal spiritual life; and refuse to limit the realm of existence to the dark and narrow confines of the material world, exerting every effort to refute the materialist ideology. Furthermore, Bahá'ís recognize the principles of prophethood, divine revelation, and the need for the advent of the Manifestations of God as fundamental tenets of their belief. They hold firm unto prayer, fasting, and worship; and regard communion with the one Beloved through prayers and devotions as a daily obligation. They recognize the ordinances governing marriage as set forth by the laws of the Holy Book; and promote goodly deeds and philanthropic endeavors.

Given that there are no prerequisites for adherence to a religion other than one's belief in the true Source of life and life after death, the acceptance of the Manifestation of God, turning unto the realm of the unseen, submission to divine Revelation, observance of acts of worship, regard for purity and chastity, and holding fast unto charitable deeds and the like, it follows that a collection of such convictions must needs be reckoned as a religious system. It can in no wise be labelled as a non-religious doctrine, nor can it be viewed as a political system, or a partisan ideology. Moreover, its followers cannot be branded as faithless, infidels, or heretics. Even those who do not acknowledge the truth of this Cause must inevitably regard it as a religion.

The Bahá'í Faith, which is counted among the independent religions, attests to the truth of all the Prophets of God; recognizes and lauds all divine religions; and extols with all respect the saints and holy figures of other faiths. It testifies that His Holiness Muḥammad—upon Him be a myriad salutations and praise—was the Lord of the Messengers, the Seal of the Prophets, and the Beloved of God. Among all the world religions, the Bahá'í Faith is the only one that acknowledges the truth of Islam, and bears witness to the prophethood of Muḥammad, the Apostle of God. When promulgating the Bahá'í Faith and promoting its Teachings among the peoples and kindreds of the world, the Bahá'ís summon mankind to recognize the validity of the Message of the Prophet Muḥammad (may the blessings of God be upon Him); they consider the recognition of the truth of Islam as a prerequisite for belief in the Bahá'í Faith, and advocate the inclusion of lessons on the Qur'án in the curriculum of Bahá'í schools throughout the world, especially in the countries of Europe and America, where the vast majority of the inhabitants are Christians.

This is because the Bahá'í Faith upholds the oneness of the foundation of Divine Religions and the continuity of spiritual beliefs, promotes all divine Faiths, and is committed to fostering spiritual principles and teachings among humankind. While considering the essential truths of religions, it disregards differences in names, designations, or titles among them, but focuses on matters of the spirit. As such, within the spiritual domain, differences are of no consequence, preventing diversities in the outward practices and conventions from ever becoming obstacles to the essential and universal divine unity. The Faith's ultimate goal is the promotion and consolidation of moral principles and virtues; the substance of its aim is to summon humankind to tread the straight path of faith and true belief. The emphasis laid by the Bahá'í Faith on moral principles, and the determination of its Central Figures to edify the souls, purify the hearts, and refine the characters of its followers, are so profound that they may be regarded as the main theme of all Their Writings and Scriptures. Countless references to such passages can easily be provided to demonstrate that the Bahá'ís are continually urged to give priority to spiritual principles and detach themselves from all matters that are incompatible with the life of the spirit. These Writings regard the acquisition of a goodly character and the undertaking of praiseworthy acts and deeds as a criterion of faith, and condemn contentment with a mere belief that is not translated into action, or a verbal confession of faith that is not heartfelt and complemented by moral virtues.

So high is the level of uprightness and truth enjoined upon the Bahá'ís that they would in no wise justify the dissimulation of their faith out of caution, prudence, or fear of persecution. Whatever may be their circumstances, and while paying the highest praise to all religions and testifying to their truth, they are not permitted to represent themselves as followers of other faiths. Neither are they allowed to deny their affiliation with the Bahá'í Faith and thereby create doubts and misgivings about their adherence. When a person considers himself a Bahá'í in his heart and according to the dictates of his faith and conscience, he should also be outwardly known as a Bahá'í, and similarly, one who does not call himself a Bahá'í, according to the same principles of faith, is not inwardly a Bahá'í either. In these cases, the Bahá'ís immediately disassociate these individuals from the Bahá'í community, so that truthfulness, integrity, and sincerity may remain a hallmark of the Bahá'ís.

Furthermore, attention to spiritual matters is stressed so pointedly by the Bahá'ís that they completely avoid any involvement in political affairs; they do not participate in partisan politics, keep away from promoting any political course of action, and refrain from commitments and posts that would, in whatever way, require engaging in political matters.² Consequently, they abstain from assuming any position of service as minister, ambassador, member of a legislative assembly, and the like; undertaking such posts would inevitably be seen as an indication of their non-affiliation with the Bahá'í Faith.

This, of course, does not mean that Bahá'ís are unmindful of the welfare of their country, or neglectful of promoting the best interests of their homeland through social, cultural, or development services. On the contrary, consistent with their faith and belief, they are called on to render service; they regard work as worship, and consider diligence, activity, and engagement in occupations as an obligation, while discouraging all forms of seclusion and isolation. Not only are they fully concerned with the common weal and the welfare of the nation, but they are further commanded to act with selfless commitment in that path. It is moreover incumbent upon them to obey the government, be respectful of the laws of the land, and maintain social order. They dedicate themselves, willingly and wholeheartedly, to any task that involves obedience to the government and the law, centering their energies in that which will reconstruct the world and rehabilitate the fortunes of mankind through the promotion of Divine teachings and the promulgation of spiritual principles.

Bahá'ís throughout the world revere Iran and glorify its sanctified soil, considering it a place of pilgrimage. They regard that blessed country as the Cradle of their Faith, as the altar of sacrifice and the field of martyrdom of their holy ones. They hasten from the remotest parts of the planet to visit that land and cherish the hope, one and all, that through God's irresistible decree and according to the promise made by 'Abdu'l-Bahá, this bounteous land that has "from its earliest days been musk-scented, soul-stirring, knowledge-bearing, and jewel-laden"³ may flourish and become the most prosperous of lands, endowed with the most respected of all governments of the world.⁴

As a result of the spread of the Bahá'í Faith to all corners of the world, the fame of the land of its birth was noised abroad, promoting its spiritual repute, and calling the attention of the world to that country. As time went by, the Faith's divine teachings were promulgated from country to country, and progressively from one region, tribe, and nation to another. At the present time, the Bahá'í Faith has been established in 80,000 centers in the world, has been represented by 1640 tribes, races, and people, and its Writings are translated into 685 languages.[5] The Bahá'í International Community is recognized as a non-governmental organization by the United Nations. The adoption of the International Covenant on Civil and Political Rights by most of the countries of the world, including Iran, and the acknowledgement and acceptance of the validity of human rights in these countries, have provided the Bahá'ís with legal protection.

We hope that the themes presented above will acquaint the just and the fair-minded with the true state of affairs and the reality of the Bahá'í Faith. May they bring awareness about the way of life and the conduct of the followers of this religion, preventing the spread of false statements about the Bahá'ís—those who through a worldwide propagation of their Faith have brought the blessed country of Iran to the attention of the world. Finally, it is our hope and wish that these themes will be conducive to unity and concord, and to ever-increasing harmony and fellowship, irrespective of the differences in beliefs, customs, and habits.

NOTES TO CHAPTER ONE

1   The Bahá'í Faith was founded in the year 1260 AH (1844 CE).

2   For an explanation of the Bahá'í perspective on politics, see the 2 March 2013 letter of the Universal House of Justice to the Bahá'ís of Iran (www.bahai.org/library/authoritative-texts/the-universal-house-of-justice/messages/20130302_001/1#063389421)

3   'Abdu'l-Bahá, *Makátíb-i-'Abdu'l-Bahá*, vol. 2, ([Cairo]: Kurdistánu'l-'Ilmíyyih, 1330 A.H. [1911/1912]), 82–83; provisional translation.

4   Fáḍil-i-Mázindarání, *Amr va Khalq*, vol. 4, (Hofheim-Langenhain: Bahá'í-Verlag, 1986), 441.

5   This essay was written in 1970s and the statistics cited reflect the reality of that time. By 2001, Bahá'ís resided in 127,381 localities in 190 countries and forty-six dependent territories; 2,112 tribes, races, and ethnic groups were represented in the global Bahá'í community; and Bahá'í literature was translated into 802 languages. See, *The Bahá'í World, 2000–2001* (Haifa: Bahá'í World Centre, 2002), 277.

Chapter 2

Denying and Proving the Existence of God

Translated by Azita Vahdat Mottahedeh

Rather than trying to prove the existence of God, as is usually done, let us start our discourse by denying His existence. The purpose here is to reflect on the viewpoints and reasoning of those who deny or reject God, bearing in mind that their numbers as well as the diversity of their rationales have probably increased in the last two centuries.

There are several causes—or, more precisely, several reasons—for denying the existence of God; such reasons have always been current and present among people. In other words, the denial of God is nothing new, but previously it might have not been as widespread as it is now. In the modern world, there are both general and specific reasons leading to such a denial that should be briefly mentioned.

One such reason is that some do not find God in a form that would satisfy them, or God may have been portrayed to them in a way that is unacceptable to them. That is, such a God does not fulfil their quest and does not quench their thirst for His knowledge. These people yearn to acknowledge the existence of God and to believe in Him; the only issue is that they cannot accept God in the form in which He is represented. That form does not match the God that they are seeking, and as such, it does not satisfy their search. They are left with an unfulfilled desire and are consumed away in their longing to attain their unattainable goal. Though they deny God, they are not content with that denial, but the fact remains that God was presented to them in a manner that did not convince their mind, nor fulfil the object of their quest.

Another reason for denying God stems from the fact that those who believe in God generally fall into two categories. In the first category are those who worship God through their ideals and their deeds, their words and their hearts, and as such, their speech and conduct confirm their faith. The second category are those who recognize God only theoretically and through human learning, and aim to prove His existence. They regard themselves as believers, yet keep their deeds and actions in a sphere separate from their belief. Their faith in God has no effect upon their actions, and as such, while considering themselves believers, they see no need to refrain from misdeeds, wrongdoing, and even crime. The result is that those who observe the behavior and conduct of such so-called believers attribute the deeds of these people to their belief in God, for they cannot separate action from faith. They say that if faith in God does not transform a person, if it does not improve his or her behavior and conduct, and if it does not exert such influence as to demonstrate its creative power, of what use is such a belief? Indeed, if it yields no result, why should one hold on to it?

The harm inflicted by the vast number of those who are non-believers in their deeds, and whose faith consists of mere lip service is that, through their ungodly conduct, they cause others to become weary of any faith and belief in God.

Another reason for denying God is that there are some people who want to know, understand, and comprehend God in the same way that they know, understand, and comprehend any worldly object or matter (be it material or spiritual). By this is meant that they try to know God by the same criteria with which their minds perceive the things of this world. For example, they distinguish objects through the sense of touch, and with their circumscribed minds, they observe and comprehend the world. But such sensory perception of God is totally impossible; it is unreasonable and self-contradictory. Consequently, they find themselves incapable of accepting His existence. The reason we say that it is self-contradictory is that God is a limitless Existence—He is the Infinite, the Absolute—and naturally, such a Being cannot be fathomed by a limited and finite mind, or be comprehended by an imperfect intellect. A God who can be understood by us would no longer be God, for we have limited Him to our own understanding, and by that very limitation we are denying Him the attribute of Godhead.

In our view, and in that of any person who reflects upon his own innate nature, it is meaningless to deny God. Yet, if we consider the views of those who deny Him along with those who believe in Him, we would declare that should God exist, He could not possibly be fathomed by a finite mind or be comprehended by a limited understanding. For, otherwise, He would cease to be God and would simply be the product of one's finite mind as conditioned by its own limitations. This is why those who deny God say that they cannot comprehend Him. In fact, they are seeking to understand and accept a being who is not God, for were He to be comprehended, He would have to descend from the station of the Absolute and Infinite, and would fall into the category of the relative and the limited. Consequently, we must dispel the misconception that we can deny God because we cannot perceive Him and comprehend His Being. For, were we to comprehend His Essence, He would not be God. This is a fundamental tenet to be accepted and kept in mind.

One further reason for denying God, one that perhaps started gaining momentum in the Renaissance, is that in modern times humankind perceives itself to have attained a kind of maturity, and believes that it has grown and developed in such a way that it can place its complete trust and reliance on its own powers and abilities. This is the movement known as Humanism that emerged in Europe in the early Renaissance period: a philosophical stance that emphasizes the individual and the agency of the human being, and advocates his autonomy and freedom from the religious dogma of the Middle Ages. This view states that the individual is an independent being, self-reliant and free from all others. It further adds that throughout the Middle Ages and all down the former centuries human beings were controlled by, and their lives and affairs were governed in the name of, religion; God ruled over humans and their duties were determined in the heavens. But now, the individual wants to be free, to make his own life decisions, to be self-directed, to depend only upon his own mind and thought, and to personally choose the course of his life rather than to have it defined by God or by a religion, prophet, holy book, priest, or mullah. Naturally, this ideology grew strong; and in tandem with the advances in science and technology in this era, man's desire to be in the forefront rather than secondary to God and religion gradually gained greater importance.

When we say that advances in science and technology led man to give more attention to his own self, it is because of the astonishing results brought about by these advances. Through the power of thought and reflection, things previously unknown and totally unimaginable became known to man. Now that he could achieve so much through the power of the mind—could discover the unknown, turn life around, alter the sources of its livelihood, and benefit from these newfound powers—he questioned the need for him to submit to a religion or have his path in life determined by any entity external to his own mind.

Consequently, scientific discoveries and technological advancements exercised a powerful influence on a gradually increasing and more adamant denial of God. This process was a direct result of Rationalism, a view that places reason and science in the center, and aims to prove everything by means of reason and the knowledge resulting from it. As a result, rationalism permeated all domains, demanding that man apply reason even in his emotions, beliefs, and sentiments, draw conclusions based on the dictates of scientific reasoning, and accept the ruling of reason and intellect.

As scientific discoveries led to technological advancements, man began to assume that he could achieve anything and everything through science, and that rational and scientific reasoning are the absolute criterion. He further presumed that the only valid concepts were those substantiated by scientific deduction, and that all else was unworthy of attention. This rationalistic assumption opened the way for the denial of God to be extended to the scientific communities as well as to those of literature and philosophy. Some people even regarded this denial to be the hallmark of an enlightened mind, and considered it a distinguishing characteristic of scientific thought and intellectualism.

Such a mindset, however, was flawed from the start, for science has its own specialized domain, and reason applies to particular objects. It is not only in matters of religious belief that the range of the intellect is limited, but its scope is also circumscribed in aesthetic, artistic, emotional, and affective matters. This does not imply that the intellect is defective, for that faculty is complete within its own boundaries. The intellect is a valid criterion provided it be limited to its own confines. Yet, if it oversteps those bounds, if it intends to interfere in areas unrelated to it, to enter arenas out of its reach, and to pass judgment on matters outside of its authority, that is when it will err. This is where man was misled during the Early Modern period and the Renaissance era; the mistaken view gradually became so widespread that it came to be regarded by some as self-evident and incontrovertible.

Another factor that exacerbated this process was that when God was denied, religion was also disavowed, and this resulted in the idea that by setting religion aside, man would be unrestricted in his opinion and could rely entirely on his intellect and reason; furthermore, he would free in his actions, and at liberty to follow his own sensual desires. In other words, he cast off the shackles that religion, in the name of God, had bound him with, and emancipated himself from the fetters that the church had placed about his neck in the name of Christ. Consequently, he felt free to do as he pleased, and to unleash his heart with unbridled passion. So, when one denies God, constraints are removed from one's actions, allowing one to act free from the fear of being observed. This fact, fully compatible with man's selfish desires, had undesirable ramifications, and ultimately ended in his disadvantage. It is analogous to a child who, reaching adolescence, wishes to be free in his actions; and once unrestricted by parental rule he assumes that he is at liberty to follow his impulses and pleasures. At that moment and stage in life, he cannot conceive where that will lead to, what the outcome will be, and how he will later feel about it.

This was the very same situation in which humanity found itself at the beginning of modern times. By removing God from its life, it felt at liberty to act according to its whims and desires; and finding it delightful and pleasurable, it followed that course. Now, gradually during this century, humanity is recognizing where that path has led to, its ramifications, the menacing decline and breakdown of all order, and the manifold afflictions resulting from drugs, alcohol, lustful appetites, and crime, as well as psychological intemperance and perversions.

These results might not have been initially conceivable for humankind, and for this reason the denial of God was regarded as a welcome removal of obstacles. Towards the end of the nineteenth century, writing about the condition of the world, Bahá'u'lláh asserts that, "[i]ts face is turned towards waywardness and unbelief."[1] A world that has directed its attention towards irreligion and unbelief will not easily turn its gaze in another direction. It was necessary for humanity to continue on its path until it reached a dead-end or stumbled and faltered, in order for it to realize that the path chosen was not the correct one. This reality needed to be demonstrated in practice; merely demonstrating it in theory or purely through reason would not have borne results. Naturally, humanity needed to tread this path in order to experience its inherent consequences—that is, to come to the realization that man should not be considered as a self-reliant and self-sufficient being with full trust in his own reason and judgement. It is misleading to think that we can comprehend everything and can prove all things through the intellect.

It must be noted that this does not imply, in any measure, a denial of the intellect's distinction and virtue. There is probably no other religion in the world that has placed as much emphasis on the value of the mind, reason, and the intellect as the Bahá'í Faith has done. This is reflected in its explicit spiritual principle that religion must be in conformity with science and reason. Nonetheless, reason should not be conceived as an absolute measure. While much has been written demonstrating the distinction and excellence of the human mind, 'Abdu'l-Bahá, in explaining the *Four Criteria of Comprehension*, also discusses the imperfection of reason as an absolute criterion.[2]

By saying that the mind or reason is not an absolute criterion we mean that it is not a criterion for comprehending everything. Reason itself is limited by specific confines, and it may be called upon only in certain matters. Reason is the power to comprehend universal concepts; and the reasoning power is the means by which one is led to a conclusion from a given premise. The greatest act that can be expected of the faculty of reason is for it to combine multiple premises in order to arrive at a conclusion. Reason's function is to discover the unknown through the known, and to discern the connection that may exist between the known and the unknown. This ability is a tremendous distinction, for by it man's rational soul is distinguished from all other beings; it is the hallmark of the nobility of the mind.

But when it becomes impossible to formulate a general concept; when a notion cannot be incorporated in such a way as to create a theorem leading to a universal theory, reason then is rendered incompetent. We cannot, for example, use reason as a criterion to determine or measure sentiments, emotions, and feelings. These modalities are not rational; they are responses that at their climax reach love, which transcends reason. So, in this arena reason is lame, in the sense that one cannot tread the path of love with rational feet. In the words of Ḥáfiẓ, "That watchman is of no use in our town";[3] that is to say, reason is inadequate to the task.

This point equally applies to the inability of the intellect and of reason to prove the existence of God. For God is a universal concept. He is not a conclusion that can be inferred through the process of logically investigating certain premises or propositions. In this case, the premises would take priority over the conclusion and would be superior to it. If it were possible to logically arrive, from given premises, at the conclusion that God exists, and to apply reason to verify His existence, those premises and reasoning would need to be more obvious, more evident, and prior to the conclusion, whereas nothing can be prior to God. This is analogous to trying to perceive the sun in the light of something else, whereas it is through the light of the sun that everything can be visually perceived. Everything is seen by means of sunlight, but that light is self-evident. There is no defect in that radiance; it is perfection. To see the light, vision is all we need, but in order to see anything else, in addition to vision we also need light. Consequently, seeing everything else requires an intermediary which is light, but light can be perceived by itself and without an intermediary. This of course is simply an example to illustrate the subject, and it can only be viewed as such and is not to be taken too literally.

By this is meant that all things are known through God, but God can only be known through His own Self. It is not possible to attain to that knowledge through any other means, for then God would be made secondary to that means, in which case He would no longer be God. It is for this reason that the sages and the wise have always expressed their powerlessness to prove the existence of God, and regarded the statement, "O Thou Whose Essence alone can lead to His Essence"[4] to be the best evidence of His being. Similarly, a Persian poet wrote:

The sun itself is the proof of the sun,
If proof you need, turn not away therefrom.[5]

That is to say, if you need evidence of the existence of the sun, all you need to do is not turn your face away from it. We can only perceive the sun if we take our gaze away from all else and turn towards it. There is no other way, for all else is seen in the light of the sun, but the sun itself can only be seen by turning towards it. Similarly, the existence of God is not a conclusion to be deduced. Such a process of proof is based on reason, science, and logic, all of which function within specific contexts; if we try to apply them beyond those contexts, we in fact harm reason and science, while failing to prove the existence of God.

This is equally true about the soul. If we were to attempt to logically prove the existence of God or the soul by means of the intellect, we would be taking the intellect out of its sphere of function; moreover, the God and the soul thus proven would also cease to be God and the soul as they ought to be known. Any such attempt would thus be futile. As mentioned earlier, one of the causes of irreligion has been the attempts to know God through reason, a path that will not lead to Him and will not attain to that knowledge. The existence of God should be felt, not demonstrated; rather than accepting Him by means of the intellect, we should seek Him in the heart. Unless we find Him in the heart, there is no use in trying to prove His existence with the mind. In fact, God must first be perceived in the heart, and following such a firm foundation, all else can be built upon it, and proven.

In logic there are statements known as axioms or common notions that are taken to be true, that are regarded as self-evident, and serve as a premise or starting point for reasoning. Were it not so, that is if the premises were not regarded as well-established or accepted without controversy, any process of reasoning, even in mathematics, would continue indefinitely without reaching a conclusion. That is to say the proof of any hypothesis would depend on the proof of the premise preceding it, with no end to the process, leaving the conclusion indefinite and conditional.

Consider how mathematics, the most precise and disciplined of all sciences, is based upon this principle that not everything can be expected to be proven. This is why reason must necessarily start from premises, accept those premises as axiomatic, and then prove the truth of a proposition. It is possible, of course, to change the premises and take other premises as evident. In such a case the conclusion would naturally become different, giving rise to other propositions. Thus, one must first evaluate whether some common notions other than those that are accepted can be proposed, and then, if possible or necessary, the premises can be changed. The absolute necessity of the existence and the validity of a self-evident premise is indisputable. It follows that all else can be proven based on the accepted and evident premise. This is the case with every rational inference; it is necessary to accept certain fundamental axiomatic rules without having to demonstrate their validity. Such rules are called "laws of thought"; they include the law of non-contradiction, and the principle of causality that states that every effect has a cause that precedes it, and that every cause should always lead to the same effect. This principle is not one to be proven. The law of non-contradiction states that contradictory propositions cannot both be true at the same time and in the same sense; either one or the other should be accepted. This principle is also not rationally inferred. If we decide to disregard these two axiomatic rules, the validity of no proposition can be proven or demonstrated. We say that contradictory propositions cannot both be true. Why is that? And why do we not aim to prove it? The reason is that it is an axiomatic fact, so clearly obvious that it does not require any proof. This is why we say that to expect everything to be rationally proven is rationally absurd. There comes a point at which the process must stop and the premise must be accepted as a basic principle. This is true about particulars, and more especially so about universals; that is, we should not require that every hypothesis be proven.

The chain of hypotheses must, inevitably, lead to a basic premise that we accept as the original premise and as the presupposition of all things, without having to prove its validity. This will be the basis of the inferences that will follow. If we look carefully into this matter, God is, in a sense, essentially this inevitable Initial or Absolute Source upon which all else is conditioned, without Him being conditioned upon anything else. We must not imagine God as a strange or bizarre being. If we instead think of God as such a source—that is, recognize Him as the starting point that our intellect needs in order to be able to build all else upon it—then there will be no obstacle to accepting Him; it will even become a necessity. In other words, God can be regarded as that source, as that essence, from which the chain of all proofs and reasons originates. That original source cannot be proven, but all other proofs depend on it. The intention here is not to make this subject a philosophical issue, but simply to clarify it for laypersons.

A matter of interest here is that many divine sages in the past, and during this blessed era, Bahá'u'lláh and 'Abdu'l-Bahá Themselves, have set forth proofs to demonstrate the existence of God; yet we have just said that God cannot be proven by means of rational proofs, a notion confirmed by divine teachings. The essence and significance of the verse "O Thou Whose Essence alone can lead to His Essence," cited from an Islamic prayer, is attested by, and even elaborately explained in many of the Bahá'í Writings.[6] 'Abdu'l-Bahá clearly affirms that the theoretical arguments set forth to demonstrate the existence of God are adduced for weak souls; inasmuch as such arguments do not prove His existence, but serve to satisfy the weak souls who require a proof for everything.[7] God is not a hypothesis to be proved or denied through rational arguments. In fact, the arguments are presented in order to refute the objections of the deniers and not to demonstrate the essence of Divinity. So, by presenting arguments to prove His existence, we can establish that God cannot be denied. A careful attention to the arguments provided to prove the existence of God will show that they are only compelling arguments and as such cannot engender faith and belief. Faith in God is granted through discernment and insight, and it is the means for transforming one's life into a spiritual one. In brief, the reasons given for proving the existence of God or, to put it better, for refuting the denial of God, simply disprove the arguments of denial, and prepare the heart to accept God.

There are several such arguments. For example, when we say that every effect has a cause, or every contingent and originated thing has an origin or source, it follows that the world of being—which is originated and caused—must needs have an origin and a cause. We clearly see that the contingent world is originated and that its beings did not always exist; that they came into being gradually, or that they existed in a different form and then took on a new appearance. So, it is necessary for a pre-existent being to have preceded these contingencies, in order for origination to find meaning. There must exist a motive force, an animating principle to have preceded these effects.

The most compelling argument for the existence of God—affirmed by 'Abdu'l-Bahá and ultimately arrived at by the philosophers of the West—is to prove His existence as the source of a perfection that is deduced by the presence of the deficiencies in the contingent world.[8] To be more precise: It is an undeniable fact that there are deficiencies and imperfections everywhere, and it is evident that conceiving of anything as imperfect would be meaningless unless it be compared to a perfection. So, if we feel that all around us there exist deficiencies, that feeling is evidence of the existence of an absolute perfection in the world compared to which imperfection would have meaning. Imperfection by itself is an outward and existential matter and therefore, as an effect, it cannot be considered an originating cause.

These arguments show that it is neither necessary nor possible for us to deny the existence of God. This conclusion is the axiom for reason and rationality, in the sense that it is impossible to either prove or refute it unless we totally change the method of reasoning and the bases of rationality through adopting new principles as axioms.

It is clear and evident to me that never in the past has anyone succeeded in proving that God does not exist, and no one will ever be able to do so in the future either. This statement might seem strange, because we started by saying that there are some who are persistently determined in their denial of the existence of God, and we proceeded to explain the reasons behind this. We can now return to that subject and say that it is a misconceived notion to think that they are denying God. They imagine that they are denying God, whereas if we were to delve into the matter, we see that they are instead denying that which they cannot conceive as being God. They accept some other concept, with another designation, as their God. Their notion of God is indeed different from that common among the generality of the people. Consequently, they cannot accept such a God, for they assume God to be that which people have imagined Him to be. This is an erroneous view from the start. Religions have, from the beginning, testified that no two people can be found to conceive of God in a like manner. Every individual envisions God in some way and can understand and accept Him accordingly. However each one conceives Him to be and comprehends and recognizes Him is acceptable. That is why it has been said: "The paths to God are as numerous as the number of created souls."[9]

A tale relates that if an ant were to imagine and envision its God, it would conceive Him in the form of a huge, winged ant with two large antennae, for no one can overstep the boundaries of his own imagination. So, every individual has a God of his own. Even those who deny God have their own notion of Him, for it is not possible to ignore or dismiss the concept of God. The reason is that according to the exigencies of man's distinctive nature he is conditioned to seek and to turn his attention to something. The powers of thought, reason, love, zeal, and all his other qualities and conditions never come to a halt; they never become rigid and inert. This is a distinguishing feature of man, singling him out in the world of creation and separating him from the animal. The animal has a one-faceted existence bound by specific limitations that it cannot transgress. This is not the case with the human being, the meaning and value of whose life requires constant flow and progress. It is, therefore, never possible for man to say that he has found everything that is to be found, that he has completed his search, and that there is nothing else to be sought. There is, and always will be, something to be sought. If we remove this characteristic from man, we can no longer regard him as a human being. The moment that man regards himself to have become complete, to have achieved all, and to have nothing remaining for him to seek—in that very moment, his distinctive human life will come to a halt. By nature, man needs to constantly search after something. He seeks, finds, and then realizes that what he has found is not complete, and consequently, he continues his quest. This process is a continuous one. It is as if there always exists an unknown, a mystery, that will remain unfathomed. Even if parts or aspects of it become known, there will remain other parts and aspects that continue to be unknown and need to be discovered. In other words, the eternal quest for that mystery is a characteristic of man. A human being cannot be satisfied merely with sleep, food, desire, and passions. Contentment with those elements of life alone corresponds to decline as a human being. Those who say we want nothing in life but to eat, sleep and satisfy our passions reach a stage in life where they eat, sleep and self-indulge, but they never attain that which they truly seek. So, the true object of their quest is not a self-centered one, for that is attained, but it is found to be inadequate. It is a requirement of human existence, therefore, to always quest for the undiscovered in the intellectual, emotional, and practical aspects of life. Even when the object of the quest is achieved to a relative degree, it is impossible to fully attain unto that which is sought. As such, there exists an absolute mystery in the life of man, one with which he communes, to which he is attracted, towards which he strives—yet which he cannot reach. This mystery is that which gives meaning to human life.

So it is that man cannot be content with what he has. He is constantly seeking something that is unattainable and distanced from him, and he is constantly making efforts to reduce that separating gap. Man's attention on an absolute goal, one that is endlessly remote, yet constantly sought, plays a major role in his life. Such a remote goal is his supreme purpose and highest wish, yet it is not attainable, for if it were within reach, it would no longer be a supreme purpose. This is indeed what is implied by belief in God. That is, we conceive God as the ultimate Purpose, as the Supreme Goal, as the highest attainment of man's journey towards the unknowable Absolute. This journey is the endless quest for the unknown, Who, from a certain viewpoint, is also known. This statement—"the unknown Who, from a certain viewpoint, is also known"—may require clarification. Plato explains that inquiring about something that is already known to us would be meaningless. If we already know it, what would we be trying to inquire about? Likewise, if something is unknown to us, inquiring about it would likewise be meaningless, for what would we be inquiring about if we do not know the very object of the quest? Accordingly, when we are searching for something, we should know what we are seeking, and it should at the same time be a mystery, unknown to us; it should simultaneously be within our reach, yet unachieved; it should be with us, while distanced and separate from us. So, man turns his attention to a mystery that is concealed and yet manifest. Why do we say that it is manifest? Because if it were not, the quest for it would lose its meaning. On the other hand, we say it is concealed, for if it were not, what would man be searching for? This is an object of quest that is at once hidden yet manifest, one that we cannot disregard or ignore. A human being cannot ignore something that is an unknown mystery, and leave it to remain unknown. As soon as one does that, one loses that fundamental innate component of human life, without which one becomes like an animal. Upon realizing that there exists a mystery, an unknown, man needs to follow and seek it, even if he never attains it. The reason why we say "never attains" is that the moment one attains all, one has completed the process of life, and there remains no more quest and search. So, one can disregard the existence of God only if one can leave aside the unknown, can stop searching for it, and not seek an ultimate purpose and goal in life.

Some sects and denominations that disbelieve in God nevertheless attest to a latter time—a time when all that they seek will be achieved, when they will attain the object of their devotion. That day has not yet come, and might never come; but the idea of it is an animating force for their minds and an ultimate purpose for their desires. To outward seeming, these groups do not profess a belief in God, but they do have an object of adoration in His stead, one that they worship and for which they give up their all. They do not appear to believe in an afterlife, they do not believe in God, and regard everything to be confined to matter and to the physical and visible world. Despite this, they offer up their lives to serve the ideal that they glorify. We see, therefore, that even such individuals cannot ignore or set aside the search for that which is unattainable. It is evident that the existence of such a thing is not an actual and outward condition for our physical life, yet it cannot be disregarded. We need to turn toward it, even if only in a distant future. So, even for these sects and belief systems, to pay heed to an ultimate purpose is a necessity that leads them to have an object of their adoration and to maintain a set of beliefs and an absolute goal for which they will readily give up everything. Their attention is focused on that ultimate aim, and they advance towards it, considering its achievement to be the highest attainment of human life. They do not refer to it as God, and that does not matter at all, for we are not bound by name and fame. Our God is One to Whom no name is ascribed. If we wish to truly be a believer in Him, we must negate all name and fame, all description and identification, from Him and from ourselves.

NOTES TO CHAPTER TWO

1   Bahá'u'lláh, *Gleanings from the Writings of Bahá'u'lláh* LXI, Bahá'í Reference Library www.bahai.org/r/907560389.

2   'Abdu'l-Bahá, *Some Answered Questions*, chapter 83, Bahá'í Reference Library www.bahai.org/r/380246685.

3   Shamsu'd-Dín Muḥammad-i-Shírází, *Díván-i-Khájih Shamsu'd-Dín Ḥáfiẓ-i-Shírází*, (Ṭihrán: Iqbál, 1990/91), 46.

4   From a prayer of Imám 'Alí.

5   Jalálu'd-Dín Rúmí, *Kullíyát-i-Mathnavíy-i-Ma'naví* ([Ṭihrán]: Nashr-i-Ṭulú', 1991), 9.

6   See: Bahá'u'lláh, *The Call of the Divine Beloved*, Bahá'í Reference Library www.bahai.org/r/680099234.

7   'Abdu'l-Bahá, *Some Answered Questions*, chapter 2, Bahá'í Reference Library www.bahai.org/r/584292313.

8   Ibid.

9   See, for instance, Muḥammad-Báqir al-Majlisí, *Biḥáru'l-Anvár*, vol. 64 (Beirut: Dáru Iḥyá'i't-Turáthi'l-'Arabí, 1983), 137.

Chapter 3

Confessing the Sanctity of the Divine Essence

Translated by Vargha Bolodo-Taefi

Part One

We always strive to present discourses that demonstrate, establish, and affirm. In other words, when articulating, however inadequately, the Bahá'í view of a subject, we aspire to convey themes that are necessary and beneficial. We are rarely required to formulate an argument that negates or disproves a point. This is because, as a matter of principle, we regard it as unbefitting the station for the people of Bahá to devote their attention and time to removing the misgivings of those who reject them or to deliberating on the objections levelled against them. To be sure, this will occasionally be required, because those who oppose the Faith periodically misrepresent matters and obscure the truth before the masses to such an extent that it is necessary to clear up those misconceptions. Among the misunderstandings they have propagated—with great emphasis—is that Bahá'u'lláh has claimed the station of Divinity. They have caused so much confusion about this matter that to enlighten the minds is not an easy task, although the truth of the matter is in itself simple and quite clear.

They condemn the Bahá'ís concerning this subject, and yet anyone who reads the Writings of Bahá'u'lláh will be astonished by the unfairness of those who spread such doubts among the people. Very few Writings of Bahá'u'lláh can be found in which He does not attest the existence of God, the sanctity of His Essence, the exaltation of His attributes, and the oneness of His existence, and in which He does not view Himself as occupying a station of absolute servitude.

When reciting their Long Obligatory Prayer, Bahá'ís say: "I testify unto that whereunto have testified all created things, and the Concourse on high, and the inmates of the all-highest Paradise, and beyond them the Tongue of Grandeur itself from the all-glorious Horizon, that Thou art God, that there is no God but Thee."[1] Following the divine teachings received through Bahá'u'lláh, every Bahá'í is required to declare in this Prayer, concerning the Essence of God, that "Thou art God, that there is no God but Thee," and then to confess "that He Who hath been manifested is the Hidden Mystery, the Treasured Symbol."[2] Bahá'ís thus testify explicitly and unequivocally in their Obligatory Prayer to the oneness of God and then acknowledge that the Manifestation of God Who has appeared was a Hidden Mystery that God has revealed.

In their Medium Obligatory Prayer, similarly, Bahá'ís recite: "God testifieth that there is none other God but Him. His are the kingdoms of Revelation and of creation. He, in truth, hath manifested Him Who is the Dayspring of Revelation, Who conversed on Sinai."[3] Here, Bahá'ís first testify that God is one, that there is no God but Him, and that the kingdoms of Revelation and creation are His, and then profess that this God has revealed Him Who is "the Dayspring of Revelation" and "Who conversed on Sinai." In other words, every Bahá'í specifies clearly and plainly that the one true God is that unseen God and that it is He Who has manifested Bahá'u'lláh.

In some of His prayers, Bahá'u'lláh teaches the people of Bahá that, when turning towards God, they should first confess the oneness of God and the sanctity of His Essence and then recognize that Bahá'u'lláh has come by the Will of God, inasmuch as Bahá'u'lláh is a Manifestation invested with a revelation and sent forth by the Will of God. For instance, in a prayer, Bahá'u'lláh writes:

> Say: Glorified art Thou, O Lord of all beings, both visible and invisible! I beseech Thee, by Thy name which hath caused the earth to tremble, the heavens to be cleft asunder, the mountains to pass away, and every land to be shaken, to grant that I may remember Thee and celebrate Thy praise in such wise that I may not be hindered by the veils of such

people as have turned away from the Dawning-Place of Thy Revelation and the Dayspring of Thine inspiration.[4]

Nothing could convey the distinction between the Manifestation of Divine Revelation and the Essence of God in more certain and precise terms than this passage. This subtlety reaches its highest expression in a statement in which God addresses Bahá'u'lláh, refers to Him as His Servant, and instructs this Servant to warn and acquaint the people with the things God has sent down to Him and to fear no one. Bahá'u'lláh is further exhorted to place His trust in God, turn away from those who reject the truth, and let God be His sufficing help. In this address, God assures the Manifestation of His Cause of His victory and triumph, and even reminds Him of a time in Constantinople when He took no notice of the rulers and the dignitaries and was therefore censured by the seat of the Caliphate. This is the exact passage in which God addresses Bahá'u'lláh:

> Warn and acquaint the people, O Servant, with the things We have sent down unto Thee, and let the fear of no one dismay Thee, and be Thou not of them that waver. The day is approaching when God will have exalted His Cause and magnified His testimony in the eyes of all who are in the heavens and all who are on the earth. Place, in all circumstances, Thy whole trust in Thy Lord, and fix Thy gaze upon Him, and turn away from all them that repudiate His truth. Let God, Thy Lord, be Thy sufficing succorer and helper. We have pledged Ourselves to secure Thy triumph upon earth and to exalt Our Cause above all men, though no king be found who would turn his face towards Thee.[5]

> Call Thou to remembrance Thine arrival in the City (Constantinople), how the Ministers of the Sulṭán thought Thee to be unacquainted with their laws and regulations, and believed Thee to be one of the ignorant. Say: Yes, by My Lord! I am ignorant of all things except what God hath, through His bountiful favor, been pleased to teach Me. To this We assuredly testify, and unhesitatingly confess it.[6]

In many of His prayers, Bahá'u'lláh extols God, stresses His oneness, and testifies to His own servitude before the grandeur of God. For example, He writes:

> O God, my God! I bear witness to Thy unity and Thy oneness, and that Thou art God, and that there is none other God but Thee. Thou hast everlastingly been sanctified above the mention of any one but Thee and the praise of all else except Thyself, and Thou wilt everlastingly continue to be the same as Thou wast from the beginning and hast ever been.[7]

He states in another prayer:

> Glorified is He Who hath revealed His Cause and gave voice unto all creation to testify that there is none other God except Him, the Truth, the Knower of things unseen. This Wronged One beareth witness unto His oneness and His singleness. From time immemorial He hath been known through His own Self, transcendent in His sovereignty, and manifest through His signs. No God is there but Him, the One, the Protector, the Self-Subsisting.[8]

He similarly writes in another Tablet: "God testifieth that there is none other God but Him, and that He Who now speaketh is, in truth, the Speaker on Sinai, Who shineth above the horizon of Revelation . . . ."[9]

In yet another Tablet, He stresses: "God testifieth that there is none other God but Him, and that He Who is come through the power of truth is, verily, the Lord of all being and the King of the seen and the unseen."[10]

Numerous Writings of Bahá'u'lláh are replete with passages that introduce Him as a Messenger of God, a servant of God, the Glory of God, and the Son of His servant. In several such Writings, Bahá'u'lláh regards Himself as a servant who has believed in God and His verses, views Himself as worthy of nothing else but servitude, and seeks no other appellation. It is God Who has manifested Him, and what Bahá'u'lláh utters is likewise from God Who has raised Him up and not from Himself. Where Bahá'u'lláh summons the people to obey Him, He is in fact beckoning them to obey God Who has created and sent Him forth. His Writings are not from Him, but from God Who has chosen Him. To deny Him and to challenge His authority is to deny God and to challenge the authority of God. Therefore, He pleads His sufferings and afflictions to God and calls God to witness that His utterances are not His own, but are from God Who has sent down the verses to Him, just as divine verses were sent down to the Prophets before Him.

Elaborating on these themes, He affirms in one of His Writings: "Testify thou in thine inmost heart that there is no God but Him, the Almighty, the Best-Beloved, and bear witness that He Whom God hath sent forth is His servant and His Glory."[11] Just as the followers of Islam confess in their testimony of faith, the *Tashahhud*, that Muḥammad is the servant of God and His Messenger, we have also been instructed here to testify that Bahá'u'lláh is the servant of God and His Glory.

Bahá'u'lláh also writes in another Tablet: "O Mihdí! Bear thou witness even as God hath testified for His own Self ere the creation of the heavens and the earth that there is none other God but Him, and that this Youth is His servant and His Glory."[12]

Further, Bahá'u'lláh stresses in the Súriy-i-Mulúk: "Certain ones among you have said: 'He it is Who hath laid claim to be God.' By God! This is a gross calumny. I am but a servant of God Who hath believed in Him and in His signs, and in His Prophets and in His angels."[13]

Likewise, Bahá'u'lláh states in another Tablet:

This is a Book which proclaimeth the truth: 'No God is there but Him, the Help in Peril, the Self-Subsisting' . . . He it is Who hath arisen to demonstrate His absolute servitude unto God, your Lord, could ye but perceive it, and desireth naught save servitude unto the One True God. Unto this all things bear witness, even if ye were to deny it.[14]

He also writes in an epistle: "I am, O my Lord, Thy servant and the son of Thy servant. I bear witness unto Thy unity, and Thy oneness, and to the sanctity of Thy self and the purity of Thine Essence."[15]

He reiterates in yet another Tablet: "Verily, I am a Servant Who hath believed in God and in His signs, and have sacrificed Myself in His path. Unto this bear witness the woes which now beset Me, woes the like of which no man hath ever before sustained. My Lord, the All-Knowing, testifieth to the truth of My words."[16]

He states in another Tablet: "God hath called Me forth and entrusted Me with verses with which all the Prophets and Messengers of God were invested."[17] He further writes: "By God! This thing is not from Me, but from Him Who hath sent Me with the truth and made Me to be a mercy unto all created things."[18]

In another Tablet, Bahá'u'lláh clarifies: "In raising the call 'Come unto Me, come unto Me, O people of the world,' I have sought only Thy behest by which Thou didst make Me manifest and raise Me up."[19]

Bahá'u'lláh affirms, in yet another Tablet: "Say: Do ye cavil at Him Who hath come unto you bearing the clear evidence of God and His proof, the testimony of God and His signs? These things are not from Himself; nay, rather they proceed from the One Who hath raised Him up, sent Him forth through the power of truth, and made Him to be a lamp unto all mankind."[20]

In one of His Writings, Bahá'u'lláh also states:

> O thou who art sunk in the sea of evil suggestions! Know thou that thy repudiation and denial return not to Me, but to God, My Lord, thy Lord, and the Lord of our forefathers. For, verily, I am a Servant Who hath believed in Him and in His Messengers and His chosen Ones. I find Myself to be altogether nothing for He hath called Me forth with the power of truth and sent Me unto all mankind. Shouldst thou wish to raise objections, go thou unto Him and say: "Wherefore didst Thou send down Him Who hath caused mine essence and the realities of the infidels to tremble?"[21]

In yet another Tablet, Bahá'u'lláh elucidates: "Were they to ask: 'Why doth He reveal verses?' I am not He Who is their Author, but Thou didst and dost reveal them as Thou pleasest, even as Thou didst reveal them before Me unto Thy Messengers and chosen Ones."[22]

Likening Himself to a man who was asleep, Bahá'u'lláh specifies in His Writings that He was lying asleep on His bed when the breezes of Divine Revelation were wafted over Him, wakened Him, and bade Him arise and voice His call to all that are in heaven and on earth. At times, Bahá'u'lláh stresses this argument by calling God to witness, that it may be made clear that without a Divine decree directing Him to break His silence and endowing Him with speech, He would not have revealed Himself. Rather, He would have remained silent like other people and would have been spared from the claws and fangs of the ravening wolves that have set upon Him. But now that He has arisen at the command of God, torn the veil of the people's heedlessness, raised His call, and spread His Message, He does not relent, nor submit to the people's desires—even under the threat of the sword.

In this regard, Bahá'u'lláh writes:

I was asleep upon My couch, when lo, the breezes of My Lord, the All-Merciful, passed over Me, awoke Me from My slumber, and bade Me lift up My voice betwixt earth and heaven. This thing is not from Me, but from God. Unto this testify the dwellers of His Dominion and of His Kingdom, and the inhabitants of the cities of His unfading glory.[23]

This theme also appears in another Tablet of Bahá'u'lláh:

By God! Verily I was asleep, when lo! the breezes of Revelation bestirred Me. I was silent, and thy Lord, the Almighty, the All-Powerful, caused Me to speak forth. Were it not for His behest I would not have revealed Myself. Verily His Will prevailed over My will and raised Me up to establish a Cause which hath made Me the target of the darts of the infidels. Read what We have revealed to the kings that thou mayest be assured that this Servant speaketh as bidden by the All-Knowing, the All-Informed.[24]

In yet another Tablet, Bahá'u'lláh affirms: "O King! I was but a man like others, asleep upon My couch, when lo, the breezes of the All-Glorious were wafted over Me, and taught Me the knowledge of all that hath been. This thing is not from Me, but from One Who is Almighty and All-Knowing."[25]

In another Tablet, Bahá'u'lláh addresses the people of the Bayán:

> Say: O people of the Bayán! Kill me not with the swords of aversion. By God! I was asleep, when lo, the hand of the will of your Lord, the All-Merciful, awoke me and bade Me lift up My voice between earth and heaven. This thing is not from Me, could ye but comprehend. If another soul were to be found who would proclaim and stand firm in the Cause, He would not have raised Me up, caused Me to utter any word, or made Me manifest among these people. Unto this beareth witness the Book whose verses have been inscribed by the Pen of God, the Lord of all that hath been and shall be.[26]

Here Bahá'u'lláh asserts that Divine revelation is not reserved for Him alone, insofar as the Holy Spirit has an essentially equal relationship to every human being. But when It finds one of the members of the human race serving and worthy of receiving the Holy Spirit, It illumines that soul with the light of Its revelation. He then specifies: "The Unconstrained seized the reins of volition from My grasp, raised Me up as He ordained, and caused Me to speak in accordance with His good pleasure."[27] He further reiterates this point:

> Say: O people of the Bayán! Had it been in My power, I would not have consented to reveal Myself amongst the people. Fear ye God and refrain from rising up against Him Who is come invested with that which ye possess of the testimonies of the Messengers. I was seated, when lo, your Lord, the Almighty, the Most Powerful, raised Me up. I was silent, when His mighty and unassailable command caused Me to speak. I was asleep, when lo, He awakened Me and rained down upon Me verses whose number no man of understanding can appraise. Say: Peruse that which hath been sent down by the Most Sublime Pen and that which ye possess; then be fair and be not of the transgressors. I plead

My grief and My sorrow to God: Pour out patience upon Me, O My Lord, and render Me victorious over the people of tyranny.[28]

Bahá'u'lláh has similarly written in another Tablet:

He is the Ever-Abiding, the All-Knowing, the All-Wise. Blessed is He Who raised Me up to proclaim this Revelation when I was seated, caused Me to speak His praise when I was silent, and manifested Me despite My concealing Myself. We testify that He, verily, is powerful to do what He willeth and He is the Help in Peril, the Self-Subsisting.[29]

Addressing one of the princes of Persia, Bahá'u'lláh states:

He is the All-Knowing, the All-Informed. O Prince! Thy Highness didst see Me in the past when I was but a man like others. Wert thou to visit in this day, thou wouldst see Me shining forth with a light whose Revealer no man discerneth and ablaze with a fire whose Enkindler none distinguisheth. This Wronged One, however, knoweth and comprehendeth, proclaiming: "The Hand of the Will of God, the Lord of all worlds, hath revealed this light and the Hand of Power hath kindled this fire the flame of which crieth out: 'By God! The promise is fulfilled and the Speaker on Sinai speaketh in the Burning Bush, and yet the people, for the most part, are heedless.'"[30]

He continues to addresses this Prince, Farhád Mírzá, the Mu'tamidu'd-Dawlih:

O Prince! I had concealed My Cause, when lo, My Lord manifested Me. I was asleep, when the Breeze of God wafting over Me roused Me from My slumber. No sooner had I raised My head than I heard these words from every direction: "O Thou Who speakest in the Burning Bush! Blessed is the spot that is ennobled by Thy footsteps, the soul who hath attained Thy call, and the face that hath turned towards Thee. Arise, and say: 'O peoples of the earth! My thoughts are not your thoughts, nor do I walk in your ways. Call ye to mind that which ye were promised in the verses that were revealed aforetime[31] and in My manifest Book.'" Thereupon I arose and uttered that whereunto I was bidden. This thing is not from Me, but from One Who is the Almighty, the All-Powerful.[32]

I have cited many passages on this theme so that in Bahá'u'lláh's own words the relationship between Him and the Divine Essence can be made clear and it will be appreciated that the views expressed in this essay are substantiated by Bahá'u'lláh's Writings.

In yet another Tablet, Bahá'u'lláh writes:

O people! I was asleep in My home, withholding My tongue from extolling His virtues, when lo, the breezes of God passed over Me, and quickened Me with the truth, and caused Me to speak His praise, and made Me His guidance and monition unto all mankind. Every time I choose to hold My peace, lo, the Holy Spirit, through the power of truth, causeth Me to speak forth, and the Most Great Spirit stirreth Me up, and the Immortal Spirit moveth the Pen of Bahá, could ye but know it. O people! Fear ye God, and be abashed before His Beauty, and speak not that for which ye shall be accursed of all the atoms of the earth and beyond them the Tongue of God, the King, the Truthful, the Faithful. This thing is not from Me, but from Him, did ye but perceive it. By God! Had it been in My power, I would have concealed Myself from your eyes and not have surrendered My heart to the clutches of the wolves of the earth. To the truth of My words God Himself doth bear witness.[33]

By this passage, Bahá'u'lláh means that He is entrusted with a mission by God and cannot transgress His divinely prescribed mission. He utters in a prayer: "Thou didst, O My God, waken Me by Thy grace, and raise Me up to occupy Thy throne, and cause Me to speak forth Thy praise, and command Me to rend asunder the veils."[34] He further states in this prayer:

Thou knowest, O My God, that had it been in My power, I would not have consented to reveal Myself amongst men, nor would I have allowed one word to fall from My lips before them. Every time I desired to conceal Myself from the wolves of the earth, Thou didst make Me manifest by Thy power and Thy sovereignty, and every time I desired to retire and live in seclusion, Thou didst purpose for Me to be revealed and made manifest. Thy desire prevailed over My desire and Thy will overruled My will till at last Thou didst raise Me up to occupy Thy seat and cause Me to cry out amidst Thy creatures.[35]

In one of His Tablets, Bahá'u'lláh addresses His pen in the following words: "O My pen! Bewail My plight and the things that have befallen Me at the hands of the rebellious among My creatures, and say: 'O God, My God! I was asleep, Thou didst awaken Me, and raise Me up, and cause Me to speak, and didst then abandon Me in the clutches of hatred.'"[36] To be sure, notwithstanding Bahá'u'lláh's earnest and sincere description of the circumstances, in order to ensure that no one would venture to presume that He is complaining about the clutches of the ill-intentioned and the malicious, He immediately asserts: "O Thou the Object of My heart's desire! Were the powers of the whole earth to gather together to harm Bahá, His tongue would never cease to utter Thy glorification and praise, nor hesitate for less than the twinkling of an eye to proclaim amidst Thy people that which Thou hast enjoined upon Him."[37]

A point which merits reflection is that, when describing the manner in which pilgrims are to present themselves before Him, Bahá'u'lláh emphatically forbids the people from bowing down before Him, falling at His feet, kissing His hands, or prostrating before Him when entering His presence. Bahá'u'lláh avers that these principles should govern His followers' behavior and pilgrimage and instructs them to exemplify a spirit of joy and radiance when attaining to His presence and to present themselves before Him with a bearing befitting the noble station of a human being. Bahá'u'lláh stresses that no one is allowed to abase himself before another, prohibits the kissing of hands as well as prostration and bowing down before any human being, and asserts that one may prostrate oneself only before God, the Invisible. In other words, prostration is permissible only during prayer, when one's attention is directed towards God. Otherwise, one must never throw oneself to the ground and prostrate before a visible being. One who bows down before a visible being must repent, because bowing down is permissible only before the Invisible Essence.

Notwithstanding all the emphases and provisions in the Writings of Bahá'u'lláh in relation to confessing the oneness, transcendence, and sanctity of the Invisible Essence of God, how strange that some should attribute Divinity to Bahá'u'lláh! How unfair! Bahá'u'lláh asserts conclusively and emphatically that one must not even bow to Him when attaining to His presence because one can only bow before the One Invisible God. Can a claim to Divinity be attributed to the Author of such words? Bahá'u'lláh's own words in this regard are cited below so that, when considering and studying this question, the matter will be made abundantly clear. Bahá'u'lláh writes:

> Whoso seeketh to attain unto the ultimate Purpose and the presence of the Lord of creation must needs follow that which the Pen of the Most High hath enjoined upon him, as bidden by Him Who is the Almighty, the All-Knowing. He, verily, hath forbidden you from bowing down and falling at My feet or the feet of others. This is that which hath been revealed in the Book, as bidden by Him Who is the All-Knowing, the All-Wise. Say: O ye beloved of the All-Merciful! If ye desire to meet Me, it is incumbent upon you to present yourselves in a spirit of joy and radiance according to such manners as are seemly adornings unto the temple of man. Fear ye God and be not of the heedless. He, verily, ordaineth as He pleaseth and enjoineth that which shall guide the people unto this Most Great Light before Which, as soon as It appeared, the Faithful Spirit bowed down in worship.
>
> Kiss not anyone's hands, nor bow down when entering anyone's presence. He, verily, enjoineth upon you what is right. He is the Ordainer, the Answerer of prayers. To none is given the right to abase himself before another. Such is the command of God when He, with manifest sovereignty, established Himself upon the throne. Ye have been forbidden

to commit that which We have mentioned here. Take ye hold of the precepts of God and His command and follow not the ways of the ignorant. Whoso attaineth My presence will be regarded by God, the Lord of this glorious habitation, as one of them that have been privileged to behold His Face, and whoso gaineth admittance is numbered with them that have attained unto that which hath been recorded in the Books of God.

Kissing of hands, prostration, falling to the ground, and bowing down have been forbidden unto you. Thus have We set forth Our verses and sent them down as a token of Our grace. I am, verily, the All-Bountiful, the Ancient of Days. Prostration is befitting only before Him Who is the Unknowable, the Unseen. He who is seen is, verily, of them unto whom hath testified the Manifest Book: It is not for anyone to fall prostrate before him. Should one prostrate himself, it behoveth him to return and repent unto God. He is, in truth, the Ever-Forgiving, the Merciful. It hath incontrovertibly been made evident that prostration is befitting before none save the Unseen Lord. Ponder this in your hearts, O people of the earth, and be not of such as have turned aside.[38]

In short, in the above passages, Bahá'u'lláh explicitly prohibits bowing down, falling to the ground, prostration, and the kissing of hands, and regards prostration as befitting only before the Threshold of an Essence Which is Unknown and Unseen—that is, the Divine Essence.

Some people of malice allege that Bahá'ís prostrate themselves before the Shrine of Bahá'u'lláh, whereas prostration before Bahá'u'lláh is permitted to no one according to the above passages. Although our Qiblih is outwardly the Holy Shrine of Bahá'u'lláh, in truth we face this Point of Adoration as a means of directing our attention towards God. God is free from habitation and direction, yet we must inevitably turn towards a direction—one that occupies the most noble, the most precious, and the most exalted station of existence in the world of being. This direction is the location of the Manifestation of God.

In the foregoing passages quoted from the Writings of Bahá'u'lláh, it is explicitly demonstrated that He has sought no station except servitude to the Divine Essence; He has insisted that He be recognized as the servant of God, the Glory of God, and a Messenger of God; He has emphasized that His Cause be regarded not as His own, but as the Cause of God, and His Will as the Will of God; and He has stressed that no one should prostrate himself, bow down, or fall to the ground before Him. When Bahá'u'lláh sees or hears that notwithstanding all these emphases some accuse Him of denying the Invisible Essence of God, He regards this accusation as the greatest tyranny and cruelty towards Himself and laments this injustice.

Concerning the words of these unfair individuals, Bahá'u'lláh writes in a Tablet: "And amongst the people are those who claim that He hath disbelieved in God—yet every member of My body testifieth that there is none other God but Him; that those Whom He hath raised up in truth and sent forth with His guidance are the Manifestations of His most excellent names, the Revealers of His most exalted attributes . . . ."[39]

He writes in another Tablet:

> Amongst the faithless are those who claim that He hath denied the Invisible Essence. Say: silence thy tongue, O thou who hast joined partners with God! The Invisible Essence doth verily speak forth with this most wondrous, this incomparable tongue. All the atoms of the earth testify that there is none other God but Him and He Who now speaketh is, in truth, the Manifestation of His Essence, the Dawning-Place of His signs, the Dayspring of His Revelation, and the Fountainhead of His Cause amidst all peoples.[40]

He states in yet another Tablet:

> Amongst the people are those who claim that He hath denied the Invisible Essence. Say: woe betide thee, O thou embodiment of tyranny! He, in truth, hath offered up His life, and His soul, and all His possessions, that He might vindicate the truth of the Invisible Essence; and yet behold how ye reject Him in your habitations, though ye perceive it not. Verily, He hath been made to dwell within the most

desolate of cities in the path of the Invisible Essence; and yet ye dwell in palaces, though ye recognize it not.[41]

In His Writings, Bahá'u'lláh describes His state by likening Himself to a leaf that finds itself at the mercy of onrushing winds, compelled to move at their bidding. He writes:

> This is but a leaf which the winds of the will of thy Lord, the Almighty, the All-Praised, have stirred. Can it be still when the tempestuous winds are blowing? Nay, by Him Who is the Lord of all Names and Attributes! They move it as they list. The evanescent is as nothing before Him Who is the Ever-Abiding. His all-compelling summons hath reached Me, and caused Me to speak His praise amidst all people.[42]

He also states: "By My life! Not of Mine own volition have I revealed Myself, but God, of His own choosing, hath manifested Me."[43]

He asserts in yet another Tablet:

> Thinkest thou that I speak as Mine own soul prompteth or that I subsist through Mine own being? Nay, by Him Who is the Lord of all worlds! The winds of His will stir Me as He ordaineth, in accordance with His good pleasure. Every understanding heart will perceive through My stirring the motive force of God, the Sovereign, the All-Powerful, the All-Subduing, the Almighty. Canst thou remain still by thine own will when an ague which causeth every limb of thy body to tremble holdeth sway over thee? Nay, by Him Who hath created thee by the power of truth, wert thou of them that perceive. Even as it stirreth thee and transcendeth thy capacity to be still, so do the winds of the will of God stir Me in like manner. And if it be thy wish to dispute, then dispute with Him. Verily, I am but a Servant Who repaireth unto Him and I find for Myself no rest, nor stillness, nor any motion save at His behest. None can deny it unless he be a malevolent transgressor and sinner.[44]

A similar theme is found in a prayer revealed by Bahá'u'lláh:

> Every time I hold my peace, and cease to extol Thy wondrous virtues, Thy Spirit impelleth me to cry out before all who are in Thy heaven and on Thy earth; and every time I am still, the breaths wafted from the right hand of Thy will and purpose pass over me, and stir me up, and I find myself to be as a leaf which lieth at the mercy of the winds of Thy decree, and is carried away whithersoever Thou dost permit or command it. Every man of insight who considereth what hath been revealed by me, will be persuaded that Thy Cause is not in my hands, but in Thy hands, and will recognize that the reins of power are held not in my grasp but in Thy grasp, and are subject to Thy sovereign might.[45]

These passages have their counterparts in numerous Writings of Bahá'u'lláh, but we limit ourselves to the few examples cited above. This selection would suffice those who are endued with insight and discernment to recognize the truth that the invisible and inaccessible Essence of God is entirely distinct from the physical body of Bahá'u'lláh which was chosen as the place of manifestation of a divine revelation.

We close this discussion with the following prayer of Bahá'u'lláh:

> I am well aware, O my Lord, that I have been so carried away by the clear tokens of Thy loving-kindness, and so completely inebriated with the wine of Thine utterance, that whatever I behold I readily discover that it maketh Thee known unto me, and it remindeth me of Thy signs, and of Thy tokens, and of Thy testimonies. By Thy glory! Every time I lift up mine eyes unto Thy heaven, I call to mind Thy highness and Thy loftiness, and Thine incomparable glory and greatness; and every time I turn my gaze to Thine earth, I am made to recognize the evidences of Thy power and the tokens of Thy bounty. And when I behold the sea, I find that it speaketh to me of Thy majesty, and of the potency of Thy might, and of Thy sovereignty and Thy grandeur. And at whatever time I contemplate the mountains, I am led

to discover the ensigns of Thy victory and the standards of Thine omnipotence.

I swear by Thy might, O Thou in Whose grasp are the reins of all mankind, and the destinies of the nations! I am so inflamed by my love for Thee, and so inebriated with the wine of Thy oneness, that I can hear from the whisper of the winds the sound of Thy glorification and praise, and can recognize in the murmur of the waters the voice that proclaimeth Thy virtues and Thine attributes, and can apprehend from the rustling of the leaves the mysteries that have been irrevocably ordained by Thee in Thy realm.[46]

NOTES TO CHAPTER THREE, PART ONE

1 Bahá'u'lláh, *Prayers and Meditations by Bahá'u'lláh* ch. CLXXXIII, Bahá'í Reference Library, www.bahai.org/r/693883235.
2 Ibid.
3 Ibid., ch. CLXII, Bahá'í Reference Library www.bahai. org/r/170377886.
4 Bahá'u'lláh, *Áthár-i-Qalam-i-A'lá*, volume 2 (Hamilton: Association for Bahá'í Studies in Persian, 2002), 34; provisional translation.
5 Bahá'u'lláh, *Gleanings from the Writings of Bahá'u'lláh* ch. CXVI, Bahá'í Reference Library, www.bahai.org/r/786607255), .
6 Ibid., ch. LXV, Bahá'í Reference Library www.bahai.org/r/594333508.
7 Bahá'u'lláh, *Epistle to the Son of the Wolf*, Bahá'í Reference Library wwww.bahai.org/r/253750144.
8 Bahá'u'lláh, *Majmú'iy-i-Alváh-i-Mubárakih*, (Cairo: Maṭba'atu's-Sa'ádah, 1920), 219; provisional translation.
9 Bahá'u'lláh, *Ad'íyiy-i-Ḥaḍrat-i-Maḥbúb*, (Bundoora: Century Press Publications, 2004), 269; provisional translation.
10 Ibid., 274–275; provisional translation.
11 Bahá'u'lláh, Iranian National Bahá'í Archives, volume 36 (n.p.: n.p., 1976), 115; provisional translation.
12 Bahá'u'lláh, "Súriy-i-'Ibád," in *Áthár-i-Qalam-i-A'lá*, volume 4 ([Ṭihrán]: Lajniy-i-Millíy-i-Intishárát va Muṭáli'át, 1976/77), 24; provisional translation.
13 Bahá'u'lláh, *The Summons of the Lord of Hosts*, Bahá'í Reference Library www.bahai.org/r/653697684.
14 'Alí-Murád Dávúdí, *Rahá'í* (Hofheim: Bahá'í-Verlag, 2010), Vahid Rafati, ed., 169; provisional translation.
15 Bahá'u'lláh, *Epistle to the Son of the Wolf*, Bahá'í Reference Library www.bahai.org/r/992766841.

16   Bahá'u'lláh, "Tablet to Náṣiri'd-Dín Sháh," in *The Summons of the Lord of Hosts*, Bahá'í Reference Library, www.bahai.org/r/159246174.
17   Bahá'u'lláh, *Kitáb-i-Badí'* (Hofheim: Bahá'í-Verlag, 2008), 142; provisional translation.
18   Ibid., 159; provisional translation.
19   Bahá'u'lláh, *Majmú'iy-i-Alváḥ-i-Mubárakih*, (Cairo: Maṭba'atu's-Sa'ádah, 1920), 228; provisional translation.
20   Bahá'u'lláh, "Tablet to Napoleon III," in *The Summons of the Lord of Hosts*, Bahá'í Reference Library, www.bahai.org/r/157306287.
21   Bahá'u'lláh, *Kitáb-i-Badí'*, 69–70; provisional translation.
22   Bahá'u'lláh, *Ad'íyiy-i-Ḥaḍrat-i-Maḥbúb*, (Bundoora: Century Press Publications, 2004), 25–26; provisional translation.
23   Bahá'u'lláh, "Tablet to Náṣiri'd-Dín Sháh," in *The Summons of the Lord of Hosts*, Bahá'í Reference Library, www.bahai.org/r/159246174.
24   Bahá'u'lláh, provisional translation qtd. in Nader Saiedi, *Logos and Civilization: Spirit, History, and Order in the Writings of Bahá'u'lláh* (Bethesda: University Press of Maryland, 2000), 35.
25   Bahá'u'lláh, "Tablet to Náṣiri'd-Dín Sháh," in *The Summons of the Lord of Hosts*, Bahá'í Reference Library, www.bahai.org/r/159246174.
26   Bahá'u'lláh, *Áthár-i-Qalam-i-A'lá*, volume 2, 53–54; provisional translation.
27   Ibid., 54; provisional translation.
28   Ibid., 56–57; provisional translation.
29   Ibid., 179; provisional translation.
30   Bahá'u'lláh, *Ishráqát va Chand Lawḥ-i-Dígar*, 143–144, Bahá'í Reference Library reference.bahai.org/fa/t/b/I/i-143.html); provisional translation.
31   See Isaiah 55:8.
32   Bahá'u'lláh, *Ishráqát va Chand Lawḥ-i-Dígar* 144, Bahá'í Reference Library reference.bahai.org/fa/t/b/I/i-144.html); provisional translation.
33   Bahá'u'lláh, *Kitáb-i-Badí'*, 63; provisional translation.
34   Bahá'u'lláh, *Ad'íyiy-i-Ḥaḍrat-i-Maḥbúb*, (Bundoora: Century Press Publications, 2004), 16; provisional translation.
35   Ibid., 26; provisional translation.
36   Bahá'u'lláh, *Áthár-i-Qalam-i-A'lá*, volume 2, 68; provisional translation.
37   Ibid.; provisional translation.
38   Ibid., 7–78; provisional translation.
39   Bahá'u'lláh, "Tablet to Náṣiri'd-Dín Sháh," in *The Summons of the Lord of Hosts*, Bahá'í Reference Library, www.bahai.org/r/159246174.
40   Bahá'u'lláh, *Áthár-i-Qalam-i-A'lá*, volume 1 (Dundas: Mu'assisiy-i-Ma'árif-i-Bahá'í, 1996), 99; provisional translation.
41   Ibid., 5:3; provisional translation.

42   Bahá'u'lláh, "Tablet to Náṣiri'd-Dín Sháh," in *The Summons of the Lord of Hosts*, Bahá'í Reference Library, www.bahai.org/r/159246174.

43   Ibid.

44   Bahá'u'lláh, *Kitáb-i-Badí'*, 70; provisional translation.

45   Bahá'u'lláh, *Prayers and Meditations by Bahá'u'lláh*, ch. CLXXIX, Bahá'í Reference Library, www.bahai.org/r/639614090.

46   Ibid., no. CLXXVI, Bahá'í Reference Library, www.bahai.org/r/129964059.

Chapter 3

Confessing the Sanctity of the Divine Essence

Translated by Vargha Bolodo-Taefi

Part Two

It is clear from a study of the Writings of Bahá'u'lláh that He refers to Himself as having been made manifest by God, as the servant of God, the son of the servant of God, and the Glory of God. He confesses that He has no will in the face of the Will of God. He explicitly declares that He only desires what God desires; He reveals nothing of His own accord; He is at all times like a corpse in the embalmer's hands and a leaf before onrushing winds; and what proceeds from His tongue is what God decrees. He emphasizes these themes to such an extent that to attribute to Him a claim to Divinity would evidently be a false accusation.

In this discussion, the tenets of the Bahá'í belief in God—as an invisible, inaccessible, and unknowable Essence—are explored in order to demonstrate how we regard Bahá'u'lláh and what station we attribute to Him.

One of the themes that is emphasized extensively in the writings of the Bahá'í Faith is the principle of confessing the sanctity of God. According to the Writings of Bahá'u'lláh and 'Abdu'l-Bahá, God is inaccessibly exalted and ineffably transcendent. In other words, God is sanctified from all association, tie of direct intercourse, likeness, or kinship. In a sense, it is evident that He is beyond the reach and ken of His creation and above any claim by any creature to the possibility of reunion with Him. Nor can anyone profess nearness to Him such as would entail His appearance in the visible plane.

God is absolute oneness; He is not God if He is not one. Accordingly, to confess His oneness is a prerequisite of faith. This is because we can believe in God only inasmuch as we can accept a unity beyond plurality—a unity that expounds and reconciles the plurality. We can think of God as the point where all beings relinquish their attributes of diversity and plurality and return to their original unity and oneness. Our reason is in need of accepting, and tending towards, such a point; it is inclined to accept such a unity. Therefore, it recognizes God and believes in Him. By "recognizing" God we mean discerning His existence; otherwise, it is impossible to know God befittingly. Consequently, monotheism is prerequisite to recognition of God, in the sense that one who does not recognize God's oneness does not, in fact, recognize Him.

Monotheism—that is, confessing God's oneness—requires that we extend no form of plurality to God and attribute no division to His Essence. The reason for this is that any form of plurality and division is tantamount to multiplicity, and multiplicity runs counter to oneness. A true believer in the unity of God cannot accept that God has attributes, inasmuch as every attribute has a meaning which is distinct from the meaning of another attribute. When we characterize God as possessing some attributes, therefore, we ascribe to Him attributes that are different from each other and extend plurality to Him. This plurality of attributes is contrary to confessing God's unity and singleness, which is the prerequisite of believing in God. It also follows that no names or attributes can be ascribed to God, because with every name by which we call God we convey an attribute. As a result, neither attributes nor names are worthy of God. God possesses neither any attribute nor any name. In order to avoid the plurality of names and attributes, we might propose that all names and attributes are only one in relation to the Divine Essence. Many philosophers submitted to this view, defined all attributes in relation to God as "knowledge," and stipulated that God's only attribute is knowledge. According to this view, then, we should consider whether this attribute is distinct from the Essence of God, is an accident predicated upon the Essence of God, or is identical with the Essence of God. Some may consider the attribute to be distinct from the Essence of God, just as the attributes are distinct from the essence in all creatures. For instance, any attribute that I ascribe to myself is distinct from my essence, because the attribute is predicated upon the essence as an accidental property which is not identical with it. For this reason, the distinction between the attribute and the Essence leads to multiplicity. Therefore, not even a single attribute can be ascribed to God unless that attribute is understood to be identical with His Essence.

All that remains, then, is the Essence of God, as it is mentioned in an Islamic tradition: "God was alone; there was none else besides Him."[1] Since the verb "was" (*kána*) in this sentence is modal, rather than temporal, this statement conveys that God is ever alone and there is nothing else besides Him.[2] This signifies that the incomparable Essence of God has neither any attributes nor any names. To be sure, some understand this tradition to indicate that once upon a time God existed with no creation and none else besides Him. We, however, do not understand this tradition in this manner, but rather believe that God has ever been and will forever be, and that there never was, nor will there ever be, anything else besides Him. He is an inaccessible and unknowable Essence with neither any attribute, nor any name, nor anything else that can extend multiplicity to His Essence.

So it is that confessing God's oneness requires that we ascribe to Him no name, attribute, or quality. On the other hand, we must also admit that there is no direct tie of association or relationship between God and other beings. If in any respect we associate God with another being, we thereby create a relationship and, in so doing, we relegate God from His non-delimitation to the realm of delimitation and impair the absolute non-delimitation of His Essence. Insofar as created beings are diverse and plural, were every being to find a path to God and form an association or relationship with His Essence, plurality would characterize the Essence of God, this plurality would lead to division, and with division God's Divinity would be contradicted.

Bahá'u'lláh states that no tie of association binds God to His creation, no relationship can be formed with God, no direction can be taken to turn towards God, and no connection can be created with the Divine Essence. Such matters are entirely among the properties and exigencies of the contingent world and inconsistent with the reality of the invisible world of God. One of these associations and relationships, which some believe can be established between created beings and God, is knowing or understanding

God. However, since God has no attribute, name, direction, or association, it is not possible to know Him, inasmuch as to know is, by definition, to establish an association or a relation between the knower and the object of knowledge. Were we even to consider knowledge not in its philosophical sense, but as a specific category, still we could not regard God as "known" by created beings and maintain that His creatures know Him.

'Abdu'l-Bahá's utterances that interpret the Writings of Bahá'u'lláh and the Báb are replete with statements in this regard. In one such statement, for example, 'Abdu'l-Bahá asserts that we cannot know the reality of anything, because so long as a thing is distinct from the knower, it is impossible to know it through its essential reality and inherent nature; and once it becomes one with the knower and the separation is eliminated, the knower no longer exists as a separate entity in order even to lay a claim to knowledge. This is because the knower is, in fact, transformed into that thing. However, if this transformation does not take place and the knower is not transformed into that thing, that thing is so separate from the knower that the separation prevents the knower from knowing it, and its essential reality and inmost being remains unknowable.[3]

There are also other reasons why the Essence of God cannot be known; for instance, no inferior being can comprehend a superior being. Plants cannot be expected to comprehend animals, nor can animals comprehend the human aspect of human beings. Animals can see human beings through their animal senses; nevertheless, human beings, in the sense of their human characteristics, are beyond the comprehension of animals. Human beings, likewise, cannot comprehend the Being Who is superior to them—the Essence of God. This is not the occasion to elaborate on this statement and to demonstrate its truth. Since on this occasion only the beliefs of the Bahá'ís concerning the station of Bahá'u'lláh are being conveyed, for now there is no need to prove the truth of this statement.

Moreover, God is infinite and unlimited. Unless an object of our knowledge is encompassed within the bounds of the mind, we cannot comprehend it; and if it is encompassed within the bounds of the mind, then it cannot be the non-delimited Essence. Rather, it will be a finite being that is limited within the bounds of the human mind, not the infinite and invisible Essence of God.

Accordingly, neither do we attempt to contain God within our minds, nor does God fit within the human mind. That is to say, God cannot be known by us; otherwise, if He were to fit within our minds and be comprehended, that very fitting would be tantamount to being limited, and a god that can be limited cannot be God. Consequently, those who believe that they know God in fact know a thing that they have contained within their minds, a thing that can no longer be God. They have contrived and invented, and then known, a god that is not God. In this relation, Bahá'u'lláh and 'Abdu'l-Bahá stress that there is no difference between this form of worshipping God and idolatry. Idolaters shape and mold their idols with their own hands, and then know and worship them. Those who worship God in this way similarly fashion a god in their imagination and then worship it. Inasmuch as that object of worship is contained within their minds, or rather their imaginations, in that very containment it becomes confined to limits and ceases to be God.

It is, therefore, one of the axiomatic beliefs of the Bahá'ís that the Essence of God cannot be known. Since God cannot be known, the question of how the commandment to worship God is to be understood and practiced arises. Clearly, confessing the existence of God is an undisputable requirement of our belief. To be sure, the aspects of this question that pertain to reason and faith merit a separate examination. In the current exploration, however, we should address the following question: Given that on the one hand we confess the existence of God, yet on the other hand we cannot know Him, what, then, is our duty?

An analogy can facilitate our investigation of this question. Imagine that you have no access to an individual in order to know her, owing to her existence in a time or place distant from yours. For instance, she lived some centuries ago and has now passed away; or she is alive but lives far from you and you have no access to her. In these scenarios and under these circumstances, your direct path to knowing that individual is barred. But other paths to knowledge are open; they include knowing her through her works, creations, and whatever other fruits of her existence are available to you.

For example, the individual in question might be a painter who is out of your reach but whose paintings you can access. By examining these paintings, reflecting on their characteristics, and contemplating their features, you can come to know their painter to some extent. There can be no doubt that in these situations the essence and the innermost reality of the painter cannot be known, but the closest objects to the painter, her noblest creations, are accessible to you and can be known. This knowledge, at this level, is the highest limit of the knowledge of the painter that you can possibly achieve.

Similarly, the person who is the object of your knowledge might be a poet who is beyond your reach: you cannot see him, converse with him, hear his voice, or get to know him in person. But an alternative path to knowing him is to study his poems and works of literature that he has left behind or that are within your reach. These writings, stories, epics, and poems are means by which to understand him. You peruse his works, reflect upon them, memorize them, and through these means form an understanding of the poet's personality and identity. In this way, that which replaces knowing the poet is that which is closest to him and, at the same time, available to you. For otherwise how can one travel to the time of Firdawsí, or bring him to the present time, to know him? How is it possible to journey to the time of Homer and gain an understanding of his state and condition? Although Firdawsí and Homer are beyond our reach, yet the _Sháhnámih_ and the _Iliad_ are available and make it possible to know those personalities. We grow familiar with these works, we experience joy and excitement when we read the _Sháhnámih_, and by contemplating and reflecting on it we discover the identity of Firdawsí to the extent possible. This is because the _Sháhnámih_ is the closest thing to Firdawsí's character, inmost reality, and essence, and is, at the same time, something that is accessible to us and that provides us with the means of knowing him. Since the person of Firdawsí is not within our reach, we inhale his fragrance in the _Sháhnámih_, which is to him as the scent is to the flower.

In considering these matters, a point that must be borne in mind is that the means of knowledge are subject to proximity and remoteness. For instance, in one sense, the final painting of a painter could represent the closest means of attaining to a more complete knowledge of him, insofar as it manifests his artistic perfections more evidently. Our attention, therefore, is drawn to it as it portrays the painter's work, intuition, and creativity more fully. Naturally, the painter's other works that are further away from the pinnacle of his artistic performance can also represent him, although they are less perfect and more distant.

We shall not expatiate further on this analogy, but return now to our exploration of God's Divinity. The entire world of existence is the work of God. The whole creation is a poem composed by God and a handiwork fashioned by Him. Therefore, although we have no access to the Essence of God, yet His composition and handiwork are within our reach. Of course, as mentioned earlier, there is a difference in station between God's creatures. In other words, one of God's handiworks and creations expresses His reality more fully than the others. When we observe the differences of degree in creation, we notice that the human being is the most perfect and the noblest of God's creations. And among human beings, Those singled out as the Manifestations of the Cause of God and specially favored with the divine revelation are the noblest, the most exalted, and the most perfect creation of God. Even among the Manifestations of God—and as expressed in the Qur'ánic verse "Some of the Apostles We have caused to excel the others"[4]—the One occupying the highest station among Them is the latest Manifestation of God in every prophetic cycle, Who, owing to the progressive development of the world of creation, manifests a greater extent of perfections. This excellence, this distinction, is not His essential property, insofar as all the Messengers of God occupy the same station and are the bearers of the same reality. Instead, the station that the Manifestation of God for this age occupies is more perfect and nobler than the stations of the previous Manifestations of God owing to the comparative excellence of the age in which He has appeared. It is He Who can be recognized in place of God: since God Himself is inaccessible and invisible, God's inner Reality is made manifest and can be seen in the Manifestation of His Cause and recognized in Him Who is the most perfect creation of God.

As specified previously, one reads the *Sháhnámih* and knows it as a representation of Firdawsí. Those who love poetry might in fact admire, even worship, Firdawsí's poetry more than they do Firdawsí's personage. In the same manner, we recognize Bahá'u'lláh, Who is God's most exquisite composition, as a representation of God, and likewise we worship Him, love Him, and turn to Him. Indeed, inasmuch as we unequivocally confess God's sanctity and regard Him as inaccessible, and consider His Essence as occupying the loftiest heights of transcendent sublimity and as being exalted far above the reach and ken of the entire creation, we instead turn to Bahá'u'lláh—Who represents the Godhead and is the Manifestation of His Cause in this age—since Bahá'u'lláh is the noblest being and the most perfect Messenger in this cycle.

This assertion, however, is in relation to the station of the temporal limitations and distinctions of the Manifestations of God, insofar as perfection is relative in the cycles of the Manifestations of God. Nevertheless, each Manifestation of God is the most perfect of all human beings. And since the human species is the most perfect of all created beings, we recognize this most perfect Creation as standing as the representative of God's own Self. We see God as manifest within Him, and since, as mentioned earlier, we have no way of seeing God, we recognize the invisible God in the human temple of His Manifestation. Similarly, since we have no way of worshipping the Divine Essence, we worship God in His Manifestation.

Why do we have no way of worshipping God? Because worship requires certain customs and forms. In worship, one must turn one's face in a specific direction and face a particular location; otherwise, worship has no meaning. Now, what should be this direction and where should be this location of God? Unquestionably, none of the directions that one may choose can be towards God, Who is placeless. God has neither direction, nor location, nor place, as He is beyond direction and place. What, therefore, can be that place to which we direct ourselves in worship? Surely, that place must be the noblest of all locations and directions. What makes it the noblest of all locations and directions? Its association with God's noblest Creation. That is why Mecca was chosen as the Qiblih of the followers of Islam and the Ka'bih has become the place turning towards which is regarded as turning towards God, because that city and that house are associated with the noblest Beings, namely Abraham and Muhammad. They both raised the call of the Oneness of God and hoisted the banner of Divine Unity; for this reason, They are the noblest members of the human race and the noblest of God's creation. The call of God was raised through Their call. So, turning towards that Spot is regarded as turning towards God and allows one to worship Him.

Thus, it can be recognized that on the one hand, we worship God; and on the other hand, since His Essence is beyond our reach, immensely sanctified, utterly invisible, immeasurably exalted, and absolutely transcendent, instead of worshipping His Self, we center our attention on His noblest Creation. Let us now call to mind the unfairness of some skeptics who allege that the Bahá'ís regard Bahá'u'lláh as God since in their Obligatory Prayers they face the place where the Remains of Bahá'u'lláh are laid to rest. They voice such objections because they fail to understand the station and the significance of recognizing God. Our very turning towards the Resting Place of Bahá'u'lláh indicates that God has no place towards which we may turn. Thus, inevitably, the spot we face must be the location of one of God's creatures that is chosen as the point and direction of our turning towards God. When the noblest Creation of God and the noblest Spot associated with this Creation have been chosen as the place turning towards which represents turning towards God, then why should this be perceived as contradicting the Oneness of God? Does facing a house made of brick and mortar mean that we—God forbid—worship stones and mud? If the brick and mortar used in building a house can, instead of God, act as the Qiblih in our worship and adoration, then why would the physical parts and members forming the human temple of the Manifestation of God—which are undeniably nobler than the physical parts of other created things—not be accepted as the focal point of such adoration? How can this belief be said to contradict the Oneness of God? On the contrary, such manner of worship and adoration is in fact the condition, the prerequisite, and the requirement of confessing the Oneness of God. This is because in order to confess God's transcendence we must admit that we cannot face towards Him in any direction or regard Him as having a place. For this reason, Bahá'u'lláh states in the opening paragraph of the Kitáb-i-Aqdas: "The first duty prescribed by God for His servants is the recognition of Him Who is the Dayspring of His Revelation and the Fountain of His laws, Who representeth the Godhead in both the Kingdom of His Cause and the world of creation."[5]

In this passage, the recognition of the Dayspring of God's Revelation and the Fountain of His laws—Who stands in place of God's Self in both the Kingdom of God's Cause[6] and the world of creation—precedes the recognition of the Essence of God. Beyond the Kingdom of God's Cause and the world of creation is the world of God. These three worlds are referred to in the writings of mystics and philosophers, so a detailed explanation is not necessary here.

Why does Bahá'u'lláh assert in the first paragraph of the Kitáb-i-Aqdas that in the Kingdom of God's Cause and in the world of creation the recognition of the Dayspring of the Revelation of God substitutes for the recognition of God? Because in the world of God, He is inaccessible, unknowable, and exalted above all understanding. We cannot gain access to His world, and His transcendence necessarily implies our inability to know Him. Therefore, in the Kingdom of God's command and in the world of creation recognizing the Manifestation of God instead of recognizing God is acceptable. In this way, God is exalted to a station that is sanctified from all relationship, association, and kinship, and whoever claims to have known God is an idolater, because he or she has understood only that which is contained within the confines of his or her thought, reason, understanding, and illusion, and has worshipped this mental creation rather than God. A physical idol is similarly something that one fashions and worships instead of God. But this mode of worshipping God is worse than worshipping idols, because, as explained by 'Abdu'l-Bahá, in idolatry, that which is the subject of comprehension at least has a sensible existence, whereas a god that is fashioned in one's mind exists only in one's fancy and imagination.[7] Therefore, by the recognition of God is meant the recognition of His Manifestation. All the Manifestations of God are equal in rank in this respect, inasmuch as they are one single reality. In relation to us, however, insofar as the cycle of each Manifestation is characterized by a relative perfection manifested in the people of that age, the recognition of the most recent Manifestation of God Who is associated with our age represents the highest limit of the recognition of God that is possible in this age.

I would like to draw your attention now to several verses of the Qur'án. These verses indicate that we shall attain to the Presence of God, that we long to meet our Lord, and that the promised day of this meeting shall come. For instance, Qur'án 13:2 states: "It is God who hath reared the heavens without pillars thou canst behold; then mounted His throne.... He ordereth all things. He maketh His signs clear, that ye may have firm faith in the Presence of your Lord."[8] Qur'án 29:5 similarly says: "To him who hopeth to attain the Presence of God, the set time of God will surely come. And He is the Hearer, the Knower."[9] Qur'án 29:23 further states: "As for those who believe not in the signs of God, or that they shall ever attain His Presence, these of My mercy shall despair, and these doth a grievous chastisement await."[10] The Qur'án is replete with verses such as these, yet, to be sure, God cannot be seen, known, or comprehended. So, inevitably, attainment to the Presence of God must be understood as attainment to the presence of the Manifestation of God when He appears. This is because, as mentioned before, neither can God be lowered to this world for human beings to attain to His Presence here, nor can human beings ascend to a station where they can meet God.

Therefore, meeting God or attaining to His Presence, mentioned in numerous verses of the Qur'án, has a different meaning. On the one hand, the reality of attainment to the Divine Presence is confirmed by the explicit text of the Qur'án and must be accepted. In the Qur'án, God has warned against denying, denouncing, or doubting its truth, as seen in the verse cited above. He has cautioned the people not to hesitate in accepting the truth of these verses, nor to deny them or lose hope of meeting God. On the other hand, the transcendence of God, the powerlessness of the human mind to understand Him, and the difference in stations of existence prevent human beings from attaining to the Presence of God and knowing Him. There is no alternative except to believe that meeting God, or attaining to the Divine Presence, has a specific meaning. And what meaning is there nobler and deeper than meeting God in the highest station of His creation—His Manifestation?

In the time of Christ, in place of meeting God, the people met God in Christ, while they were also promised that they would attain to God's Presence in the Revelation of Muḥammad in a more perfect and nobler meeting. During the cycle of the Qur'án, humanity met God in the beauty of Muḥammad and was simultaneously bidden to expect the Presence of God again at the End of Days and on the Day of Resurrection prophesied in the Qur'án. That is why, on the one hand, we are promised attainment to the Presence of God and, on the other hand, seeing ourselves so distant from the station of God—the realm of Divinity—we consider such attainment impossible.

If by Divine Presence is meant the revelation of God in His own Essence, attainment to this Presence is impossible for any being in the world of creation. But if we understand Divine Presence to be the revelation of God in something other than Himself, then, evidently, the highest form of this revelation is God's revelation in His Manifestations. Bahá'ís confess this principle—that attainment to the presence of the Essence of God, and to the World of God, is impossible. To believe that one can attain to the presence of the Essence of God requires one either to lower God from His station of transcendence, or to elevate oneself to the heights of His glorious Threshold—both of which are incompatible with a belief in the sanctity and transcendence of God. If Divine Presence is to take place in the world of creation, however, it must inevitably be fulfilled in the highest station of the world of creation, that is, in attaining to the presence of the Manifestation of God.

Be that as it may, whether we understand Divine Presence to be a physical event or interpret it as recognizing God and seeking to know Him, these conceptions cannot be fulfilled except in the form of meeting and recognizing the Manifestation of God. Several passages from the Writings of Bahá'u'lláh are provided here for further reflection on this theme. In the Kitáb-i-Íqán, Bahá'u'lláh writes:

> Therefore, whosoever, and in whatever Dispensation, hath recognized and attained unto the presence of these glorious, these resplendent and most excellent Luminaries, hath verily attained unto the "Presence of God" Himself, and entered the city of eternal and immortal life.[11]

He further writes in the Kitáb-i-Íqán:

> Reflect for a while upon the behavior of the companions of the Muhammadan Dispensation. Consider how, through the

reviving breath of Muḥammad, they were cleansed from the defilements of earthly vanities, were delivered from selfish desires, and were detached from all else but Him. Behold how they preceded all the peoples of the earth in attaining unto His holy Presence—the Presence of God Himself. . . .[12]

In another Tablet, He states:

In short, sanctify your inner and outer eyes from all save God that ye may attain unto His beauty in every Revelation and partake of His presence, which is the Presence of God Himself. This is a word of truth which no other word can surpass and which shall never be abrogated.[13]

Bahá'u'lláh also writes in His Tablet to Shaykh Muḥammad-Taqíy-i-Iṣfahání, known as the Epistle to the Son of the Wolf:

In all the Divine Books the promise of the Divine Presence hath been explicitly recorded. By this Presence is meant the Presence of Him Who is the Dayspring of the signs, and the Dawning-Place of the clear tokens, and the Manifestation of the Excellent Names, and the Source of the attributes, of the true God, exalted be His glory. God in His Essence and in His own Self hath ever been unseen, inaccessible, and unknowable. By Presence, therefore, is meant the Presence of the One Who is His Vicegerent amongst men.[14]

According to these passages, insofar as the Divine Essence is invisible, inaccessible, and unknowable, whether we understand attainment to the Divine Presence to be a physical experience in the form of an outward vision or we do not believe in such a physical experience, attainment to the Divine Presence is possible only by attaining to the presence of the Manifestation of God.

Bahá'u'lláh writes in the Kitáb-i-Íqán:

For the highest and most excelling grace bestowed upon men is the grace of "attaining unto the Presence of God" and of His recognition, which has been promised unto all people. This is the utmost degree of grace vouchsafed unto man by the All-Bountiful, the Ancient of Days, and the fullness of His absolute bounty upon His creatures. Of this grace and bounty none of this people hath partaken, neither have they been honored with this most exalted distinction. How numerous are those revealed verses which explicitly bear witness unto this most weighty truth and exalted Theme! And yet they have rejected it, and, after their own desire, misconstrued its meaning. Even as He hath revealed: "As for those who believe not in the signs of God, or that they shall ever meet Him, these of My mercy shall despair, and for them doth a grievous chastisement await." Also He saith: "They who bear in mind that they shall attain unto the Presence of their Lord, and that unto Him shall they return." Also in another instance He saith: "They who held it as certain that they must meet God, said, 'How oft, by God's will, hath a small host vanquished a numerous host!'" In yet another instance He revealeth: "Let him then who hopeth to attain the presence of his Lord work a righteous work." And also He saith: "He ordereth all things. He maketh His signs clear, that ye may have firm faith in attaining the presence of your Lord."

This people have repudiated all these verses, that unmistakably testify to the reality of "attainment unto the Divine Presence." No theme hath been more emphatically asserted in the holy scriptures. Notwithstanding, they have deprived themselves of this lofty and most exalted rank, this supreme and glorious station. [15]

The space of our current exploration is inadequate to accommodate the magnitude of Bahá'u'lláh's extensive explanation that follows these passages. Suffice it to say that our purpose in emphasizing this theme is that we regard Bahá'u'lláh, or any Messenger of God within His own cycle, as the Manifestation of the Inaccessible God; we recognize Him as invested with God's own title; we worship Him, pray to Him, and obey Him in place of God; and we ascribe to Him the names and attributes of God. This is because God has no name or attribute; He is pure, absolute, and uncompounded Essence. Then where do names and attributes find individuation and specification? In the most noble, the most perfect of His creatures, that is, the Holy Spirit—and the dawning-places of the Holy Spirit are the Manifestations of God. That is where God can be known. That is where names and attributes can be ascribed to God. Indeed, names and attributes ascribed to God pertain to His Manifestation.

In light of the foregoing, this—rather than a claim to Divinity—is the intention and the meaning when divine names and attributes are ascribed to Bahá'u'lláh in some of His Writings. Were such attributions to signify a claim to Divinity, then Bahá'u'lláh would not have provided such emphatic, explicit, and cautionary statements concerning the transcendence and the sanctity of the Divine Essence as examined in our previous exploration of this topic. Therefore, where Bahá'u'lláh ascribes to Himself, in some of His Writings, some divine names and attributes, He does so in absolute servitude and evanescence so that the sanctity and the transcendence of the Divine Essence may be preserved. In His view, to confess the sanctity and the oneness of the Divine Essence requires that names and attributes be removed from the Inaccessible and the Unknowable Essence of God and that all names and attributes return to the Manifestation of God.

It bears emphasizing and repeating that where Divine names and attributes are ascribed to Bahá'u'lláh in some of His Writings, these Writings should not be understood as Bahá'u'lláh making a claim to Divinity. They rather indicate that God is inaccessible; He is absolutely transcendent; He is exalted above, and sanctified from, all understanding; we abide by His bidding and He is near us, because we are His creation; yet we are far from Him, because He is not in our station or within the bounds of our perception and understanding. How befittingly has the poet of Shíráz, Sa'dí, expressed this:

> Wonder not, if my Best-Beloved be closer to me than mine own self;
> wonder at this, that I, despite such nearness, should still be so far from Him.
> What am I to do? To whom shall I unburden myself;
> for He is by my side, yet I am far from Him.[16]

Therefore, while God is near to us, we are far from Him since we emanate from Him, and we are separate from Him since we are created by Him. He is the animating source, the origin, and the wellspring of our existence. Thus, the fulfilment of the purpose of our existence is to return to Him, just as we emanate from Him, so that we may be realized in Him. This requires that we recognize the noblest of God's creations, the One closest to Him, and the noblest member of the human race, that is the Manifestation of God. And the noblest Manifestation of God is the most recent Manifestation in every age.

In this manner, on the one hand, God is "the Hidden," which is the station of His absolute transcendence, and, on the other hand, He is "the Seen," that is, He occupies a station to which we have access and can plead. The Qur'án states: "He is the First and the Last; the Seen and the Hidden; and He knoweth all things!"[17] Where is God seen? "The Seen" requires a dawning-place in order to be seen. This dawning-place is His creation, His handiwork. Which creation and handiwork can it be? All of God's creatures and handiworks, in the sense of the Universal Revelation, are this dawning-place; but among them, the perfect dawning-place is humankind; and among the human race, the most perfect are Manifestations of God; and among Them, the most recent Manifestation of God is the most perfect dawning-place of the Revelation of God.

NOTES TO CHAPTER THREE, PART TWO

1   See, for instance, Muḥammad-Báqir al-Majlisí, *Biḥáru'l-Anvár*, vol. 54 (Beirut: Dáru Iḥyá'i't-Turáthi'l-'Arabí, 1983), 198. Translated in *Gleanings from the Writings of Bahá'u'lláh*, chapters XCIII and LXXVIII.

2   The verb "was," like its Arabic equivalent, *kána*, is used in some contexts, particularly in theological discourse, to signify existence or a state of being that transcends temporal constraints without being tied to a specific moment in time.

3   See, for example, *Some Answered Questions*, chapters 37 and 59.

4   Qur'án 17:55; qtd in Bahá'u'lláh, *The Kitáb-i-Íqán*, Bahá'í Reference Library www.bahai.org/r/093854815.

5   Bahá'u'lláh, *The Kitáb-i-Aqdas* ¶1, Bahá'í Reference Library www.bahai.org/r/495703799.

Chapter 3

Confessing the Sanctity of the Divine Essence

Translated by Vargha Bolodo-Taefi

Part Three

In this last part, it would be appropriate to consider several points that complete our exploration of this topic.

One of these points is that in some of His Writings, Bahá'u'lláh utters verses such as "Verily, I am God" or "By God! Naught hath appeared save for My sake and the ocean of utterance hath not surged save through remembrance of Me."[1] Such passages, which appear to suggest a claim to Divinity, are completely justifiable when considered in light of our earlier explorations, and there is no room for any doubt or misgiving. Nevertheless, let us emphasize this matter again and, in our attempt to understand the meanings of such passages, cite evidence from the Writings of Bahá'u'lláh Himself so as to dispel the possibility of anyone entertaining the misgiving that Bahá'u'lláh, in His human station, regards Himself as God.

In the highest form of every religious belief a quality of servitude can be witnessed, indicating the evanescence of the pious adherent. In other words, one can reach such a point in one's servitude, self-effacement, and humility as to regard oneself as non-existent. In this station, all of one's being feels the existence of the Beloved. In this station, one no longer speaks in one's own voice; whatever one utters is in the voice of the Beloved, for to speak in one's own voice is to admit one's existence. In this station, the Beloved admonishes the lover, seeing the lover's existence as contrary to the prerequisites of true love. It is evident that at some stage upon the path of love and devotion, one finds the Beloved in one's own stead; the lover's self-effacement and death in the Beloved ensue. In this station, the lover sees no existence and reality in himself. If he prays in this station, he simultaneously seeks forgiveness for offering that prayer. There are prayers revealed by the Báb in which He begs forgiveness for the very act of praying, insofar as to pray implies that he who prays considers himself as existing, whereas in a state of absolute selflessness and complete immersion no existence is left to be able to pray. Saʻdí says:

> From cloud's embrace, a raindrop gently fell
> Awestruck to glimpse the boundless ocean's swell:
>
> "Amidst this sea, who am I to claim a place?
> If it existeth, indeed, I am but a trace."[2]

In such a state, the raindrop completely perishes while the ocean remains; the raindrop finds existence only through the ocean's existence and life. Some mystics and lovelorn poets have experienced this station of complete self-effacement, as well as the subsequent union of the raindrop and the ocean. Dihqán-i-Iṣfahání states:

> Love's station, a marvel to perceive:
> Though beloved's veins the blade's mark receive,
> 'Tis the lover's veins the blade doth cleave.[3]

Similarly, Ẓahír-i-Fáryábí writes:

> Upon beloved's vein the lancet's edge did bite,
> Yet the lover's blood floweth in love's desperate plight.[4]

Such is the station of the union of the lover and the beloved, of the lover's death in the beloved's life, whereby nothing remains but the beloved. This is one of the stations of the mystic journey and quest. Baháʼís believe that the highest form of this evanescence, this everlasting life and union of the lover and the beloved, is realized in the Manifestations of God. It is the Manifestation of God Who can attain to the highest station of utter nothingness. When He considers His human reality, He feels that

He is falling short in proving His love until He reaches this station. But when in the station of pure love and utter nothingness, His human reality persists no more and His human voice can no longer raise its call. For if it did, He would still be bound by His human reality, which would be inconsistent with His prophetic office and station of revelation. In revelation, it is the Prophet Who speaks, yet we state: "Thus spoke God and such is the Word of God." The voice emerges from the Prophet's lips; the words proceed from the Prophet's tongue; He is the One Who utters, and yet we state: "God said," not "the Prophet said." Does this mean that we consider the Prophet to be God? The words are uttered by the Prophet, but we recognize them as the words of God. By this logic, is the Prophet God? To be sure, these statements and inferences can be correct, as long as we understand their true meaning. What these statements signify is that in the station of revelation, it is God Who speaks—the Prophet has no separate existence in order to speak His own words. He Who speaks for the Prophet and within the Prophet is God. The Prophet and His individual, human existence are indiscernible, that is, utter nothingness. In other words, the Prophet's own thoughts, reason, and understanding are absent. He renounces His self, reduces it to naught, and surrenders it entirely so that the Will of God and His Word may be heard from the Prophet's tongue and lips.

All divine religions, including the Bahá'í Faith, mention a station that is described as utter nothingness, self-effacement, and renunciation of human reality. In this station, all that remains is God. Therefore, in the station of divine Revelation, the Manifestation of God says: "I am God." In order to avoid individual interpretation in our exploration of this theme, let us peruse the Writings of Bahá'u'lláh that illuminate the truth of this matter. Bahá'u'lláh writes:

> Men have failed to perceive Our purpose in the references We have made to Divinity and Godhood. Were they to apprehend it, they would arise from their places, and cry out: "We, verily, ask pardon of God!"[5]

He writes in another Tablet:

Statements conveying Divinity and Godhood have ever been and continue to be from God, exalted be His glory. This Wronged One uttereth these sublime words at all times: "O God, my God! I bear witness to Thy unity and Thy oneness, to Thy majesty and Thy sovereignty, to Thy power and Thy might. . . ."[6]

He also states:

The evanescent is as nothing before Him Who is the Ever-Abiding. His all-compelling summons hath reached Me, and caused Me to speak His praise amidst all people. I was indeed as one dead when His behest was uttered. The hand of the will of thy Lord, the Compassionate, the Merciful, transformed Me.[7]

He similarly asserts:

By the righteousness of God! Idle fancies have debarred men from the Horizon of Certitude, and vain imaginings withheld them from the Choice Sealed Wine. In truth I say, and for the sake of God I declare: This Servant, this Wronged One, is abashed to claim for Himself any existence whatever, how much more those exalted grades of being! … Whatever hath been said hath come from God. Unto this, He, verily, hath borne, and beareth now, witness, and He, in truth, is the All-Knowing, the All-Informed.[8]

It can be seen in the above explicit statement that Bahá'u'lláh is ashamed to claim any existence for Himself. Who then is the Speaker? It is God! Accordingly, what might be perceived as a voice of grandeur is in fact a voice of complete self-effacement, evanescence, and utter nothingness.

In another Tablet, referring to "the son of Báqir of the land of Ṣád" (Shaykh Muḥammad-Taqíy-i-Iṣfahání, son of Shaykh Muḥammad-Báqir-i-Najafí) Bahá'u'lláh states:

According to what hath been reported, in these days, the son of Báqir of the land of Ṣád hath entered the land of Ṭá, in pursuance of the order of His Majesty the S͟háh, and hath said in a gathering: "Let the Súrih of Tawḥíd be translated and delivered to every citizen of the realm, so that all may know that the one true God begetteth not, nor is He begotten, and that the Bábís believe in his [Bahá'u'lláh's] Divinity and Godhood."⁹

In another instance, in the *Epistle to the Son of the Wolf*, Bahá'u'lláh explicitly addresses S͟hayk͟h Muḥammad-Taqíy-i-Iṣfahání or whomever accuses Bahá'u'lláh of claiming Divinity:

Either thou or someone else hath said: "Let the Súrih of Tawḥíd be translated, so that all may know and be fully persuaded that the one true God begetteth not, nor is He begotten. Moreover, the Bábís believe in his (Bahá'u'lláh's) Divinity and Godhood."

O S͟hayk͟h! This station is the station in which one dieth to himself and liveth in God. Divinity, whenever I mention it, indicateth My complete and absolute self-effacement. This is the station in which I have no control over mine own weal or woe nor over my life nor over my resurrection.¹⁰

In the Kitáb-i-Íqán, Bahá'u'lláh provides a more elaborate explanation of this matter:

Thus in moments in which these Essences of being were deeply immersed beneath the oceans of ancient and everlasting holiness, or when they soared to the loftiest summits of divine mysteries, they claimed their utterance to be the Voice of divinity, the Call of God Himself. Were the eye of discernment to be opened, it would recognize that in this very state, they have considered themselves utterly effaced and nonexistent in the face of Him Who is the All-Pervading, the Incorruptible. Methinks they have regarded themselves as utter nothingness, and deemed their mention in that Court an act of blasphemy. For the slightest whispering of self, within such a Court, is an evidence of self-assertion and independent existence. In the eyes of them that have attained unto that Court, such a suggestion is itself a grievous transgression. How much more grievous would it be, were aught else to be mentioned in that Presence, were man's heart, his tongue, his mind, or his soul, to be busied with anyone but the Well-Beloved, were his eyes to behold any countenance other than His beauty, were his ear to be inclined to any melody but His voice, and were his feet to tread any way but His way.

In this day the breeze of God is wafted, and His Spirit hath pervaded all things. Such is the outpouring of His grace that the pen is stilled and the tongue is speechless.

By virtue of this station, they have claimed for themselves the Voice of Divinity and the like, whilst by virtue of their station of Messengership, they have declared themselves the Messengers of God. In every instance they have voiced an utterance that would conform to the requirements of the occasion, and have ascribed all these declarations to Themselves, declarations ranging from the realm of divine Revelation to the realm of creation, and from the domain of Divinity even unto the domain of earthly existence. Thus it is that whatsoever be their utterance, whether it pertain to the realm of Divinity, Lordship, Prophethood, Messengership, Guardianship, Apostleship or Servitude, all is true, beyond the shadow of a doubt.[11]

Bahá'u'lláh explicitly elucidates in these paragraphs that whenever the words and utterances of the Manifestation indicate Divinity, the reason is the complete self-effacement and utter nothingness of the human reality of the Manifestation. Bahá'u'lláh explains this point in another Tablet in the following words:

Moses, Who ranketh among the greatest of the Prophets, after a period of thirty days—during the first ten days of which, as described by the mystics, He surrendered His deeds to the deeds of God; during the second ten days, His attributes to the attributes of God; and during the third ten days, His essence to the Essence of God—insofar as a remnant of existence yet lingered within Him, was addressed: "Thou shalt never behold Me!"[12]

This passage suggests that the Manifestation of God must be the essence of absolute selflessness and utter nothingness in order for that which speaks through Him—within His heart and soul, and in His tongue—to be recognized as God. Our purpose in citing these passages is to emphasize that the existence of the Writings of Bahá'u'lláh uttered in the voice of God should not be understood as suggesting that Bahá'ís equate Bahá'u'lláh with the Godhead. Such Writings indicate, according to the explicit statements of Bahá'u'lláh Himself, that Bahá'ís consider Bahá'u'lláh in that station to be utter nothingness and sheer non-existence—that any such utterance and summons proceed from the Divine Essence and that it is God Himself Who raises the call of Divinity.

Another topic that should be addressed in this last part of our investigation of this theme is that in some Sacred Scriptures human properties are attributed to God. Specifically, many physical properties of human existence are ascribed to God. For instance, God is depicted as having a face. It is stated in the Qur'án: "Whichever way ye turn, there is the face of God."[13] Similarly, the Qur'án states: "All on the earth shall pass away, but the face of thy Lord."[14] In one passage, God is described as having hands: "'O Eblis,' said God, 'what hindereth thee from prostrating thyself before him whom I have created with mine own hands?'"[15] In the Qur'án, having a side is also attributed to God: "'Oh misery! for my failures in duty towards God!'"[16] In subsequent verses of the same súrih it is written: "The whole earth shall on the Resurrection Day be but His handful, and in His right hand shall the heavens be folded together. Praise be to Him! And high be He uplifted above the partners they join with Him!"[17]

Similarly, it is stated in the Qur'án that in order to accept their pledges of allegiance, Muḥammad placed His right hand over people's right hands and such was the symbol of allegiance. In relation to this practice, God addressed Muḥammad: "In truth, they who plighted fealty unto thee, really plighted that fealty unto God."[18] In this same verse, it is stated: "The hand of God is above their hands,"[19] implying that it is God's hand, not Muḥammad's, that is above their hands. In other verses it is written that in one of His military expeditions, Muḥammad threw a handful of sand or pebbles toward the enemies and God addressed Him: "Those shafts were God's, not Thine!"[20]

It can be observed in verses such as these that human physical characteristics are attributed to God. To be sure, these verses do not seek to incarnate or personify God. God's divine unity and sanctity are emphasized in the Qur'án to such an extent that no one can accuse it of seeking to incarnate or personify God. It is clear that the logical and accurate way of appreciating these verses is to know and recognize God as manifested in His noblest creation. God's noblest creation is the human being, and the noblest member of the human race in each age is the Manifestation of God for that age. It is for this reason that when speaking of God it is as though the Qur'án is speaking of a human being. In fact, the human being, which is the noblest creation of God, serves as the medium of descriptions that pertain to the Divine Essence. Similar expressions can also be found in the writings of the Bahá'í Faith. This is because it is God's method to utilize such a mode of description, and the Sacred Scriptures use such expressions to communicate their themes. Therefore, as is the case with the writings of all other religions, these kinds of analogies and expressions can also be found in the writings of the Bahá'í Faith.

Nevertheless, some question why descriptions that are only fitting for human beings are attributed to God, arguing that one who does so in fact regards himself as God. Such a criticism is manifestly unfair, inasmuch as once God is described with human attributes, or a face or a head is attributed to Him, then one might as well perceive Him as possessing hair; once He is symbolically described as possessing a hand, it is also conceivable that His hands may be described as "chained."[21] It is unfair to portray the necessities of imagery, the properties of a metaphor, or the requirements of a description as personification or materialization of God. One should not commit such injustice.

Some, for instance, have criticized Bahá'u'lláh for having spoken in His Writings of inhaling God's sweet fragrance or perfume. They have voiced their objection to this metaphor, protesting attribution of any smell to God. They are ignorant of the truth that the writings of litterateurs and mystics are replete with such words as "smell," "fragrance," and "perfume" to convey, figuratively, an inner meaning.

Among the Islamic traditions cited in *Biḥáru'l-Anvár*,[22] as well as in *Safínatu'l-Biḥár* which serves as a subject index of

Biḥáru'l-Anvár, it is stated: "Verily, I perceive the Self of your Lord from the direction of Yemen."[23] Likewise, passages such as "Verily, I perceive the fragrance of the All-Merciful from the direction of Yemen," and, "The fragrances of Paradise waft from the direction of Arabia," can be found in several works of mysticism.

Rúmí, whose greatness and station are indisputable, writes in his *Mathnaví*:

> Cast off all doubt from out thine ear
> That the celestial voice thou mightst hear
>
> Purify thine eyes from error's touch
> That unseen meadows thou mightst watch
>
> Cleanse thou the rheum from out thine head
> And breathe the breath of God instead[24]

In the following verses, he similarly describes this "breath of God," this Divine fragrance mentioned in the above traditions:

> To me hath come a marvelous scent
> Like to the Prophet, from Yemen it went
>
> Thus He spoke: "In the breeze's hand,
> From Yemen, the scent of the Divine land!"
>
> The aroma of Rámín from the soul of Vays
> Divine fragrance too, cometh from Uvays
>
> From Uvays of Arabia, a wondrous scent
> Into ecstasy and rapture the Prophet was sent
>
> As Uvays dissolved into the selfless embrace
> The earthly transformed to celestial grace.[25]

Such expressions can be found in the works of many a poet and mystic who cited them—unsurprisingly so, since they encountered similar expressions and metaphors in the Qur'án and the traditions of Muḥammad and the Imáms and were inspired by them.

Those unfair slanderers who insult and vilify the Bahá'í Writings for their use of similar expressions are clearly unaware of the rich history of this imagery in Islamic literature, poetry, and mysticism. In religious traditions, often certain associations are made to God that relate to human anatomy. Similarly, not infrequently, actions are attributed to God that befit a human station. The Qur'án, for instance, speaks of "those who war against God."[26] It is evident that, in this verse, warring against the Prophet of God, and not against the Divine Essence, is intended. Similarly, the Qur'án asserts that "God shall scoff at them," referring to "they who traduce . . . the faithful . . . and scoff at them."[27]

In yet another verse, the following statement, referring to Pharaoh and his supporters, is attributed to God: "And when they had angered Us, We took vengeance on them, and We drowned them all."[28] Evidently, "angered Us" represents a reactive response and befits human beings. But when such a purely reactive action is attributed to God, in this scenario "God" should clearly be perceived as a conception that fits the human station. This is because no means of conveying these expressions is available to us beside the human being, which is the noblest creation of God. It is revealed in the Qur'án: "Who is he that will lend a generous loan to God?"; and then a few verses later: "Verily, they who give alms, both men and women, and they who lend a generous loan to God,—doubled shall it be to them—and they shall have a noble recompense."[29] It is evident that neither is God, the All-Possessing, in need of borrowing, nor do His feeble and needy servants possess any wealth to lend Him. A created being whose every possession is bestowed by God is in no position to lend anything to Him. Verses such as this, therefore, symbolically refer to one human being's lending to another as lending to God. They do not suggest that the Divine Essence is actually a borrower.

It is striking that notwithstanding such verses in the Qur'án and Islamic traditions some Muslims hurl insults and show disrespect when they come across verses such as "No God is there but Me, the Prisoner, the Peerless" in the Bahá'í writings. Yet the meaning and significance of these expressions in the revealed Text is perfectly clear in all these instances, as it is in the Quranic verses. Just as the Divine Essence does not suffer pain, fight a battle, throw pebbles, borrow, or get angry, but rather all these conditions return to the perfect human being, the Manifestation of God, by the same token the concept of God's imprisonment also finds its application and realization in His Manifestation. The choice of words and register in these passages is to convey and explicate the significance, the nobility, and the greatness of these acts by attributing them to God. To refer to Bahá'u'lláh's imprisonment, God is described as imprisoned. Why is that? Because imprisonment impedes one's connection to the outside world and the connection between humanity and God is through the utterances of the Manifestation of God. When the Manifestation of God is imprisoned, communication of the Word of God to the people is likewise confined and restricted. In this sense, God is imprisoned. Therefore, just as people can war against God or give a loan to Him, in that same sense they can also imprison God.

Another point is that in the Qur'án mention is made of the "colour of God" and that no color is better than the color of God.[30] Now when the Qur'án speaks of the "colour of God," the *Mathnaví* of the "breath of God," and the Bahá'í writings of the "fragrances of God," in all these instances the voice and the language that are employed to convey spiritual truths by no means degrade the Divine Essence or cause It to descend from the heights of Its pure sanctity or essential exaltation.

To be sure, those who are acquainted with the truth of the matter in the study of religion are not surprised by such a voice and language. These explanations are rather presented to help remove the misunderstandings and the doubts of the general public. Our purpose in laying out these arguments is to contribute to an understanding of the true foundations of the study of religion. Such an understanding encompasses the foundations of all divine religions and unifies beliefs and faiths. It is revealed in the Qur'án: "Say: O people of the Book! Come ye to a like determination between us and you."[31] In this verse, all the people of the Book—every follower of all religions—are called upon to follow a belief they all hold in common. Insofar as the foundation of all divine religions is one and all religions originate from the same source, there are beliefs and principles that they all share, but that are conveyed and understood differently. If this reality is understood correctly, it will lead to the unity of the followers of all religions. It is hoped that our deliberations in these three sessions have dispelled some misrepresentations that have caused divisions.

In this session, I would like to address the question of the Qiblih again so that any trace of misunderstanding may be dissipated. Some oppose the Bahá'ís and criticize them for prostrating themselves before Bahá'u'lláh. In our first session exploring this theme a passage from the Writings of Bahá'u'lláh was cited in which He explicitly states that should one throw oneself to the ground or bow down before Bahá'u'lláh, he or she must repent because prostrating before Bahá'u'lláh is forbidden.

We are, therefore, prostrating ourselves not before Bahá'u'lláh, but before the Invisible Essence. But, as expressed previously, insofar as the Invisible Essence has no location or direction, one cannot consider Him to be the Qiblih towards which one turns in adoration, but must inevitably face the noblest Spot which is associated with His Manifestation—the Spot from which the call of divine unity was raised. If it is permitted in Islam to turn towards a House built of clay and stone as the Qiblih of the worshippers of God, then it must also be permitted, all the more so, to turn towards a Being Who is composed of the noblest elements of the physical world. It bears noting that in the Bahá'í Faith it is not the physical body that is the object of adoration; the body is rather the means through which the Bahá'ís focus their attention on the Divine Essence. Since the Divine Essence is in the inaccessible heights of sanctity and too exalted for humanity to approach, we turn towards the Dawning-Place of His splendor.

It is astonishing that a similar criticism to that levelled against Bahá'ís—that is, similar to, "Why do Bahá'ís prostrate themselves before Bahá'u'lláh?" even though they really do not—also appears in the Qur'án. According to the Qur'án, God created Adam and commanded the angels to prostrate themselves before Him: "And when We said to the angels, 'Bow down and worship Adam,' then worshipped they all, save Eblis.[32] He refused and swelled with pride."[33] It is evident, then, that to refuse to bow down before the Manifestation of God, as commanded by God, far from being a prerequisite to confessing God's oneness, is rather a sign of swelling with pride. Some commentators and authors have suggested that Eblis' refusal to prostrate himself before Adam was a sign of his belief in God's oneness. They maintain that since Eblis confessed the oneness of God, he could not prostrate himself before Adam and so he did not. They believe that this was in fact a test from God which all the angels except Eblis failed; as a result, he emerged as the foremost among believers in divine unity.

Rúzbihán-i-Baqlí writes in his *Sharḥ-i-Shaṭḥíyát*:

Moses, the blessings of God rest upon Him, chanced upon Eblis on Mount Sinai. Moses asked: "What prevented thee from prostrating thyself?" Eblis responded: "My belief that there is but one to be worshipped. And were I to prostrate myself before Adam, I would be no different from Thee. For when Thou wert bidden but once 'Behold the mountain,' Thou didst behold. I was summoned a thousand times 'Bow down before Adam,' yet I did not. My response doth accord with my belief." Moses asked: "Didst thou abandon the command?" Eblis replied: "That was a test, not a command."[34]

Note that here Eblis contrasts himself with Moses and claims that he, not Moses, is a true believer in the oneness of God, because when Eblis was summoned to bow down before Adam, he refused. When Moses asked him what caused him not to bow down, Eblis replied that it was not a command; it was a test which he passed successfully, whereas Moses failed it.

Observe in what a camp they place themselves, those who prevent people from bowing down before the Manifestation of God because they seek to preserve the oneness of God. With discernment and fairness, one will notice that such criticisms and objections are in fact voiced for the sole purpose of undermining a whole set of beliefs in the oneness of God; they are devoid of any trace of fairness, humanity, or true understanding. Those who manifest such opposition and hostility have pressed the matter to the point that where a Bahá'í poet has employed an exaggerated reference in relation to Bahá'u'lláh or 'Abdu'l-Bahá in his poetry, they have cited such a poetic hyperbole as the reason for their criticism and opposition and as representing Bahá'í belief. They are clearly unaware of the difference between belief and poetic hyperbole. Poets in all nations of the world employ stylistic hyperbole in their poetry. Exaggeration as a stylistic device is an inseparable property of some poems, because poetry manifests imagination. But imagination is completely different from reality. To be sure, some poets have utilized more intense forms of exaggeration and have taken it to extremes.

Ṭaráz-i-Yazdí praises Imám ʿAlí—who in turn described even Muḥammad with the phrase "I testify that Muḥammad is God's servant and apostle"—in the following verses:

> O noble Arabian chief, thou mirror of the unseen's grace
> Upon the ancient sovereign's crown casteth a shadow thy face
>
> In praise and homage what words to unfold?
> For thou art the very essence of praise untold
>
> Such praises spoken by eloquent tongues fall short
> That thou art foe-subduer and conqueror of army's fort
>
> Behind the curtain, veiled from mortal eye
> In ignorance, they hailed thee God on high
>
> I know not what words shall take flight
> Shouldst thou unveil thy visage fair and bright
>
> "Ṭaráz," consumed by longing, silent in despair
> No words he breatheth, to shield thee from a commoner's air.[35]

To be sure, one cannot ignore the refinement of Ṭaráz-i-Yazdí's poetry, but one must also acknowledge his exaggeration and inaccuracy. Similar overstatements about the station of Baháʾuʾlláh and ʿAbduʾl-Bahá, which are certainly far from the truth, can also be found in Nabíl-i-Zarandí's and Naʿím-i-Sidihí's poetry. The truth of the matter is expressed in the Writings of the Manifestation of God and the Interpreter of His Words, which are cited in the three explorations of this topic.

It is hoped that no one will attempt to find fault baselessly. However, if there are any misunderstandings in comprehending the truth, or if certain truths become subject to misinterpretation, it is hoped that these clarifications and a study of the sacred writings will remove all such misunderstandings and misinterpretations. One must believe that most people understand, and convey, the truth similarly. Should there be a difference, however, in how people convey the truth, it can be explained using Rúmí's parable of the ripening of young grapes:

> In clusters, brethren grapes are entwined
> Once pressed, they yield one nectar, refined
>
> Unripe and ripe, like nature's dual ends
> Once strangers, now in ripeness, intimate friends
>
> Worthy unripe grapes, with potential crowned
> Pure hearts within, by spirits pure, tightly bound
>
> Swiftly they hasten, becoming ripe with zest
> Shedding duality, strife, in ripening's quest
>
> In ripeness, skins burst, a union profound
> Characterized by oneness, unity unbound.[36]

I conclude my remarks with a passage from Shoghi Effendi's "The Dispensation of Bahá'u'lláh" that masterfully presents and does justice to the true station of Bahá'u'lláh:

> The divinity attributed to so great a Being and the complete incarnation of the names and attributes of God in so exalted a Person should, under no circumstances, be misconceived or misinterpreted. The human temple that has been made the vehicle of so overpowering a Revelation must, if we be faithful to the tenets of our Faith, ever remain entirely distinguished from that "innermost Spirit of Spirits" and "eternal Essence of Essences"—that invisible yet rational God Who, however much we extol the divinity of His Manifestations on earth, can in no wise incarnate His infinite, His unknowable, His incorruptible and all-embracing Reality in the concrete and limited frame of a mortal being. Indeed, the God Who could so incarnate His own reality would, in the light of the teachings of Bahá'u'lláh, cease immediately to be

God. So crude and fantastic a theory of Divine incarnation is as removed from, and incompatible with, the essentials of Bahá'í belief as are the no less inadmissible pantheistic and anthropomorphic conceptions of God—both of which the utterances of Bahá'u'lláh emphatically repudiate and the fallacy of which they expose. . . .

That Bahá'u'lláh should, notwithstanding the overwhelming intensity of His Revelation, be regarded as essentially one of these Manifestations of God, never to be identified with that invisible Reality, the Essence of Divinity itself, is one of the major beliefs of our Faith—a belief which should never be obscured and the integrity of which no one of its followers should allow to be compromised.[37]

NOTES TO CHAPTER THREE, PART THREE

1   Bahá'u'lláh, INBA, vol. 44 (N.p.: n.p., 1976), 51; provisional translation.

2   Abú Muḥammad Mushrifu'd-Dín Muṣliḥ ibn 'Abdu'lláh, *Bústán*, chapter 4, section 2.

3   Qtd. in 'Alí-Murád Dávúdí, ed. Vahid Rafati, *Rahá'í* (Hofheim: Bahá'í-Verlag, 2010), 191.

4   Ibid.

5   Bahá'u'lláh, *Epistle to the Son of the Wolf*, Bahá'í Reference Library, www.bahai.org/r/604805315.

6   Bahá'u'lláh, Bahá'í Reference Library, www.bahai.org/r/814067175; provisional translation.

7   Bahá'u'lláh, *The Summons of the Lord of Hosts*, Bahá'í Reference Library, www.bahai.org/r/476272255.

8   Bahá'u'lláh, *Epistle to the Son of the Wolf*, Bahá'í Reference Library, www.bahai.org/r/828250778.

9   Bahá'u'lláh, Bahá'í Reference Library, www.bahai.org/r/814067173; provisional translation.

10   Bahá'u'lláh, *Epistle to the Son of the Wolf*, Bahá'í Reference Library, www.bahai.org/r/022841646.

11   Bahá'u'lláh, *The Kitáb-i-Íqán*, ¶¶ 196–198, Bahá'í Reference Library, www.bahai.org/r/027665932.

12   Bahá'u'lláh, INBA vol. 73 (N.p.: n.p., 1976), 130; provisional translation.

13   Qur'án 2:115. Qtd. in Bahá'u'lláh, *The Kitáb-i-Íqán*, ¶ 55, Bahá'í Reference Library, www.bahai.org/r/658212558.

14   Qur'án 28:88. Qtd. in Bahá'u'lláh, *The Call of the Divine Beloved*, Bahá'í Reference Library, www.bahai.org/r/237295179.
15   Qur'án 38:75, translated by J. M. Rodwell in *The Ḳoran* (London: Bernard Quaritch, 1876), 123.
16   Qur'án 39:56, translated by J. M. Rodwell in *The Ḳoran*, 275. The Arabic phrase "janbi'lláh" literally means "beside God."
17   Qur'án 39:67. Qtd. in Bahá'u'lláh, in *The Kitáb-i-Íqán*, ¶51, Bahá'í Reference Library, www.bahai.org/r/376614958.
18   Qur'án 48:10. Qtd. in Bahá'u'lláh, *The Kitáb-i-Íqán*, ¶ 196, Bahá'í Reference Library, www.bahai.org/r/027665932.
19   Ibid., ¶ 147.
20   Ibid., ¶ 196. While some Islamic commentators suggest that Muḥammad threw a handful of sand or dust at the enemies and prayed for their defeat, Rodwell, like Shoghi Effendi, refers to "shafts" in his translation of the verse. See J. M. Rodwell, The Ḳoran, 411.
21   Qur'án 5:64.
22   *Biḥáru'l-Anvár* is a collection of Islamic traditions compiled by Muḥammad-Báqir al-Majlisí.
23   'Abbás Qumí, *Safínatu'l-Biḥár va Madínatu'l-Ḥikami va'l-Áthár*, vol. 4 (Mashhad: Ástán-i-Quds-i-Raḍaví, 2009), 883.
24   Jalálu'd-Dín Rúmí, *Kullíyát-i-Mathnavíy-i-Ma'naví* ([Ṭihrán]: Nashr-i-Ṭulúʻ, 1991), 290; the translation of the last couplet is quoted in Bahá'u'lláh, *The Call of the Divine Beloved* ¶ 40, Bahá'í Reference Library, www.bahai.org/r/225561938.
25   Jalálu'd-Dín Rúmí, *Kullíyát-i-Mathnavíy-i-Ma'naví*, 713.
26   Qur'án 5:33, translated by J. M. Rodwell in *The Ḳoran*, 543.
27   Qur'án 9:79, translated by J. M. Rodwell in *The Ḳoran*, 531.
28   Qur'án 43:55, translated by J. M. Rodwell in *The Ḳoran*, 134.
29   Qur'án 57:11, translated by J. M. Rodwell in *The Ḳoran*, 449.
30   Qur'án 2:138.
31   Qur'án 3:64, translated by J. M. Rodwell in *The Ḳoran*, 430.
32   A fallen angel in the Qur'án, sometimes analogized to the Christian Satan.
33   Qur'án 2:34.
34   Rúzbihán-i-Baqlí, *Sharḥ-i-Shaṭḥíyát*, (Ṭihrán: Institut Français d'Iranologie de Téhéran, 1981), 518–519.
35   Aḥmad Díván-Baygí, *Ḥadíqatu'sh-Shuʻará'*, vol. 2 (Ṭihrán: Intishárát-i-Zarrín, 1985), 1109–1110.
36   Jalálu'd-Dín Rúmí, *Kullíyát-i-Mathnavíy-i-Ma'naví*, 376.
37   Shoghi Effendi, *The World Order of Bahá'u'lláh: Selected Letters*, Bahá'í Reference Library, www.bahai.org/r/913442920.

Chapter 4

Breathings of the Holy Spirit

Translated by Elham Afnan

We have been trained in our academic pursuits to begin every discussion with the definition of our terms, even when it is not strictly necessary to do so. When we say that the world of humanity is in need of partaking of the breathings of the Holy Spirit, the meaning of two terms must be clarified: one is "breathings," and the other "the Holy Spirit."

A breathing refers to an outpouring from the breast. The breaths we take and the sighs we heave are breathings. The relationship of this word to the spirit is clear, for the word "breathe" has always been linked to the word "spirit." In Arabic, we read the following in the Qur'án: "He . . . breathed of His Spirit into him"[1] and likewise "I. . . breathed of My spirit into him,"[2] and numerous other verses that have the same purport. In Persian, too, the phrase "breathing the spirit" into something is a common expression. The reason is that the spirit is the source of life—of being alive—the sign of which is breathing. In fact, a living being is one that breathes, and for this reason the spirit and breathing are tied together. In general, breathings refer to emanations or effusions, but when the term is applied to the spirit, we get the breathings of the Holy Spirit. The Holy Spirit is a term found in the Bible, particularly the New Testament, and is used in Christian thought to express approximately the same meaning as the concept of the Faithful Spirit (*Rúḥu'l-Amín*) that is found in Islam.[3] The Faithful Spirit is also equated with the angel Gabriel, and the Holy Spirit occupies the same station in Christianity, that is to say it is the agent that confers distinction upon the Manifestation of the Cause of God or, in Christian terms, the Son of God.[4]

In former times, divine revelation was interpreted in a particular way and was seen as the link between God and His Messenger. It was thought that there existed an angel or a transcendent being who was fundamentally different from ordinary humans, and who was the bearer of God's message to the Prophets: he would bring the message, deliver it, and go back. Of course, it is obvious that this is a metaphor, a symbol, a vehicle for explaining the true meaning, a meaning that the mass of the people cannot—or formerly could not—comprehend. Therefore, the angel was depicted as having corporeal reality and material existence, and even as possessing wings.[5] Today, it is difficult to accept such conceptions in a literal manner and we have no alternative but to interpret them according to symbolic inner meanings.

In this new Faith, all the truths and inner meanings of the beliefs, sayings, and verses of the Holy Scriptures have been made clear. Therefore, in Bahá'í terminology, the Holy Spirit too has acquired a special interpretation. According to this interpretation, as explained in *Some Answered Questions* by 'Abdu'l-Bahá,[6] spirits are of several kinds—or belong to different degrees, each of which is reserved for a particular kind of spirit that belongs only to a specific order of beings. The spirit is nothing but a source that manifests the attributes and distinguishing characteristics and conditions of each order of beings. For example, plants, animals, and human beings are distinguished from one another by certain characteristics and attributes that spring from a source. That source is called the particular spirit of that degree or order of beings.

In *Some Answered Questions*, in order to prove the existence of the human spirit, 'Abdu'l-Bahá confines the discussion to that which distinguishes human beings from animals. He limits His proof to showing that human beings are distinct from animals, and therefore describes these distinguishing marks. Yet 'Abdu'l-Bahá's explanations make it clear that, more generally, the spirit is nothing but that source or cause that distinguishes one kind or order of being from another.

One of these spirits, occupying its own degree, is the Holy Spirit. Just as through the animal spirit the animal is distinguished from the plant, likewise, through the human spirit the human being is distinguished from the animal and, so too, through the Holy Spirit the Manifestations of God are distinguished from other human beings. Of course, we do not mean to say that the Manifestation of God is not a human being. He is human—and is indeed the Perfect Man, in the sense that the only person that can be truly human is the Manifestation of God.

Bahá'u'lláh says in one of His Writings:

> Man, the noblest and most perfect of all created things, excelleth them all in the intensity of this revelation, and is a fuller expression of its glory. And of all men, the most accomplished, the most distinguished and the most excellent are the Manifestations of the Sun of Truth. Nay, all else besides these Manifestations live by the operation of their Will, and move and have their being through the outpourings of their grace.[7]

The Perfect Man means the Manifestation of God. Therefore, when we say that the Manifestation of God is distinguished from human individuals through the Holy Spirit, we do not mean that the Manifestation is not a human being. In the same way, when we say that a human being is distinguished from an animal through the human spirit, we do not mean that the human being is not an animal; we assert that he is an animal, but an animal that has the rational faculty and is intelligent and possesses the human spirit.

In like manner, the Manifestation of God is a human being who possesses the Holy Spirit. The spirit of each degree of existence possesses all the powers and attributes of the spirits of the lower degrees, but does not have access to the higher degrees. The animal, while it is an animal, also has the attributes of the vegetable spirit: growth, respiration, intake of nourishment, and reproduction. These are all characteristics of the plant that also exist in the animal. The animal possesses, in addition, the attributes of the animal spirit, which consist of sense perception and movement. A human being, in addition to having these characteristics of the animal—sense perception and voluntary movement—also has those of the plant. And in addition to these, he possesses the human rational soul, which leads him to discover the unknown, to make deductions, and to reason from a known thing to something that was previously unknown. The Manifestations of God likewise share with the plants their characteristics, share with animals those characteristics that have to do with perception and movement just as other people do, and share with human beings the rational soul and the power of discovery. But they are distinguished from other human beings by the Holy Spirit. That is to say, they possess characteristics that distinguish and set them apart.

As clearly specified in the Writings, the foremost influence exerted by the Holy Spirit is that it quickens the world and brings spiritual revival to it. Through the advent of the Holy Manifestations, the world of being is made new and entirely transformed. Even if outwardly it remains the same world as before, yet its essence and reality are changed. Through the advent of the Manifestations of God, the meaning of "the earth shall be changed into another earth"[8] is made evident. The coming of each of these Manifestations is the Day of Resurrection for the previous Dispensation. Thus the Holy Spirit, being the spirit that distinguishes the Manifestations of God and belongs to the realm of divine Revelation, shows forth signs and tokens that we call the signs of revelation, just as the rational or human soul shows forth the signs of intellect.

In short, when the signs of the influence of the Holy Spirit become apparent in the human world, they effect the transformation of this world from one state and degree into another. When we say that the world of humanity is in need of the breathings of the Holy Spirit, we mean that that Spirit which resides within the Manifestations of God and that influence which we call the sign and token of revelation should issue forth from those Manifestations and reach humanity so that they may bring about the education and perfection of the people. The human soul cannot consider itself independent of the signs of revelation that issue from the Manifestations. This statement is based on certain premises. Outwardly, there is no great difference between the human being and the animal. Like animals, human beings breathe, walk, eat, sleep, reproduce. One may thus imagine that a human being should consider his animal life to be essential: he should only be concerned with eating and sleeping and place no importance on other matters. In other words, because he possesses the attributes of animal life, he can dispense with reason, art, and all that belongs specifically to human life. Similarly, the human race may imagine, or indeed has imagined, that because it is endowed with specifically human powers and possesses reason—possesses science, which is the fruit of reason; possesses crafts and industry, which are the fruit of science; and possesses the laws of society, which are the outcome of the application of reason to human civilization; in short, because it partakes of the results of culture and civilization—it has no need of the breathings of the Holy Spirit. We say that we are human beings, we possess reason, through reason we acquire science, through science we create crafts and industry and obtain power, and we thereby conquer the whole creation and gain dominion over all of the material world. For this reason we believe our station to be much higher than it really is. We become proud and arrogant and see nothing except our own selves as worthy of attention. In such a situation we say that, as long as we possess reason, we are in no need of revelation; that reason allows us to dispense with revelation. It should be acknowledged that those who hold this view may not even believe in the human soul. They simply say that by exercising reason, we can dispense with revelation. As long as we are human beings and have the human spirit, we have no need of the Manifestation of God. In other words, they say, we do not believe in or accept a station in creation that is known as the Manifestation of God and is distinguished from all others through the Holy Spirit.

We know that in the Bahá'í Faith full justice has been done to the high rank and station of reason, and the greatness of reason and of its considerable results—that is to say arts, sciences, crafts and industry—has been fully proven. In a number of Tablets and talks, 'Abdu'l-Bahá speaks of the benefits of reason and the necessity of its conformity with religion. Therefore, a Bahá'í cannot deny the virtues and benefits of reason and cannot believe that because he has religion he can dispense with reason. In fact, one must have both reason and religion.

We know that in the Middle Ages, man was considered to be in no need of reason because he possessed religion. This is why religion attacked reason and denounced it. In modern times, by contrast, the opposite view is upheld. They say that man is in no need of religion because he possesses reason, that the human being is in no need of the Holy Spirit, which is what distinguishes the Manifestation of God from all others. The foundation and truth of the matter, however, according to Bahá'í belief, is that we can neither dispense with reason and its fruits through religion, nor dispense with religion through reason. That is to say, we cannot, because we possess reason, consider ourselves to be in no need of the bounty of revelation, for reason has its own particular field of action, from which it cannot stray. That which reason accomplishes is noble and highly distinguished, but the work of reason and the scope of its responsibility and action are clearly delimited and do not extend to other fields. Let us give an example. Someone who has ears cannot say that he has no need of eyes in order to see, and conversely one who has eyes cannot say he needs no ears because he can use the eyes both to see and to hear. It is evident that such a claim has no merit, for the ear has the power of hearing, which is necessary, and the eye too is necessary and perfect in its own sphere. Neither the ear nor the eye has any imperfection. The fault lies with the person who wishes to use the ear to see or the eye to hear. This is where imperfection and shortcomings arise.

Religion is necessary and perfect in its own sphere, and reason is likewise necessary and perfect in its own sphere. Of course, necessity and perfection in such matters are relative. We consider the truths of religion to be relative but sufficient in their own sphere. Those who expect reason to do the work of divine revelation or revelation to do the work of reason go astray and suffer imperfection. The work of reason is nothing but to discover the unknown. It is therefore abstract and general. This is all that reason is capable of and nothing else can be expected of it. In other words, reason discovers the nature of the unknown; when it is used to solve a problem or apprehend a matter, it presents its results regardless of whether they are beneficial and good or harmful and evil. In short, reason can serve the thief and the murderer, and it can also serve a person of goodwill. It is a tool that is available to all and that everyone can use. Reason is the means of acquiring power and attaining to one's objective. But when it comes to how one should use power and what the object of desire can and should be—then reason is incapable of making such determinations.

The great sages and philosophers, who are the wise ones of the world, used their reason and understanding in order to determine the ultimate objective of human existence, but they found it in particular things, which were different from one another and even contradictory and in conflict with each other. Some saw the highest goal to be the acquisition of power, while others found it in sacrifice and self-restraint. That is to say, in determining the highest goal according to the dictates of reason, they took different directions and, relying on the mind and on philosophy and believing that they had no need for revelation, they reached different and conflicting conclusions. Thus, man's station remained unknown, and confusion arose. As a result, strange schools of philosophical, political, and social thought came into being, and humanity was pulled in contradictory directions.

For a long time, the philosophers of Europe, in their pride and reliance on reason and industrial power, claimed that they could establish the foundations of ethics and create a moral and spiritual human civilization. Thus, it took a long time for these thinkers to realize that those things that had brought them success in the arena of industry and given them the power to subdue nature and progress materially were not the means needed for success in the realms of morality and ethics or for bringing about a spiritual culture and civilization. Day by day, they increasingly lost hope in their ability to use science and philosophy to regulate humankind's ethical, moral, and spiritual relationships. They thus recognized the deficiency in their views and have today been forced to admit that, in addition to civilization, one must also pay attention to culture. The two concepts of culture and civilization are both necessary—one cannot move forward using one without the other. Today, the necessity of giving attention to spiritual matters has become clear for many thinkers.

We said that reason is a tool and it cannot determine the ideal goal and ultimate object. How then should the ideal goal be identified, and where can it be obtained? Among animals, the goal is clear according to the dictates of nature, and reason plays no part. The animal has a clear path that it follows; it is never faced with a fork in the road and thus choice and free will have no meaning for it. For the animal the goal is clear as are the means for attaining that goal, and all this is determined by instinct. For human beings, however, reason plays a part in finding the path and distinguishing the means. Reason takes the place of instinct. Therefore, reason, which is itself an instrument and a tool, shows the way to achieving the goal.

In the human being, the task of distinguishing the goal and object, which in the animal was performed by instinct, is assigned to reason. Since the human being has gone beyond the animal and instinct no longer operates in him as it does in the animal and in nature, he has turned to reason instead, and reason has become the guide to attaining his goal. Here, then, the goal can no longer be the animal's goal. But many people wish to use human tools to reach animal goals; their ultimate purpose is eating and sleeping and satisfying the requirements of wrath and lust, which inevitably result in evil and darkness. That is to say, such a human being has replaced instinct with reason but has not changed his goals. He wishes to use reason to attain the same goals that an animal has. This is where disorder, chaos, and confusion arise. A person cannot merely eat and sleep like an animal, for he is a human being and has gone further. The meaning of life has changed for him and he wants other things. Therefore, if he uses his reason in order to attain the goals of an animal, he cannot reach them because he is no longer an animal and does not have the necessary natural instincts. Even if he should attain such goals, he would not be satisfied and content with them. As a result, his life is disrupted and upset and becomes disorderly.

Therefore, when the effusions of the human or rational soul became manifest in the human being in the form of reason, they merely gave him the power to find the necessary means and instruments for reaching his goal. It is thus incumbent upon him to use another source to determine the ideal goal and ultimate object of desire. That is to say, that source would show him the goal that reason should be used to achieve, in such a way that he can lay claim to human nobility.

Some may say that we can also determine this ultimate goal using reason or using science, which is born of reason. This is again a case of someone trying to see with his ears or hear with his eyes. Reason is not capable of determining the ultimate goal and object, for you can use reason to attain any goal or ideal that you yourself have chosen. To reason, it makes no difference where you decide to go or where you wish to end up. Reason provides you with whatever you wish and gives you whichever instrument you desire, regardless of whether you want to use reason to destroy a city or to save a multitude. What you want depends on your hierarchy of values, that is to say what is the measure of your values, what is the criterion according to which you determine the value of things. There are of course different hierarchies of values. The clear and evident reason for the difference in values among the people is that philosophical, social, and political systems of belief are all built on distinct, different, and even conflicting bases. Each person has tried to define man's primary goals and secondary objectives in life, and in doing so each has chosen a path of his own and even striven to take a path that is different than those of others. It is obvious then what the outcome will be. It is with such matters in mind that 'Abdu'l-Bahá, in numerous talks, when proving the need for reason and science, states that religion cannot dispense with reason. Reason is noble, reason is lofty, we must turn to crafts and industry, we must make use of the powers and qualities bestowed upon us by God. But so that we do not make the error of thinking the following—that since reason has such a high and noble station we can, using the science acquired through reason, dispense with religion—'Abdu'l-Bahá has emphasized that the human world, with all its merits, still needs to draw upon the breathings of the Holy Spirit.

What do the breathings of the Holy Spirit bestow upon human beings? They provide us with an ultimate goal and objective. They give us an ideal that we can never fully and completely reach, but that prevents us from drowning in our material lives. The ideal goal and ultimate purpose given to us by the breathings of the Holy Spirit creates zeal, selflessness, and sacrifice; it helps us turn our gaze to a higher reality and strive to transcend selfish desires. It is through these virtues that we can remain human, attain greater perfections, and gradually overcome our selfish inclinations. Indeed, reason limits and confines a human being within himself because reason's task is to calculate profit and loss. Even moral questions, when measured according to the touchstone of reason, become linked to profit and loss. Turning to the Holy Spirit and drawing on its power allows reason to know its place and enables the human being not to be satisfied with reason alone but to don the chain of love: love of the ultimate object of desire, love for that which transcends one's individual human existence.

Love provides human beings with the source of good taste, the arts, and the appreciation of beauty. One might say that the arts have no need of religion or the power of the Holy Spirit: non-religious forms of art are numerous and extensive. The point, however, is that if no role exists within art for it to transcend itself, then that art remains sickly and trivial. If no regard is found in art for an ideal goal or for transcendence, then that art turns into a technical craft and loses its distinguishing characteristic. The beauty that is depicted in non-religious art is yoked together to carnal desires. In the fields of painting, poetry, music, and theatre, there are few examples of non-religious art that are rich and excellent. No wonder then, that when we look at the history of art, we see that the pinnacle of the arts of painting, sculpture, and architecture in Europe was reached when art drew upon faith and religion and when the Holy Spirit shone its light upon it. Art has nothing to do with reason. Art seeks beauty, while reason seeks accuracy, and these are two different things. Reason wants to know what is accurate; art wishes to find out what is beautiful. Beautiful and accurate are different things, just as in a building architecture and engineering are two different things. Reason and science are not the source of art. Art is a distinct discipline within human culture that seeks to attain unto beauty. If reason and science are not the source of art, where then can art find its source? It is human receptivity and taste that are the source of art. If a human being does not turn to a world that transcends his own world, his receptive nature inevitably takes on a carnal and selfish aspect. It is for this reason that poetry, painting, and music either partake of faith or are in the service of carnal desires. The grace and perfection of art is found where it connects the human being to the source of Revelation.

Wherever we turn, we are confronted with insufficiency. We are necessary for ourselves, but we are not sufficient. Our being—our essence—is not sufficient for us. This is not a shortcoming on our part but the source of our strength. For our essence to be sufficient for us, we would have to be minerals or plants or animals, looking at nothing save the place where we find ourselves and see nothing except the ground beneath our feet. Or else we would have to be God—which we are not—in order for our essence to be sufficient unto us. In fact, we must either wish for nothing other than what we have, or to have all that we can wish for. For the first we would need to be an animal, and for the second we would need to be God. But we are situated between the two. Our special human position requires that we both wish to have things and that we cannot have all that we wish for. Therefore we are always struggling and searching; we wish to step out of ourselves and turn somewhere else. The place to which we turn, if it does not derive from Revelation and thus occupy a station higher than the human, will inevitably occupy one that is beneath the human station. It will therefore give an animal character to all our activities, will make our art take on a carnal aspect, and will concentrate our reason on striving to fulfill our animal needs. We will become beings that have acquired great power through the exercise of reason, but who want to use this power for a purpose that we have in reality surpassed and left behind. It is as though a person who has attained physical and intellectual maturity and amassed great wealth should wish to spend all his riches on buying and eating candy and popcorn. However, in order to procure such worthless things there was no need for all that striving and effort; they could have been obtained using much lower capacities and much lesser opportunities and means.

Humanity has acquired reason, used it to devise science, used science to invent important industries, gained great power and might, and now considers itself to be in control of nature. But what does it want all this might, power and control for? To eat and sleep and procreate? These animal pursuits did not require all this struggle, search, and effort. The animal already possesses all these abilities. It is therefore a pity that humankind should limit itself to goals that belong to the animal world, but strive to achieve these goals using the human means of reason, science, and industry.

The human being has been given reason that it may lead to his upliftment and advancement to a higher degree. This ultimate goal is attainment unto the outpourings of the Holy Spirit that are manifested in the form of divine Revelation. Each new Manifestation that comes manifests a higher degree of these outpourings. We the people of Bahá know that what has been manifested at this time, and the ultimate goal that the Holy Spirit has imparted at this stage in the spiritual development of the human race, is the oneness of the world of humanity, which is the outcome of the outpourings of the Holy Spirit and of divine Revelation in this Dispensation. Turning towards this principle is the one thing that can concentrate human power and transform it into an instrument for procuring the requirements for attaining this unity. To reach this stage of unity, which is the perfect unity of the whole human race, humanity cannot content itself with its own reason, science, and industry. To attain unto this unity, with the comprehensiveness and perfection that are envisioned for it, we are required to draw upon and use the breathings of the Holy Spirit.

Notes to chapter four

1   Qur'án 32:9.
2   Qur'án 15:29.
3   *Rúḥu'l-qudus* ("the holy spirit") and *rúḥu'l-amín* ("the faithful spirit") are Quranic expressions that describe a source or means of prophetic revelations, commonly identified with the angel Gabriel.
4   "The Faithful Spirit, Gabriel, the Holy Spirit, and the One mighty in power are all designations of the same Reality" ('Abdu'l-Bahá, *Light of the World*, 7:6, Bahá'í Reference Library, www.bahai.org/r/600266177).
5   See, Qur'án 35:1.
6   See, 'Abdu'l-Bahá, *Some Answered Questions*, ch. 36: "The Five Kinds of Spirit." Bahá'í Reference Library, www.bahai.org/r/669751216.
7   Bahá'u'lláh, *The Kitáb-i-Íqán*. See www.bahai.org/r/146847552.
8   Qur'án 14:48.

Chapter 5

Prayer and Meditation

Translated by Elham Afnan

The concept of prayer has always been present in religion: emphasis has been placed on its importance, and many prayers have been revealed or composed. When I say "revealed" I mean that God has taught the people even the words of prayer, so that they may pray using those words. The Prophets, saints, holy souls, and Imáms have also uttered words of prayer, which have been preserved and passed on to others. Besides these, prayers have also been recited by scholars, orators, and poets—even in the form of long odes—and then taken up by the people. Prayer has thus become one of the most powerful customs and traditions, to the extent that no religion is devoid of the concept of prayer.

Of course, such prayers are different from obligatory forms of worship. That is to say, there are certain forms of worship that are compulsory and required, such as the obligatory prayers.[1] However, prayer in the more general sense refers to words whose recitation is not obligatory but recommended and praiseworthy, words that are considered to be elements of piety and are widely used. Prayer takes a number of forms. Some prayers are general: You ask God to grant salvation to all people and give succor to everyone who is helpless and in need; you thus show forth your love for humanity when you pray. Other prayers are more specific: You pray for yourself, you ask something of God, you ask to receive confirmation and success. Among these are other prayers that are even more specific: You pray, not only for yourself, but for a particular purpose and for a particular outcome. Of course, sometimes these requests, these supplications, are of a spiritual nature—a person prays to attain, through divine confirmations, to faith, to sincerity, to righteousness. Other times, they are of a material nature—one prays for the payment of one's debts, or for healing, or for the achievement of a certain position. Some prayers are individual, that is a person communes with God in private and alone. Others are communal, meaning that a group of people gather together, and one person prays while the others listen attentively; or they all pray together; or one person prays and the others raise their hands in supplication or say amen. Practices for communal prayer thus develop that vary according to the different religions.

Some religious believers say that man is always in a state of prayer, or should be so. In other words, whatever one does, even if it is something small and insignificant, one utters—or should utter—a heartfelt prayer, however tacitly. At times, however, such prayers also find outward expression and are recited aloud. In fact, adherence to religion has no meaning without prayer. It is not enough for a human being to recognize God as the Creator, to obey that which He has sent down, and to practice righteousness and piety. In addition, one must pray and ask what one desires from God, the Creator, the Powerful.

At this point, a philosophical and theological discussion arises, which at times has become very heated. For example, you see that in the encounter between Greek philosophy and Christian religion (that is, when Christianity spread and came into contact with Greek philosophy, which was the dominant intellectual tradition at that time), the differences between these two schools of thought became evident. One of these points of difference was the question of prayer, another that of miracles, yet another that of divine grace; there were other questions of this sort, which of course have a long history. All these differences arose out of one fundamental difference, namely that the Greeks viewed the world as following a rational, ordered, and fixed course. Most of them believed in God, but the God of Greek philosophy, the God of Plato and Aristotle, was seen as either a source or an end, positioned at the head of a constellation of beings that were all interrelated in an orderly, fixed, and logical manner. These relationships led, through a hierarchy of degrees or stations, to that source or end. We can therefore say that God, too, was a component of man's rational framework, albeit its most complete, noble, and perfect component, one that was placed above all others and could thus be considered "universal." It is obvious that in such rigid rationalism no room can be found for a number of things. For example, when we say that God has created the world—although, according to Greek thought, we cannot say that He has created it, but must say that when God is at the head of a world that has existed from all eternity according to a constant, rigid, and preordained order, and in which everything, of necessity, has been and is and will ever be as it should be—there is no room for any change to the course of events. Thus, we cannot believe in miracles, for they imply that someone can change the normal course of events. We could only say such a thing if there were room, according to logic, for changes to be made to the normal and orderly course of events. If no such room exists, then there is likewise no room for miracles; neither is there room for divine grace and mercy in such a world. This means that, according to the dictates of necessity, when an act has a reward that is the necessary consequence of the act itself, there is no room for God to exercise His grace and mercy and grant forgiveness, instead of justice, to one who is deserving of punishment (unless his good deeds necessitate God's forgiveness, which then precludes the idea of grace and mercy).

There is likewise no room left for prayer. Why not? Because when we pray, we are asking God to change the course of events to that which we wish for. Since this course of events is unchangeable, it will continue as dictated by necessity; indeed, it is best that the law of necessity be obeyed. What place, then, is there for prayer? What do we ask of God? We tell Him, "Make this matter turn out this way!" What does this mean? It means we are asking Him to change something that has been decreed—by the natural course of events, by necessity, or by His Will—in such a way as would conform to our wishes. Clearly, this is not a logical request; it is not a request that we can reasonably expect to be fulfilled. Either we believe that events in the world follow a course of logical necessity that cannot be changed, or we believe that this course of events has been decreed by the Will of God. If the latter, then we should ask ourselves: Does this Will arise from a desire for what is good and beneficial? Is it based on divine wisdom and justice? If so, why then do we expect that it be changed? How could God allow this expectation to be fulfilled or even allow us to entertain it? In either case, how can there be a place for prayer? Is something ordained by God purely on a whim, without an underlying wisdom or a basis in absolute good? If that were so, we would have to reconsider our faith in God and the very nature of our belief in Him. In that case, to what end would we ask for anything or say anything when we pray? Therefore, even if we do not say that prayer is futile, we would have to say that it is superfluous.

This type of discussion usually arises in the context of philosophical beliefs that are based on rationalism, which considers everything as purely rational and therefore ruled by necessity. It sees no value in love, sentiment, emotion, or anything that arises from the requirements of the heart. And were it to assign them a value, it would first try to justify them according to reason, that is to change them into rational propositions that it could then verify. For this reason, some of the deistic philosophers try to rationalize prayer so that it can be placed in the context of intelligible realities. Others are strongly opposed to this, saying that it destroys the spirit of prayer, for prayer must emanate solely from love and arise only from the heart. If prayer is placed at the disposal of reason, then, while praying, we will be conscious that what we are doing has already been rationalized and therefore we are calling upon our own reason and not upon God. Thus, the spirit of prayer is destroyed, and that heartfelt communion and supplication which is the requirement of prayer turns into a kind of logical and dry argument. Much has been said about this, and the discussion requires a series of theological premises that lead step by step to a necessary conclusion; this, however, is contrary to our approach in these gatherings.

Lately, some people have attempted to find scientific explanations for prayer. In the past, the problem was that people wished to verify the truth of every matter using an explanation derived from the peripatetic school of rational philosophy.[2] In the same way, today, they try to find for every matter an explanation from the sciences, particularly the social sciences, such as psychology and sociology, using these to justify and validate and commend the matter at hand. This practice has become especially prevalent among young people, who feel that everything has to be judged by the precepts of psychology and sociology before it can be accepted with confidence. Now to what extent we can validate these sciences themselves, so that we can then take them as the source of validation for other beliefs—this they do not consider. In any case, they have attempted to find a scientific explanation for prayer, and the essence of this explanation is that prayer is a form of auto-suggestion. That is to say, when you pray, you make your success dependent on confirmation from the source in which you believe; your psyche is thus strengthened, your soul gains power; and, by relying on the source towards which you have turned, you are better able to approach your goal with confidence and calm. In other words, prayer brings you hope and a sense of reliance, and these give you stability and confidence, which in turn lead to success. Those who view prayer in this way thus associate its effect, through a number of intermediaries, with a psychological phenomenon.

This is where disagreements arise; for some others, also relying on psychology, try to show that prayer has a negative and destructive effect. They think that when a person delivers his affairs into the hands of the Almighty and leaves everything to God, then his resolve is diminished, his willpower is weakened, and he sees little need for effort, for work, for struggle. When he puts his trust in God, he no longer has trust in himself. For this reason, they say that prayer is an opiate that makes one weak, removes one's power and initiative, and creates negative results. They claim therefore that, in places where matters are left to prayer, people generally become weak, lethargic, and lacking in self-esteem. They try to support this claim with historical evidence. Just as they relied on proofs from psychology, now they rely on history as a science that must confirm something before it can be accepted. This is a disease that has afflicted all who subscribe to scientism, who cannot accept anything unless it is explained by science, and who define science in a specific way that they, in fact, have accepted without argument.

You see, then, how they have tried to explain prayer in terms of psychology, and how a psychological explanation can be used to ascribe either a positive or a negative aspect to prayer. Of course, in this too, there is a truth to be found, which is that when one prays with faith and sincerity, acknowledges that the answer to the prayer is dependent on circumstances, and does not allow one's own resolve to be weakened, then one gains confidence, determination, and constancy. However, a requirement here is that, after prayer, one should accept the outcome, whatever it may be. That is to say, when one prays but does not weaken in resolve, but rather considers resolute endeavor to be a precondition for prayer; when one has faith in prayer and is prepared to accept whatever the outcome may be (so that even if one does not succeed, there is no loss of confidence and faith), then this has a strong psychological effect. According to the One toward Whom we direct our prayers, despairing of God's mercy is the greatest sin. Here, then, one derives from prayer and the religious sentiments that surround it a constancy and firm resolve that results in success. When these conditions are in place for the person who is praying, then it is obvious that prayer has a positive psychological effect. But anyone with a rudimentary knowledge of psychology realizes that something has a psychological effect only when we do not act with that effect in mind. That is to say, when you encourage a person who lacks the resolve to carry a task to its completion, if she knows that you have no confidence in her ability to do it and only wish to manipulate her, then the encouragement has no effect. When you show someone support, if she knows you are attempting to create a psychological effect upon her in order to obtain a result, then your expressions of support have no effect. Psychological influence is effective only when it is natural, indirect, and without artifice and premeditation. Therefore, people who pray while thinking that they are using prayer for the purpose of auto-suggestion naturally will not experience even that effect. Thus, for prayer to have a psychological effect, we must have faith in that universal Source to whom we pray, and have faith in the categorical and absolute power of prayer. In that case, the effect on the psyche is automatically achieved; it cannot be achieved otherwise.

Still others have tried to look at prayer from the standpoint of sociology. They say that when prayer is performed, particularly in congregation, a kind of collective spiritualization takes place—a strengthening of the collective conscience, a directing of all minds and hearts towards one source, which then strengthens the foundation of the community in which this prayer takes place. In other words, when everyone in a gathering together says, "O God!" or says, "Is there any remover of difficulties save God?" the result is a shared attention towards the same Source in which they all believe, which in turn strengthens their bond. A kind of psycho-social effect comes into being that influences the conscience of the group and strengthens the relationships within it. This is the simplest explanation. But if we turn to the views of some of the sociologists of the early twentieth century—whose thoughts are already outdated—we would have to say that the God to Whom we turn is Himself that collective conscience with which the con-sciences of individuals are trying to connect. This is a form of socio-theism that has been discredited, on which there is no need to dwell any longer.[3] Of course, we see that even if there is any truth to such a view, it can be achieved only when there is already a belief in the effect of prayer. Otherwise, if people know that they are praying only as a ritual, that there is some form of artifice and pretense in what they do so as to bring everyone together and draw on the same power, then this prayer for help and assistance will have no result, and the utterance of the words of the ritual will have no effect. Here again, we must already have full confi-dence in the power of our faith in God and in the effect of prayer for our prayer to exert its sociological influence.

Thus, in general, observe that if there were any need to analyze prayer, that analysis would be from a metaphysical standpoint, not from a psychological or sociological one. First, there must exist faith and trust in God and thereafter belief in the effect of prayer. Only then can one perform a prayer. When prayer is offered with these conditions in place, then it has both a psychological and a sociological effect. That is to say, we must first be assured that prayer is a thing in itself, in order then to have confidence in its effects on psychological, sociological, and natural phenomena.

Let us now consider the question of whether, if we believe in God, it is reasonable to believe in the power of prayer. For we have considered the argument that God, of His own Will and accord-ing to the principle of necessity, ordains that which is necessary and right. This means that, were our prayer to affect the course of events or change God's Will, then either that Will was not well-conceived to begin with and could therefore be changed, or God changed His well-conceived Will, which was originally cor-rect, for our sake—and neither of these alternatives can be right.

This was the criticism voiced by those who objected to prayer on a theological basis. But they overlook one point, and that is the relationship that human beings have with God. Of course, the Will of God in relation to the natural world operates according to the exigencies of necessity, for nature is the realm of necessity. Indeed, we define nature as the "necessary relations derived from the realities of things."[4] But, as you know, we believe that, as human beings, we have free will. God has endowed us with free will and therefore, in the words of Bahá'u'lláh, God's "unconstrained and sovereign Will"[5] operates only within human beings. We have free will, which is to say that there exists a domain for the operation of the human will. Because we have free will, we must exercise our will; and to exercise it, we must possess the capacity for good, for virtue, for righteousness, so that we can want what is good. Thus we arrive at a place where a person wants to do something, and because she possesses righteousness and virtue, she has the capacity to want a thing as it ought to be, to want that which is good. It is here that she, when exercising her free will, turns to what is good and in so doing turns to God and shows her capacity to seek that good by turning to the Source of good. This means that this free will is exercised, on the one hand, for the sake of the good and, on the other, while turning to God. This is a sign of that person's worthiness and merit, which is deserving of a reward, and God's confirmations are therefore showered upon her. You can see a logical progression here. Our prayer is answered, which is to say it is rewarded by God, when we decide to do something good and, in doing so, turn to God. This is worthy of reward, and that reward takes the form of an answer to our prayer. Thus, prayer does not change the logical and necessary course of events, nor is it contrary to divine justice. Rather, prayer is the reward that God gives us for wanting to exercise our free will in order to do good, and for remembering God and turning to Him as we do so. Those who have recognized God but do not pray are those who, in effect, believe that their own will is sufficient for achieving their purpose, without needing to turn to God. There is a form of pride in them that makes them believe they can dispense with God. Of course, if human beings were this powerful, there would be no problem. But since our power is limited, if we behave in this way, we are showing a pride and self-conceit that, in the context of religious belief, is morally blameworthy. It is here that the effect of prayer acquires a rational dimension, and the attempt to discredit prayer using reason is refuted.

So we see that a true prayer has certain conditions. First, to the extent possible, prayer should not have an overly personal aspect. Of course, it is permissible to pray for oneself because a person's own self is dear to him; we might even say that it is the dearest thing. But when we say prayer should not be overly personal, we mean that it should not be selfish and entail taking good away from others. If it is, then it will not—and should not—have an effect, for if we want something that we should not want, then there is no reward in store for us. Next, the spiritual aspect of prayer should, as much as possible, outweigh its material aspect. That is, we should ask God to confirm us in showing forth honesty, purity, truthfulness, sincerity, and servitude, that we may obtain the resulting effects as a consequence of these very qualities that we pray for. So prayer should be as spiritual as possible, but it can also have a material aspect, for even material things can be bearers of spirituality, on condition that one truly views them in this way and does not consider material pleasure to be the ultimate goal. Next, it is never seemly for prayer to turn into a form of negotiation, where one says, "O God, if you do this, then I will do that." Prayer should be accompanied by submission to and contentment with the Will of God. We should confess that what we want is that which is best for us, as determined by God, that is we should say—from our hearts, not only in words—that we wish only what is best for us: "O God! This is what I think is best for me, but do that which you deem best." One's whole being should utter these words, for otherwise prayer becomes merely an exchange or a transaction. Next, to the best of our ability, our prayer should be such that, while offering it, we do not forget others. If we wish something for ourselves, we should also wish it for others who are in the same condition. If we ask for healing for ourselves, we should also ask for it for all humanity. If we wish for happiness for our family, we should also wish it for all people.

Another condition of prayer is that we should never view it as a necessary cause for a necessary effect. What I mean is that we should not mistake prayer for sorcery and magic. Sorcerers also pray—they utter words and incantations that are accompanied by certain rituals, sometimes also collectively. But they believe that, by doing so, they gain control over the inner essence of the world, that these rituals are the instruments of their power and the means by which they can subdue the invisible, spiritual elements that influence the world to their own will. They think that they are drawing the power of these elements to themselves and making them one with themselves, and that, in this way, the sorcerers' will is now the same as the will of the God or the gods; whatever they say will happen. Thus, the ritual that is performed in the name of prayer must and will necessarily yield the result that they ask for. And if at times it does not yield that result, then they claim that the ritual was not performed correctly: a certain prayer should have been said ten times, but they only said it eight times, or the hands should have been raised this way, but someone in the congregation raised hers that way, or a shadow of doubt crossed someone's mind while he was saying the prayer. Thus, if the prayer does not yield the result they necessarily expected, then they blame it on a mistake in carrying out the ritual. There are many stories and examples and proverbs recounted in this regard. For example, there is a story that a soothsayer told a woman who asked him for a prayer, "I will write this prayer for you to say every day at a certain time and in a certain way. But to ensure that it is answered, you must on no account, when saying the prayer, think of a monkey's face." Well, it is obvious that, every time the woman began to say the prayer, she remembered these words and the image of a monkey arose before her eyes, and she despaired of ever achieving a condition in which her prayer could be answered. But these are not prayers. In prayer, we must not imagine that the outcome will of necessity be that which we have asked. We pray, not to overcome God's Will, but to prove our own capacity and our own need to attract divine confirmation, to show that, first, our intention is good; second, that in pursuing this good we are turning to God for assistance; and third, that we accept the outcome, whatever it may be, with contentment and joy. When prayer is conjoined with such faith and conviction, then it is a true prayer, an acceptable prayer, a prayer that we cannot forego.

This was a rational explanation for those who need to explain everything through reason. However, as I mentioned earlier, those of mature understanding view the justification of prayer by rational means as a way of destroying the intrinsic power of prayer, which should rather arise out of love and be as a communion between lover and beloved. If we turn our relationship with God into a rational relationship based on necessity, we grievously harm the spiritual aspect of our faith. Even though all things are in essence rational—since our belief in God is based on reason, then everything else that follows from it is also rational—yet, by trying to see everything in rational terms, we undermine the emotional character of the matter and no longer attend to the requirements of the heart. During prayer, instead of turning our hearts to God, we try to make a rational argument about why the prayer will be answered. Clearly, the metaphysical effect of the prayer, as well as its psychological and sociological effects, are thereby lost.

In the Writings of Bahá'u'lláh and 'Abdu'l-Bahá the recitation of prayers and invocations is enjoined, and their importance emphasized. The Universal House of Justice, too, recommends and emphasizes the importance of prayer, and always prays. Of course, these are prayers that do not preclude preparation, prayers that go hand in hand with reflection, prayers that set in motion endeavor and effort. If there is no endeavor, or if it is not combined with reflection and thought, then prayer, as I have explained, is not true prayer and will not exert an influence. Thus, prayer, even if it were not a religious commandment, would still be highly recommended. At the same time, it has such a great recompense that Those Who are filled with the Holy Spirit[6] reach a station wherein They consider the act of prayer as a sin, indeed as blasphemy and heresy. You see in many of the Writings of the Báb and Bahá'u'lláh that They sometimes say They are ashamed to stretch Their hands forth in prayer. Why? Because in that condition, They are asking something of God, whereas one should ask nothing of the Beloved save the Beloved Himself. The very act of asking something of Him and praying at His threshold—even if one wishes for nothing but His Will—this act places one before God as though one has independent existence. As the poet says,

> My praise is a sign of being, yet no being have I
> My very act of praise would true praise deny.[7]

The fact that I am praying indicates that God exists and I exist, and this is itself an error. For before God's existence, I am non-existent; before Him, I am nothing.

> Who may I be, where the sea has its run,
> If the sea has existence, I, truly, have none.[8]

For this reason, the Báb and Bahá'u'lláh, because They see prayer as a sign of existence and ego, consider it improper, and They repent of it and ask for forgiveness for having performed it. Of course, we must admit that this is a height to which our thoughts can scarcely reach, and not every soul can attain such a station. That which is considered a virtue for human beings is a sin for the Manifestations of God. Long has it been said: "The good deeds of the righteous are the sins of the near ones."

NOTES TO CHAPTER FIVE

1 In Arabic and Persian, a distinction is made between general prayer (*du'á*) and obligatory prayer (*ṣalát* or *namáz*).

2 The Peripatetic school was a philosophical school founded in 335 BC by Aristotle in Athens. It was an informal institution whose members conducted philosophical and scientific inquiries. It was so named because of the *peripatoi* (walkways) of the Lyceum where the members met.

3 This is likely a reference to the views of the French sociologist Émile Durkheim.

4 'Abdu'l-Bahá, *Tablet to Dr. Auguste Forel*, Bahá'í Reference Library, www.bahai.org/r/495128940.

5 Bahá'u'lláh, *Gleanings from the Writings of Bahá'u'lláh*, ch. XXVII, Bahá'í Reference Library, www.bahai.org/r/441185340.

6 For a discussion of the relationship of the Holy Spirit to the Manifestations of God, see 'Abdu'l-Bahá, *Some Answered Questions*, ch. 25, Bahá'í Reference Library, www.bahai.org/r/081192424.

7 Jalálu'd-Dín Rúmí, Kullíyát-i-*Mathnaví-i-Ma'naví*, vol. 1 ([Ṭihrán]: Nashr-i-Ṭulú', 1991), 28.

8 Abú Muḥammad Mushrifu'd-Dín Muṣliḥ ibn 'Abdu'lláh, *Bústán*, Book 4. Qtd. in G. S. Davie, trans. *The Garden of Fragrance* (London: Kegan Paul, Trench & Co., 1882), 147.

Chapter 6

Life in the Next World

Translated by Nima Rafiei

The subject of life in the next world, or alternatively, the belief in the immortality of the soul, is one of the fundamentals of religion and is shared amongst the followers of all of the world's religions. It is one of those beliefs without which religion loses its meaning. Religion requires such belief. Many issues in religions are justified, explained, and proven through this fundamental belief. On the one hand, belief in the immortality of the soul serves as the foundation of morality. This means that the morality that necessitates self-restraint, that entails forsaking pleasure and material benefit to oneself, and that calls for acceptance of hardship in this world as a pre-requisite of piety, requires that an individual endowed with such a sense of morality must also believe in life after death.

If morality were not built on this foundation, it inevitably would lead to utilitarianism— that is, a morality that is based on worldly and physical pleasures and benefits—and such "morality" is not worthy of the name. Of course, some of the philosophers and thinkers have posited that morality can be based solely on reason, without any belief in the afterlife serving as its foundation. That is, they base it on belief in an absolute ethical or moral duty, without being aware or expectant of any sort of reward. Now, such a foundation does not hold up since what they ask us to accept as an "absolute moral duty," and wish us to be compelled by and bound to, is not a matter that one can feel within oneself as a spiritual recompense or an acceptable and valid reward. If a person who in this world renounces himself and everything that pertains to him, and has no hope or expectation of something else—of another life in another world—he will conclude that his life is useless and without meaning.

Of course, turning towards far-off ideals that will come to fruition in the distant future in this world is an aspect of human nature and a higher motivator for this manner of moral renunciation. But you will agree that this has a generic and comprehensive aspect and does not provide an answer for the individual. A question such as this goes unanswered: "What does it mean that for my whole life I have experienced hardship, suffering, and trouble and that I am to pass away without a trace of me being left behind, so that I may partake of and delight in the feeling that in the distant future such a spiritual order will be established in the world?" Some beliefs and ideologies have attempted to view transcendent and ethical ideals as the sole basis for acts of sacrifice, devotion, and self-denial from individuals and consider them sufficient for human beings. Inevitably, however, they have had to resort to the exertion of brute force and tyranny in order to keep people compliant. That is, since this motive was not sufficient to restrain the individual, they deemed it necessary to seek assistance from force and tyranny to compensate for this shortcoming and inadequacy. In principle, every cause that does not consider religious conscience and belief in a spiritual life as a necessity and requirement will not constitute a source of adherence to morality, nor will it provide for human commitment to it.

We can explain this in the following manner: A person who is pious and virtuous, God-fearing and endued with a sense of morality, is obliged to be self-sacrificing and devoted to others and to set aside and forego the gifts and trappings of this world, while many of these gifts and pleasures are enjoyed by those who are not pious or bound by morality. As such, it would seem that there is no justice in the world: the pious are ill-fated, while evil-doers have good fortune. Our world is full of this. Such a state raises the question of what this all means. What can it mean that my share has been nothing but sorrow, and his nothing but pleasure, my life filled only with grief, and his with happiness and joy? One can hardly expect a person to accept morality under such circumstances.

Of course, the ultimate guarantor for morality in human beings, from which we act, is that at some point in the distant future justice will be manifested to its fullest. For those things that necessitate hardship, toil, strife, and deprivation, this is correct but not sufficient. This is not something one can accept with all one's heart. For this reason, the above question usually remains unresolved, since justice, like happiness, cannot be realized in this world if we believe that it is only in this transitory world that we exist. Yet human beings still expect an answer. This is why most of those who are not religious do not anticipate any sort of non-physical life or existence after this. They see such injustice in this world and accept that it exists, and as such, are inescapably led to the conclusion that the world is random and there is no consequence to actions. This, then, is what they say and believe: "I will die and be finished and nothing will remain of me, so why should I not strive, as much as I can, to eat and sleep and enjoy myself?" If everyone thinks this way, it is clear what a competition there will be to commit evil deeds, and what the outcome will be. Should such individuals be forcibly silenced, or should order or control be allowed to lapse? There is no other choice apart from these two.

It is here that belief in life after death and the expectation of the continuation of life afterwards, which religious belief necessitates, brings human beings hope of justice. Thus, human beings have two motivating forces for accepting suffering, hardship, self-sacrifice, and righteous action: one is a motive that pertains to the general human tendency by which the individual looks past himself, and toils and strives with the expectation that at some point in the distant future, the human race will find its ideals realized; and the other is that motivating force that the individual human being feels within himself, by virtue of an inherent, enduring belief in life in the next world, in which he will be recompensed for having suffered and toiled in this life. In addition, people can then also see justice everywhere in this world. That is, if one were told that earthquakes, storms, and volcanic eruptions must necessarily occur and that their occurrence is not due to evil, wickedness, or punishment—rather, it is an occurrence that had to and did happen—they may, confronted with such an assertion, ask: "What, then, is the fault of those who, though entirely blameless, have perished due to these occurrences and experienced injustice or misfortune?" The answer is that with belief in the next life, the idea that such events are acts of oppression against anyone loses its meaning and significance. People can accept the all-encompassing order of this world and not consider it in conflict with justice because they believe in and anticipate life in the next world for the soul. This belief and anticipation revive hope. We see people who throughout their lives have suffered and endured hardship, yet until their last moments they are happy, have a cheerful disposition, are hopeful and joyful and are never disappointed or disheartened in thinking they have lived a fruitless life and now must leave it and pass away.

Such abiding joy and devotion come from faith, and no other kind of joy can ever take its place or rival it. Not even the worst kind of pain, suffering, torture, or torment can weaken or overtake this joy. Those who do not have such belief and do not draw inspiration from it are always sorrowful, sullen, anxious, and distraught. As opposed to the thought of old philosophers such as Epicurus[1] who said that the anticipation of death invites grief and anguish, it must rather be said that grief and anguish, despair and loss arise when people think that their existence comes to an end in the final moments of their life. Conversely, the hope of life after death, that is the metaphysical belief in a future world where the life of the spirit continues, brings joy and hope to life in this world. More specifically, such belief—if true—requires that we never despair of God's mercy in relation to our sins and of our life in the next world, and that we consider such despair, if it occurs, to be itself a great sin. It is thus that by believing in spiritual life after the decomposition of this physical constitution, we accept belief in justice and ensure hope and joy for people.

Of course, apart from this, we cannot speak of anything pertaining to life in the next world. Why? Because we are at a lower plane and cannot conceive of a higher plane. And since we are incapable of conceiving of a higher plane of existence, we likewise cannot speak of it. We do not know how it is. What we do know is that it exists. If we were to speak of it, it would only show that we have pictured or imagined it, and such imagination or conception is not its reality. Any image or idea of life in that world that we entertain in this life is commensurate with the qualities or characteristics of our physical existence in this world; namely, it immediately takes on a physical color or appearance and is likened to the delights of this world. One resorts to parables, for instance, of the garden of paradise and the fire of hell; milk, wine, and delectable fruits; the snake and the scorpion, and so on. Why? Because when we want to imagine something that is not a part of our contingent world, we use these very same characteristics to describe it, and there is no other recourse. It is for this reason that the religions of the past used such comparisons and parables, but we only consider them to be metaphors and allegories, symbols for conceiving of celestial gifts that do not exist in this world.

We consider paradise to be nearness to God, both in this world and—in a more complete sense—in the next world. Likewise, hell is remoteness from God and occurs both in this world and in the next. This nearness to and remoteness from God are what constitute our heaven and hell. So, in this way, while this matter becomes personal and satisfies our individual interests and can be a motivator for us, it lacks a material, elemental, and superficial aspect related to carnal desires and base cravings. It relates to the higher values of individual life, and its merit lies precisely here; because if it merely pertained to human inclinations in general, it would not suffice as a motivator for an individual, and if it had a material and physical aspect, it would not be worthy of any place in the next world.

Considering that the primary agent in creation is love—love is the mystery of creation and the cause of existence and is, for this reason, the ultimate purpose of creation—therefore nearness to or remoteness from God are the same as nearness to or remoteness from the True Beloved. It is thus illustrated that while we indeed have a personal purpose and desire in performing our acts of kindness and piety, this personal desire is nothing but drawing near unto the Beloved and achieving His pleasure. Since love involves sacrifice and selflessness, it necessitates devotion and total surrender of the lover's self in the existence of the Beloved. Therefore, while it has a personal aspect, love also accomplishes the self-effacement of the individual, and as such, this contradiction is resolved. Through belief in life in the next world, both the personal and non-personal aspects join together. On the one hand there is a personal self that desires, while on the other, because the self who desires is a lover and that which he desires is his Beloved, in reality this requires him to be selfless.

Bahá'u'lláh has stated that His commandments should be observed only for the love of His beauty and for the sake of His good pleasure. We consider this to be a fundamental principle, both in this world and the next, and we likewise regard that which we wish for as the result of our actions, in both worlds, to be naught but attaining the good pleasure of the Beloved and drawing near unto Him; this for us is "heaven." And since this is the case, we are not among those who expect, in exchange for what they lose in this world, to receive the exact same things in the next. For instance, if we abstain from drinking wine, it is not with the expectation of drinking from the "pure wine" in the next world, with "pure" having a meaning other than in a spiritual or allegorical sense. Or if in this world we live in a confined prison or a desolate ruin or a derelict house, we do not expect that heavenly mansions in beautiful gardens and blossoming bowers, with streams of milk, and the youths and maids of paradise, all await us to compensate for what we have lost in this world. We never see or consider ourselves in this way; rather, we believe in the afterlife as a kind of unique and pure existence in another world without any trace of material or physical aspects, and it is the anticipation of this spiritual life that motivates and drives us in this world to endure suffering, make sacrifices, and practice selflessness.

We stated that any attempt to describe the next world would compromise its purity, for doing so would inevitably impose upon it the characteristics of this world. For instance, we say that souls in the next world encompass this world and that they are aware of our lives. However, we cannot say what type of awareness or knowledge this is. Sometimes we say that the deceased can see and hear us. However, this seeing and hearing is merely a simile, a way of explaining things by approximating how we perceive in this world, because a spirit, which has neither ears nor eyes, cannot see or hear in the way we do. The only thing that is real is that we say the spirit comprehends and encompasses us. This encompassment and comprehension are of a kind by which a higher being understands a lower being, in a way that the latter is unaware of. For example, an animal senses a plant, but since the plant lacks these senses, it cannot comprehend how the animal senses it because that sensation is not particular to plants. A human in this world understands and perceives animals, but since this understanding is of an intellectual type and is termed knowledge, the animal does not understand it. It only perceives through outward seeing, hearing, and making sounds, which are of its own kind. Similarly, incorporeal souls have knowledge and encompass us in this world, but since they are on a higher level, it can never be determined what this knowledge and encompassment are like. In summary, we must know that whatever is said about that world brings it closer to this one, makes it of this world's kind, and strips it of the inherent purity and clarity of that otherworldly form. Therefore, it does not befit the life of that world. Hence, we should, to the extent possible, avoid imagining the life of that world in this one. We accept and anticipate the next world on the basis of our religious belief, and this is dictated by our spiritual love for the True Beloved. This and nothing more.

Of course, this relates to human spirits, which are incorporeal, immortal, eternal, and individual. It does not relate to the animal spirit because the animal spirit is not incorporeal or immortal, nor does it relate to the Holy Spirit because the Holy Spirit does not have personal, specific, or individual characteristics. The Holy Spirit is universal and indeed eternal, it always has been, is, and will be, and it is always in the celestial and spiritual realms. However, the eternal spiritual life of individual Manifestations of God is not in relation to Their association with the Holy Spirit. Why? Because the Holy Spirit admits no specification or individuation. 'Abdu'l-Bahá states explicitly in *Some Answered Questions* that the individuation of the Manifestations of God, like that of other individuals, is owing to the human soul, but the Holy Spirit admits no individuation or specification.[2]

The afterlife, therefore, does not apply to the Manifestations of God in the way that it applies to other people. That is, the expectation of divine reward and punishment and the like does not apply to Them because They possess the Supreme Infallibility. Since they occupy this station, reward and punishment for Their deeds has no meaning. It is through the Supreme Infallibility, according to Bahá'í belief, that the Manifestation of God is infallible. When we say He is infallible because of the Supreme Infallibility, what do we mean? Our meaning is that sin has no access to His presence. Why is there no place for sin in His presence? The reason is elaborated in the Kitáb-i-Aqdas.[3] Sin is that which is counter to what is ordained by the divine Manifestation, and good is action that is in accordance with what is ordained by the divine Manifestation. The criterion for establishing right and wrong, good and evil, is the decree of the Manifestation, His action, and His word. Our actions are good when they are in accordance with the action of the Manifestation and bad when they run contrary to it. As such, sin, error, and wrongdoing have no meaning when pertaining to the actions of the Manifestation, because those actions themselves are the standards by which all other works, actions, and conditions are measured and their being good or evil, right or wrong, sinful or virtuous, is determined.

He does whatsoever He wishes, because He is the Manifestation of God's attribute, "He doeth whatsoever He willeth."[4] Since He does as He wills, sin does not apply to Him. Since we are not like this—meaning that we must do that which He wills—if we do not do so, we have sinned. Since He does what He wills and that which He wills is good, wrongdoing has no meaning that pertains to Him. It is in this station that we say He is inherently infallible—since He is the Manifestation of the divine attribute of "He doeth whatsoever He willeth." This is the meaning of the "Supreme Infallibility," and by this meaning He—Supremely powerful to do what He wills—is free of sin; He does what He wills and that which He wills is good. This Supreme Infallibility is specific to Him, specific to every independent divine Manifestation in each dispensation, specific to the one Who reveals scripture and ordains laws. Namely, it is particular to Him Who brings laws and Whose law is the standard that establishes good and evil, wrongdoing and righteousness. Therefore, this quality is specific to Him. His successor, the Center of His Covenant, the Guardian of His Cause, the Imám Who observes His decree, the prophet Who promulgates His law and does not bear his own, although they follow His command, cannot be infallible by reason of the Supreme Infallibility. This is also among our fundamental beliefs: we consider the divine Manifestation of the Cause of God to be infallible through the Supreme Infallibility, and apart from Him, no other shares this attribute. Bahá'u'lláh has admonished His followers in the Kitáb-i-Aqdas and His Tablets that if we consider any other than the divine Manifestation as infallible through the Supreme Infallibility we have grievously blasphemed. May God protect us from such egregious blasphemy. Let us pray that He protects us.

Of course, the Center of the Covenant and the Guardian of the Cause are infallible, and the one who decrees in the name of the independent Manifestation of God is infallible because 'Abdu'l-Bahá says if they were not infallible, then the Cause that has been placed in their hands would deviate, and such deviation would lead to the deviation of all people, and this would be far removed from God's justice. Thus, they are infallible—not due to the Supreme Infallibility, but because they stand within the sheltering shade of the Manifestation of the Cause of God and His Revelation. The Center of the Covenant is infallible because He abides by the command of the Manifestation of divine revelation, because He is the perfect exemplar of the teachings of the divine Manifestation; as 'Abdu'l-Bahá terms it, he has "conferred infallibility." 'Abdu'l-Bahá is infallible due to His being within the sheltering shade of the Cause of Bahá'u'lláh. This is imparted from God to Him; this infallibility is not inherent, but acquired.

It must be noted that what has been set forth in the Kitáb-i-Aqdas that is particular to the divine Manifestations is described with the adjective "Most Great." It is therefore clear that an infallibility other than the Supreme Infallibility also exists and is not subject to this superlative qualification. 'Abdu'l-Bahá explains that the Supreme Infallibility is inherent, while infallibility for the Center of the Covenant and for the Guardian of the Cause is acquired and conferred.

According to the Will and Testament of 'Abdu'l-Bahá, we consider the Universal House of Justice to be protected from error and infallible. That is, when the collective body of the Universal House of Justice carries out its functions as the Center of the Cause of the Blessed Beauty, it is infallible according to the text of the Kitáb-i-Aqdas and the Tablets of Bahá'u'lláh. It is protected from error, is free from misconduct, does not commit mistakes, and is free of fault. Of course, according to our belief, revelation ends with the Manifestation Who is the bearer of the Holy Writ and the source of command, and after Him there is no revelation until the appearance of the next Manifestation at another time. The Guardian in one of His letters has explicitly stated that divine revelation has ended with the Báb and Bahá'u'lláh until the appearance of the next Manifestation in no less than one thousand years, and that at least until such time, no one can expect a new Manifestation. As such, since Bahá'u'lláh, nobody has been the recipient of divine revelation.

Both 'Abdu'l-Bahá and the Guardian were inspired without being recipients of divine revelation. In its legislation, in issuing decrees and making decisions, the Universal House of Justice is likewise infallible. Why? Because it is inspired without being the recipient of divine revelation. It is inspired in that it decides according to the will of God and acts with the gracious assistance of God. For this reason, whatever it does is always the object of divine confirmation, and whatever it desires is always correct, without any interruption in this divine affirmation during either its decision-making or its communication as the World Centre of the Bahá'í Faith. This belief protects us, protects our Faith, and is the protector and guardian of human felicity now and in the future. In this way, attention is drawn to how we emerged from a single source and turned towards a single destination. The Prophets have striven with their teachings to bring us closer in this world to the source of unity from which we have strayed, until such time as the golden age of mankind in this world unfolds, and also draw us nearer to that center of unity so that personal happiness may reveal itself to us both in this world and in the continuation of our life in the next.

Among our core beliefs is that the kingdom of God will be established upon this heap of dust—this very world of ours—to the extent possible in this contingent world. As stated in the Gospel, may the will of God be done on earth as it is in heaven.[5] May this world, figuratively speaking, become like a mirror that reflects the order of the higher world. How would it be reflected? In such a way that it maximizes the possibility of realizing true unity in the world of multiplicity. Divine unity, pure unity, absolute unity indeed exists in the realm of God; as I have mentioned in one of my other talks, this unity can also be realized in this world, but as a unity within diversity. To the greatest extent possible, any form of difference must diminish to allow unity to be realized to the fullest extent. Of course, when we say that any form of difference must diminish, we refer to those differences that hinder unity; however, some differences are necessary for the realization of unity, which is unity in diversity. Consider a geometric shape that you have drawn: it has straight lines, curves, volume, perspective, dotted lines, angles, and hundreds of other parts. But all these different parts demonstrate a single thing that is realized in this form. Each part, wherever it goes, signifies a command, even when diverging from the others. Thus, the diversity that shows how multiple parts can come together to display a single order, a single command, a single beauty, signifies the realization of unity. Differences that must disappear are those that cause division and discord, that foster enmity and hostility based on race, gender, and class, based on differences between slave and free, rich and poor, East and West. Such discord and division must be eliminated, and the day must come when, as far as possible in this contingent world, everything reveals the signs of unity. This is what we believe will happen. However, mindful of our discussions about determinism and free will, we should note that it will unfold, but it must unfold through our actions. The divine will acts, but He has desired that His will be realized through humanity, through the sons and daughters of man, so that in the process, humanity may develop the capacity and merit for such a lofty station, and by its own volition, reach a place where it is deserving of such honor.

This means that under the divine will, our efforts are required for the fulfillment of God's will. We believe that on the one hand, the divine will operates in general, universally, through the operation of invisible means in the world, and on the other hand, a clear plan has been placed in our hands, for which we are responsible. We are free to demonstrate our worthiness to accept this responsibility. In the process of manifesting this capability, we ourselves earn the right to achieve such an order and enter such an era, which is the Golden Age of the Dispensation of the Abhá Beauty. We expect the realization of such a promised day, whose signs are already apparent; our expectation is accompanied by action, work, and activity, because it is we who, as agents, are obligated to realize such a system in the world of possibility in response to the primary and universal agent, which is the divine will.

NOTES TO CHAPTER SEVEN

1 The Greek philosopher, Epicurus, was born in 341 B.C. and passed away at the age of seventy-three in either 271 or 270 B.C. Epicurus believed that the foundation of human happiness lies in intellectual and spiritual pursuits, and that every action that a person takes should be with the intention of acquiring these.

2 'Abdu'l-Bahá, *Some Answered Questions*, chapter 39, Bahá'í Reference Library, www.bahai.org/r/905019971.

3 Bahá'u'lláh, *The Kitáb-i-Aqdas*, ¶ 47, Bahá'í Reference Library, www.bahai.org/r/235783608.

4 See Qur'án 22:18. This expression is used by Bahá'u'lláh in Epistle to the Son of the Wolf and is translated by Shoghi Effendi as "He doeth whatsoever He willeth." See www.bahai.org/r/758311257.

5 See the Lord's prayer in Matthew 6:9–13.

Chapter 7

Religion is the Truth and the Truth is One

Translated by Nima Rafiei

One of the essential teachings of the Bahá'í Dispensation is the fundamental oneness of the world's religions. It could be said that this teaching is the crowning jewel of the Blessed Beauty's dispensation. 'Abdu'l-Bahá's utterances on this theme are plentiful and quoting all of them here is not possible. Among them are the following: "The foundation of the divine religions is one. One truth, one spirit, one light. It admitteth no multiplicity."[1] He also states: "The foundation of the religions of God is one and is the truth, and the truth admitteth no multiplicity or division."[2] And: "The foundation of the religions of God is one, and the purpose of all the religions of the world and their adherents is one."[3] The sacred utterances on this subject—most of which date back some sixty or seventy years—are many, and quoting all of them here is not possible.

Basically, the concept of religion in the Bahá'í Faith necessitates the unity of religions. That is, Bahá'ís believe that the sequence of successive religions throughout various ages—from the beginning of human history to the present age, and until the end of time—constitutes a singular spiritual phenomenon whose essence is consistently preserved. Just as an individual human being remains the same person throughout her life from birth until death, despite all the developments that occur during her lifetime—that is, she remains who she ever was and will always remain who she is—likewise, the divine religions, from the beginning until the end that has no end, cannot be more than one religion in essence, although they change according to the exigencies of the time and the different stages of humanity's spiritual development. The underlying meaning is that the essence of religion, emanating from the absolute Divine Essence, is in its highest prescribed degree of perfection from the very beginning. However, as it relates to humanity within the realm of creation, it undergoes various transformations in accordance with the progression of human life through stages of spiritual growth. It is for this reason that the secondary aspects, details, laws, and ordinances of religions undergo change. Yet, beyond these variable conditions, the permanent and unified identity of religion remains intact and is preserved.

In this vein, we consider the reality of religion to be one essence whose accidental properties, like all other things, change according to the requirements of the age. The change in these accidental properties should not distract us from the essential unity of religions. Nearly seventy years ago, 'Abdu'l-Bahá said in this regard: "Observe how man, from the inception of his life until the end is one person in every way. Likewise, the religion of God is but one religion throughout all ages."[4] And likewise, He says: "These differences you observe in the religions of God are like the differences between the beginning and the end of a person's life. . . . No matter how much . . . a person . . . manifesteth differences outwardly, he remaineth but one person. Likewise, though the religion of God manifesteth outward characteristics that are different in the days of the Prophets, yet it is a single reality."[5] Bahá'ís believe that the adherents of all religions can recognize this truth, namely, the oneness of the foundations of religions, or, at the very least, prominent religious figures have repeatedly emphasized it. At this juncture, we will abstain from discussing other religions and focus solely on citing passages from the Qur'án. In this sacred Book, we see in several instances that the religions founded by Prophets before the advent of the radiant Faith of Muḥammad are referred to as *"islám"* or submission and self-surrender to God. Solomon, for instance, was lauded as an adherent of *"islám"*: "O my Lord! I have sinned against my own soul, and I resign myself, with Solomon, to God the Lord of the Worlds."[6]

Moreover, the faith of Abraham is referred to as *"islám"* and adherence to it as the true religion is considered obligatory: "Follow, therefore, the religion of Abraham, the sound in faith, who was not one of those who joined other gods to God,"[7] and "And who hath a better religion than he who resigneth himself to God, who doth what is good, and followeth the faith of Abraham in all sincerity?"[8] and "He hath elected you, and hath not laid on you any hardship in religion, the Faith of your father Abraham. He hath named you the Muslims,"[9] and "And who but he that hath debased his soul to folly will mislike the faith of Abraham, when we have chosen him in this world, and in the world to come he shall be of the Just? When his Lord said to him, 'Resign thyself to me,' he said, 'I resign myself to the Lord of the Worlds.'"[10] Jacob and all of his sons are referred to as Muslims: "And this to his children did Abraham bequeath, and Jacob also, saying, 'O my children! Truly God hath chosen a religion for you; so die not unless ye be also Muslims'"[11]; and similarly, "Were ye present when Jacob was at the point of death, when he said to his sons, 'Whom will ye worship when I am gone?' They said, 'We will worship thy God and the God of thy fathers Abraham and Ismael and Isaac, one God, and to Him are we surrendered (Muslims).'"[12] Jesus Christ and His apostles are also mentioned as Muslims: "And when Jesus perceived unbelief on their part, He said, 'Who my helpers with God?' The apostles said, 'We will be God's helpers! We believe in God, and bear thou witness that we are Muslims.'"[13] These verses clearly show that the religions of Abraham, Isaac, Jacob, Solomon, and Jesus, which appeared hundreds and thousands of years before the advent of the religion of Muḥammad, were different in terms of the names of the Prophets, the titles of the Books, and the details of the laws; but that all of them can, nevertheless, be called by the single name of *"islám."* This itself is proof that all religions, despite the differences in their laws, ordinances, and accidental properties, are various stages of the same singular truth, and with regard to this oneness of meaning, according to the Qur'án, the general title for all of them can be *"islám."*

Bahá'ís consider this to be true in this time too, that is, at the time of the Revelation following that of Muḥammad. They do not deny that, according to one of the essential truths of the teachings of the Qur'án, *islám* is the true religion and choosing any other religion beside it cannot be accepted by God: "The true religion with God is Islam,"[14] and "Whoso desireth any other religion than Islam, that religion shall never be accepted from him, and in the next world he shall be among the lost."¹⁵ Bahá'ís confess that Muḥammad—the salutations and blessings of God be upon Him—was the Seal of the Prophets and that both prophethood and messengership were fulfilled through Him, just as they began through Him in time immemorial and will perpetually continue through Him for evermore. They agree with <u>Sh</u>ay<u>kh</u> Farídu'd-Dín 'Aṭṭár, who said of the Prophet Muḥammad:

> All Prophets, all Messengers, in every guise,
> Through countless paths, Your faith They realize.
>
> Both before and after, in worlds You stand,
> First and the last, by Your own command.
>
> None came before You, this truth is plain,
> Nor will another after You remain.¹⁶

One should study the blessed words of Bahá'u'lláh, written some one hundred and twenty years ago in the Kitáb-i-Íqán, to understand that, according to the belief of the Bahá'ís, just as before the appearance of the Prophet Muḥammad every religion was His religion and every Messenger embodied His essence, so too after His Advent every religion is that same religion in its foundation, since the essence of religion is one—though differences in outward forms, laws, and circumstances arise according to the requirements of the time. Every Messenger Who is sent forth is associated with the same Holy Spirit that is none other than the blessed self of the Seal of the Prophets, though there be differences in name, appearance, nationality, or tribe. For this reason, Bahá'ís believe that with the advent of the Bahá'í Faith, the luminous religion of Islam remains valid in its essence and that there is never any question of opposition to it. When Bahá'ís mention the name of Bahá'u'lláh, they are, in truth, mentioning the names of Muḥammad and other Manifestations of God. When they proclaim the Bahá'í Faith throughout Europe, Africa, Asia, Oceania, and the Americas, they are, in essence, calling people to the principles of Islam, which are aligned with the truths of all religions. This is because they see the essence of these two, and all other, religions as one and the same: "Say: 'We believe in

God, and in what hath been sent down to us, and what hath been sent down to Abraham, and Ismael, and Isaac, and Jacob, and the tribes, and in what hath been given to Moses, and Jesus, and the Prophets, from their Lord. We make no difference between them. And to Him are we resigned (Muslims)."[17]

The Bahá'ís of Iran deeply lament the accusation of opposing Islam that some levy against them, and consider it impossible for any fair-minded person to entertain such a notion.

The fact that it has been necessary for certain secondary laws or matters related to the outward forms of religious practice, customs, or temporal and spatial conditions to undergo changes—changes that were inevitable due to the demands of the time, for any phenomenon that takes place within the bounds of time inherently entails motion and change—in no way implies that any contradiction can be perceived between the Bahá'í Faith and Islam, or other religions. 'Abdu'l-Bahá says: "The religion of God consists of two parts: One is the very foundation . . . This part suffers neither change nor alteration. . . . It will never be abrogated . . . but will remain in force and effect for all eternity. . . .The second part of the religion of God, which pertains to the material world . . . is changed and altered in every prophetic Dispensation and may be abrogated . . . according to the exigencies of the time."[18] He also states: "Every religion is comprised of two parts. One part is primary ... which is one and in no wise subject to change. The other part is secondary . . . In every dispensation, it changeth according to the exigencies of that age."[19]

The purpose of this detailed explanation is to ensure that the spread of misinterpretations does not hinder non-Bahá'í friends from understanding the beliefs of the Bahá'ís, and to firmly establish that if, at any time, a Bahá'í were to think, even momentarily, that the Bahá'í Faith is in opposition to the truths of any divine religion, he could no longer consider himself a Bahá'í. If he were not to reconcile such views, the Bahá'í Faith would distance itself from them.

This explanation has been given in general terms and with consideration of the shared truths and oneness of the principles of all religions. However, regarding the specific relationship with Islam, numerous evidences can be drawn from the writings of Bahá'u'lláh, 'Abdu'l-Bahá, and Shoghi Effendi, demonstrating—through the explicit texts of the Author of the Bahá'í Faith and His appointed Interpreter—how the Bahá'ís regard the resplendent religion of Islam. In the Writings revealed by the Pen of Bahá'u'lláh that the Bahá'ís recite when praying to God, one repeatedly observes that they commune and associate themselves with the name of Muḥammad, the Chosen One, and remember that Lord of the Prophets. According to the teaching of Bahá'u'lláh, they even beseech God not to be deprived of Muḥammad's intercession. In one of Bahá'u'lláh's prayers, we read:

> Salutations and blessings upon the Dawning Place of God's most excellent Names and most exalted Attributes, Him in every letter of Whose name all names are treasured and through Whom the whole existence, both seen and unseen, is adorned, Him Who is named 'Muḥammad' in the Kingdom of Names and 'Aḥmad' in the heaven of immortality.[20]

And also:

> I testify, O my God, unto that whereunto have testified Thy Prophets and Thy chosen Ones, and unto that which Thou didst reveal in Thy Books and Thy Scriptures. I beseech Thee by the mysteries of Thy Book and by Him through Whom Thou didst open the portals of knowledge before Thy creation and raised up the standard of divine Unity amidst Thy servants, to bestow upon me the intercession of the Prince of the Messengers, Him Who is the guide upon every path, and graciously assist me to do that which is pleasing and acceptable unto Thee.[21]

And:

> O Thou Who causest the dawn to appear and subduest the winds! I beseech Thee by Thy Prophets, Thy Messengers, Thy chosen ones, and Thy loved ones, whom Thou hast made to be the standards of Thy guidance amidst Thy creatures and the signs of Thy victory throughout Thy realm, and I beseech Thee by the light that dawned from the horizon of Ḥijáz and illumined Mecca and Medina, and all that

is in the world of creation, to graciously assist Thy servants to remember and to praise Thee, and to observe whatsoever Thou hast revealed in Thy book.[22]

Many statements like this can be cited, each testifying to how the Bahá'ís refer to the Prophet Muḥammad and the exalted station in which they hold Him. Among the necessary beliefs of anyone who adheres to the Bahá'í Faith is the acceptance of Islam, recognizing this luminous religion as the religion of God and regarding the Prophet Muḥammad as the Chief of the Pure Ones. Shoghi Effendi, in a book titled *The Advent of Divine Justice* addressed to the Bahá'ís of the United States of America, explicitly states that the Bahá'ís of that region must study the Qur'án, must properly understand Islam, and must dispel the misinterpretations about this radiant religion that are widespread in the West. Since that time, in many Bahá'í schools in America and Europe, the teaching of the Qur'án, discussions on Islamic beliefs, and explanation of those beliefs has become a primary part of their curriculum.

In the Writings of 'Abdu'l-Bahá, in His talks, letters, and addresses, we repeatedly observe how He sought to defend Islam before non-Muslims, how He endeavored to demonstrate the truth of Muḥammad's mission with clear and conclusive explanations, how He strove to show that the glorious Qur'án is filled with moral and scientific truths, and how He undertook to dispel every accusation levelled against Islam and its Holy Prophet out of prejudice in the West. In synagogues and churches across Europe and America, He devoted some of His addresses entirely to explaining the truths of Islam and proving the prophethood of He Who is the Best of Creation [Muḥammad].

One can refer to the Tablet of visitation revealed by Bahá'u'lláh for the Prince of Martyrs (Imám Ḥusayn—may the spirit of all of existence be sacrificed for his sake) to see to what heights He raised the station of that great Imám. He states that there are none in the world who could compare to Imám Ḥusayn's blessed being: "There was none to equal or to match him in the world."[23] Moreover, He calls for the souls of the Concourse on high to be sacrificed for the tribulations endured by that offspring of the Divine Lote-Tree and hidden mystery of the exalted Word: "May the souls of the entire Concourse on high be sacrificed for thy tribulation, O thou offspring of the Divine Lote-Tree, and hidden and inscrutable mystery of the exalted Word."²⁴ Elsewhere, He states that through the martyrdom of that pride of the Imáms, the Pen of His Decree was stilled and the very foundations of the earth were made to tremble: "By thy tribulation, the Pen of Decree was stilled . . . and the foundations of the earth trembled and all of existence was nearly reduced to utter nothingness."²⁵ He also states that Imám Ḥusayn is the fruition of the appearance of the Prophets: "Were it not for thee, the All-Merciful would not have revealed Himself to the son of 'Imrán [Moses] in the Sinai of certitude."²⁶

These brief excerpts suffice to prove that no one claiming to follow the Bahá'í Faith could regard himself as being in opposition to the radiant religion of Islam, a religion whose essence is the essence of all religions. This essence has been, is, and will remain eternally unchanging, one, and enduring. "There is no change in the words of God! This, the great felicity!"²⁷

NOTES TO CHAPTER SIX

1   'Abdu'l-Bahá, qtd. in 'Abdu'l-Ḥamíd Ishráq-Khávarí, *Payám-i-Malakút*, (New Delhi: Bahá'í Publishing Trust, 1986), 196; provisional translation.
2   Ibid., 166.
3   Ibid.
4   Ibid., 189; provisional translation.
5   Ibid.; provisional translation.
6   The Quranic terms *islám* (submission) and *muslim* (one who submits) are semantically flexible and context-dependent. While some commentators understand these terms as referring specifically to the institutional religion of Islam and its adherents, many scholars and commentators note that in the Qur'án itself, *islám* more accurately denotes a spiritual disposition of wholehearted surrender to God's will. It is this attitude of wholehearted surrender and devotion to God that the Qur'án attributes not only to the followers of Muḥammad, but also to earlier figures like Solomon, Abraham, Jacob, and Jesus.
    Qur'án 27:44, translated by J. M. Rodwell in *The Koran* (London: J M Dent & Sons, 1909), 177. The verbal noun *islám* is derived from the Arabic verb translated as "resign" in this verse.

7   Qur'án 3:95, translated by J. M. Rodwell in *The Koran*, 395.
8   Qur'án 4:125, translated by J. M. Rodwell in *The Koran*, 424. The verbal noun *islám* is derived from the Arabic verb translated as "resigneth" in this verse.
9   Qur'án 22:78, translated by J. M. Rodwell in *The Koran*, 460.
10 Qur'án 2:130-131, translated by J. M. Rodwell in *The Koran*, 351. The verbal noun *islám* is derived from the Arabic verb translated as "resign" in this verse.
11 Qur'án 2:132, translated by J. M. Rodwell in *The Koran*, 351.
12 Qur'án 2:133, translated by J. M. Rodwell in *The Koran*, 351–352.
13 Qur'án 3:52, translated by J. M. Rodwell in *The Koran*, 391.
14 Dávúdí's broader theological point here is to underscore the spiritual continuity of the world's revealed religions and to illustrate that the unity of divine revelation is a Quranic truth as well as a Bahá'í one. That all revelations of God throughout history constitute a single, progressive religious reality—referred to as *islám*, the spiritual disposition of submission to God as described in the verses quoted from the Qur'án here—is a central teaching of the Bahá'í Faith. The Bahá'í teachings affirm the essential oneness of all religions and recognize that each Manifestation of God has revealed teachings according to the needs of the time and capacity of the people. From this perspective, all divine religions can be seen as successive stages of a single Faith of God, expressed in the Quranic lexicon as *islám*. Yet the Bahá'í Faith also regards itself as an independent religion, not a sect or continuation of Islam as a socio-historical system.

Qur'án 3:19, translated by J. M. Rodwell in *The Koran*, 387. For a discussion of this verse, see the next note.
15 Qur'án 3:85, translated by J. M. Rodwell in *The Koran*, 394. The absence of capitalization in Arabic allows for a broader reading of the word "islám" in its original language. The introduction of capitalization as an orthographic convention in the English language, however, has imposed doctrinal boundaries that restrict the semantic flexibility of this word in Arabic. What is now recognized as Islam, with its legal, theological, and institutional structures, had not yet fully emerged at the time the Qur'án was being revealed. The Quranic use of "dín" and "islám" in the seventh century predates the emergence of Islam as a structured religious system. For a discussion of this concept, see Nicolai Sinai, *Key Terms of the Qur'an: A Critical Dictionary* (Princeton: Princeton University Press, 2023), 293–300. Sinai writes that "the Qur'anic religion is deemed to be more than one peculiar manifestation of human religious practice and is labelled 'the true mode of religious worship' or even 'the true religion'" and that Qur'án 3:19 "equates this true religion, 'the mode of religious worship that is valid before God'. . .with al-islām, an attitude of total devotion or self-surrender to God that is understood to entail

full recognition of his prophetic emissary Muhammad" (Ibid., 299–300)..

16   Farídu'd-Dín 'Aṭṭár, *Manṭiqu'ṭ-Ṭayr*, (Ṭihrán: Intishárát-i-Kitábfurúshíy-i-Ṭihrán, 1975), 24.

17   Qur'án 3:84, translated by J. M. Rodwell in *The Koran*, 394.

18   'Abdu'l-Bahá. *Some Answered Questions*, ch. 11, Bahá'í Reference Library, www.bahai.org/r/337609919.

19   'Abdu'l-Bahá, qtd. in Ishráq-Khávarí, *Payám-i-Malakút*, 185; provisional translation.

20   Bahá'u'lláh, Bahá'í Reference Library, www.bahai.org/r/586510811; provisional translation.

21   Bahá'u'lláh, *Majmú'iy-i-Alváḥ-i-Mubárakih* (Cairo: Maṭba'atu's-Sa'ádah, 1920), 407–408; provisional translation.

22   Ibid., 406–407; provisional translation.

23   Bahá'u'lláh, *The Kitáb-i-Íqán*, Bahá'í Reference Library, www.bahai.org/r/711028028.

24   Bahá'u'lláh, Bahá'í Reference Library, www.bahai.org/r/524834627; provisional translation.

25   Ibid.; provisional translation.

26   Ibid.; provisional translation.

27   Qur'án 10:64, translated by J. M. Rodwell in *The Koran*, 280.

Chapter 8

The Oneness of Religion

Translated by Vargha Bolodo-Taefi

You may know that Shoghi Effendi has stated that the spiritual teachings of the Bahá'í Faith can be summarized in a single principle: the unity of humankind.[1] All other teachings are secondary, peripheral, or ancillary to this fundamental and essential principle. Based on this statement of Shoghi Effendi's, and by extending it to encompass the entirety of the Bahá'í Faith—viewing the Bahá'í Faith as an integrated whole, as a unity, or a singular entity—we can unequivocally assert that the Bahá'í Faith is the religion of unity: unity at the beginning, unity at the end, and unity between the beginning and the end. This means that the essence of the Bahá'í Faith is to restore unity to a world, or an individual, severed from it—and thus, disconnected from its own origin—and to realize again at the end the unity that existed at the beginning.

The unity at the beginning is an absolute, pure, and unconditioned unity. The unity at the end is also a unity whose ultimate ideal and desired perfection is absolute unity. Between the two, however, in this visible world, humanity is subject to multiplicity. The Bahá'í Faith declares, openly and unequivocally, that this entire spiritual enterprise—that is, this Faith along with all the religions that have preceded it and those that will succeed it—is an endeavor to introduce unity into this multiplicity. The objective is to attribute unity to the existing multiplicity, to relate unity to it, and to reveal unity within it, so that unity will manifest itself within multiplicity to the fullest extent possible, to the highest degree that is feasible and conceivable for multiplicity to embody unity. The hope is that this endeavor may lead to a state where it can be said that the primal and original unity has reappeared, has resurfaced, and has been realized anew.

The unity at the beginning, the pure unity and absolute oneness, is the world of God, a realm inconceivable to us within the world of multiplicity. Not only is it impossible to realize such unity, but it is impossible to even imagine it. It is evident that the trace of the Untraceable cannot be sought in a realm replete with traces, where nothing is found but traces. For this reason, those who have sought to see God in the world of creation or equated creation with God have erred and strayed from the path. Creation cannot be God, nor can God manifest Himself in creation in such a way that the distinction between Creator and creation is eliminated. Such a phenomenon is impossible. That creation has emanated and come into being itself indicates that God did not intend for only Himself to remain. He willed to bring forth a creation apart from Himself, so that His beauty might be reflected in the mirror of His creation, and—although this creation is other than Him—a pathway to Him might be found within this world of distinction.

For this reason, we hold that creation is distinct from God. Yet this creation, though distinct from God, has emanated from Him. This emanation signifies that pure unity and absolute oneness, the hallmark of the Divine realm, has inclined toward multiplicity. There are, however, intermediary stages in this process. Absolute oneness does not transform into absolute multiplicity abruptly, without stages, steps, or a path marked by successive stations. God willed that this oneness should gradually don the garment of multiplicity and take on its hue. Consequently, an intermediary realm is necessary—a transitional reality between the absolute oneness of the Divine realm and the absolute multiplicity of the world of creation. This intermediary realm is the realm of Divine Revelation.[2] In other words, a realm has come into being and appeared that, on the one hand, bears a connection to God and, on the other, maintains an association with creation. Without such an intermediary, the Absolute Oneness—Who could have no relation, connection, or association with absolute multiplicity, as such a relationship would contradict the very nature of His oneness—would make it incumbent upon Himself and direct His will either to refrain from creating altogether or, if He were to create, to make the path to creation pass through the intermediary of the realm of Divine Revelation. In this intermediary realm, unity—while it is neither absolute unity nor absolute multiplicity—begins to become the recipient of multiplicity. In this realm, we find signs and traces of a unity that is transitioning into multiplicity. Accepting the existence of the realm of Divine Revelation as an intermediary realm and transitional reality between absolute unity and absolute multiplicity, one that bridges the world of God and the world of creation, is a fundamental tenet of our beliefs.

Since the fundamental principles of religions are one, we do not claim that this principle began with us—that is, with the Word of Bahá'u'lláh in this age. Religions existed prior to the Bahá'í Faith, albeit all of them were the Bahá'í Faith. Indeed, from another perspective, we might even say that all of them were Islam, or were Christianity, or Judaism. These names and titles do not alter the essence of the matter. The diversity of names and labels never diminishes the oneness of the essence of religions or the oneness of their foundation. It is for this reason that we assert—and can substantiate the assertion—that this principle is among the fundamental and universal truths of all religions, such that the absence of this principle in any religion is inconceivable. We firmly believe that it has always been thus, and that sound belief has always necessitated recognizing the existence of a realm called the realm of Divine Revelation as the intermediary between the absolute oneness of the Absolute Reality and the absolute multiplicity of the absolute creation. We further hold that it is this realm of Divine Revelation that is the origin of the created world, or that, in the terminology of the ancient sages, serves as the intermediary of creation. It is the first creation and the means through which all other creations have come into being. It is the first effect, the first emanation to emerge, to proceed, to be made manifest from the Absolute Reality. By this virtue, it can relate to multiplicity and associate with creation, or, in another sense, serve as the creator—or the intermediary for the creation—of the world of multiplicity. This is because this realm can relate to multiplicity while also maintaining its relationship with oneness. This Divine Revelation, which is but one Revelation, this Word of God, which is but one Word, this Divine Manifestation, which is but one Manifestation—which is at once the first and the last Manifestation, though, in the strictest sense, even the terms "first" and "last" cannot be attributed to it—is the foundation of religion.

You may have heard that we Bahá'ís often prefer to refer to the totality of our teachings and beliefs as the "Bahá'í Revelation," although we do not hesitate to call it the "Bahá'í Religion" either. By this designation, we mean to underscore the idea that religion, for us, serves as an intermediary for manifesting unity within multiplicity. Similarly, the realm of the Divine Revelation is a reflection of the same principle and spirit, a testament to the same unifying spirit seeking to manifest itself within the body of multiplicity to gradually guide it toward unity. Because we recognize this principle as the defining character of our belief, we emphasize identifying and referring to the Bahá'í Faith as the "Bahá'í Revelation" and promote this terminology. In its relation to this world and to the system of laws and ordinances that govern human conduct, this singular Revelation is termed religion. It is for this reason that we recognize divine religions as one religion. The essence, or the truth, therefore, is the "Revelation"; and the laws and ordinances may more accurately, and in common terminology, be referred to as "religion." The truth and the laws together constitute for us a path that may serve as a force to continually realize unity in diversity and oneness in multiplicity from the beginning to the end.

Since Divine Revelation—or, in common terminology, the religion of God—serves as the means of realizing unity in diversity, it necessarily follows that Revelation itself cannot be manifold; it cannot possess multiplicity. How can something that is itself multiple serve as the agent of unity? Consequently, the Revelation of God must be regarded as one: "Our Cause is but one."[3] The Word of God must be considered one. The religion of God must be understood as one. In this way, we must affirm the oneness of the foundation of all religions. We must hold that from the beginning that has no beginning to the end that has no end, emanations of the Word of God—which is the same as Revelation and religion—that pertain to this world can only ever be one. In relation to its essence, its meaning, and its intension, the Word of God is one.[4] Any multiplicity or diversity pertains solely to its extension.

It is evident then that one of the fundamental tenets of the Bahá'í Faith is the belief that Revelation is the first emanation from God. When we speak of it as "first," we do so from our own perspective, for otherwise, the term "first" does not apply in this context. This is because this emanation, like God Himself, is pre-existent—even if it is only temporally pre-existent. The first emanation of God—namely Revelation, which serves as the intermediary of creation—is one both in its essence and in its meaning and intension. That is to say, the reality that emanates from God, within which Divine Revelation is made manifest—and for this reason, we refer to it as the Manifestation of God—is only ever one in the world of existence. It has ever existed, it will forever exist, and it is always permanent and immutable. Though it does not share the same nature as the eternal and everlasting Essence of God, it is nevertheless both pre-existent and everlasting, meaning it can neither come into existence nor cease to exist.

There is but one Manifestation of God. There is, however, no contradiction in referring to what we term the Manifestation of God using the terminology of other religions—such as Messengers, Prophets, or Lawgivers. The terminology we use aligns with a specific meaning we emphasize in this relation. But we have not invented it; it has always existed. We emphasize it in light of the exigencies of this age in which the Bahá'í Faith has appeared. It is not our terminology to refer to the Founders of religions—or Those known as such in the eyes of the world—as Messengers, Prophets, or Lawgivers. Rather, we use the term Manifestations of the Cause of God. If, on occasion, the term Prophet or Messenger is employed, it is in the context of other religious traditions to facilitate mutual understanding and agreement in terminology. That we do not use these common terms does not imply, God forbid, that we deny prophethood or messengership. It rather reflects the fact that in previous dispensations, the terms prophethood and messengership were used because Divine Revelation was perceived through the specific lens of those religions; and today, Divine Revelation is regarded from the perspective of the Bahá'í Faith. As indicated earlier, we use the term Manifestations of the Cause of God to underscore this particular understanding. It is rare to find in the Writings of Bahá'u'lláh instances where He refers to Himself as a Prophet or Messenger, unless it is in the context of discourse or dialogue with others in order to discuss, converse, or convey His meaning. In such cases, He would inevitably adopt the terminology familiar to His audience to convey His meaning. And the reason was to draw attention to this same understanding, to allow us to state and demonstrate that what is revealed by these Holy Beings is Divine Revelation itself and that Divine Revelation serves as the intermediary between God and His creation. It is the means by which oneness is conferred association with multiplicity, just as Revelation acts as the intermediary between God, Who is absolute oneness, and creation, which is absolute multiplicity. It is this understanding that the Bahá'í Faith has emphasized.

All the Manifestations of God, or, as others may term Them, the Prophets, Lawgivers, Messengers, or Founders of religions—titles which we, too, have no objection or hesitation to use, for we find them valid as they convey the same meaning, and a diversity of terms is unimportant—are, from beginning to end, one and the same. They are but one essence. This is because Revelation is the first emanation from God. And nothing except one can emanate from one. This is an axiomatic principle of reason and philosophy.[5] Nothing except oneness can emanate from oneness. If we perceive multiplicity emanating from oneness, it is inevitably because we have been able to consider that oneness from various perspectives and recognized it as the source of diverse effects. Therefore, if we are to preserve the absolute oneness of God, we must necessarily regard what emanates from Him as truly one. The first emanation from God is Revelation, and the Manifestation of Divine Revelation; therefore, it can be no more than one, from the beginning to the end.

The sages of past religions have alluded to this notion in various ways. In Christianity, this first emanation is referred to as the Word of God, which is the same as the Holy Spirit that partakes in the effusion of grace from the being of Christ. It both shines forth from God unto Christ and simultaneously receives from Christ the power to shine throughout the world; it is none other than the Holy Spirit. It is singular, one and the same. Similarly, Muslims have named this first emanation the "Muhammadan Spirit," the sacred reality of the Seal of the Prophets. They, too, are correct, for in truth, there is no Muḥammad or Jesus. Insofar as this emanation is from God, it is but one Revelation, one Word, one being, and one essence. It does not admit plurality; its essence is incompatible with multiplicity. It only admits plurality inasmuch as it becomes related to the world of multiplicity and appears among the creation and for the creation.

For this reason, we regard the Manifestations of God, from the beginning to the end, as one and the same: one essence, one nature, one reality, one identity. One may choose any term. Whatever term is more precise may be employed, provided we affirm Their oneness, for oneness is Their very reality. Without our acknowledgment of the truth, which is Their oneness, the foundation of our belief would not remain solid, and our convictions would not be established upon a firm basis. That is why we assert that Bahá'u'lláh, from the perspective of His divine, spiritual, and celestial identity, did not appear in the nineteenth century. Likewise, Muḥammad, from the perspective of His true spiritual essence, did not come into being in the sixth century. Jesus, insofar as the reality of the Holy Spirit manifested in Him and radiated through Him—that is, in His spiritual identity—did not come into the world 622 years before the migration of Muḥammad, on the day reckoned as the beginning of the Gregorian calendar. This is because that singular reality transcends time altogether.

It has always existed, it always exists, and it always will exist. This reality, in other words, is "not begotten."[6] It is not born. We use "not begotten" in relation to both God and the Manifestation of His Revelation. And there is no issue with this assertion, for the Manifestation of God manifests the divine attributes. The unbegotten nature of God is manifested in the unbegotten nature of His Manifestation, to the extent possible in this world and as it relates to the realm of multiplicity. Therefore, what is regarded as the spiritual reality of the Manifestations of God is never born at a specific time, such that it could be said not to have existed prior to that moment. Rather, it has always existed, for Revelation is one. There is no Moses, Jesus, Muḥammad, the Báb, or Bahá'u'lláh; They are all a single reality: one essence, one identity, one truth. There is but one. To be sure, since we do not regard Their human souls, insofar as They are human beings, as one and the same, there is no question of reincarnation in our beliefs. We categorically reject reincarnation and 'Abdu'l-Bahá has explicitly repudiated it from the Bahá'í point of view.[7] The spiritual reality, the singular essence, of the First Emanation from God, of the Manifestation of God's Revelation, remains eternally the same, singular, and one in its own realm. Although it is not the embodiment of Supreme Singleness—a station reserved for the Essence of God alone—it is nevertheless one, and thus it admits of no multiplicity.[8] This principle is emphasized in the Persian Bayán and the Kitáb-i-Íqán, as well as in all Bahá'í writings where the subject arises.

We regard this unity as a foundational tenet of our belief. Yet, beyond this station of essential unity, we also believe in the station of distinction, as termed in Bahá'í parlance: distinction in relation to conditions of time and place. This means that the singular reality, when manifested amid diverse settings and situations, surrounded by multiplicities, and encompassed by material conditions, which are necessarily diverse, reflects diversity in its outward appearance. For example, it is exactly comparable to the sun whose precise moments of rising and setting vary as it appears on Sunday, Monday, and Tuesday. Its visibility differs depending on whether it is obscured by clouds. Atmospheric conditions may cause its heat to reach us with greater or lesser intensity. Yet, in relation to itself, the sun remains but one and accepts no multiplicity. This multiplicity we witness pertains to the horizons from which the sun rises and sets, as well as to the conditions, circumstances, and intermediaries through which its light and warmth reach us. Thus, what we receive embodies multiplicity. This multiplicity manifests itself commensurate with the appearance of that singular sun from multiple horizons, in multiple conditions and settings. It is in this context that Moses differs from Jesus, Jesus differs from Muḥammad, Muḥammad differs from the Báb, and the Báb differs from Bahá'u'lláh.

Any diversity of religions then pertains to diversity of laws. A diversity of laws is an essential requisite of the diversity of requirements, conditions, settings, and circumstances. And the diversity of requirements, conditions, settings, and circumstances is, in turn, an essential property of the realm of multiplicity. The diversity of religions, therefore, has a significance only within the realm of multiplicity. From the perspective of the reality of religions, a diversity of religions is utterly insignificant. Its only validity is relative to humanity and in relation to the aspect of religion that pertains to laws and ordinances. Clearly, when religion is considered from this perspective, its truths become relative. This is explicitly stated in the writings of Shoghi Effendi.[9] Religious truth is relative. It is important to note, however, that by religion, what is meant here is the aspect that pertains to laws and ordinances—the body of laws addressing the needs of daily life and the education of the peoples of the world, in accordance with their capacity and readiness to receive such education. Such truths are relative, contingent, and dependent upon time, place, circumstances, requirements, and conditions. It is in this station—the station of distinction—that diversity pervades religion, and religions assume multiplicity.

From our perspective, therefore, there is no difference between the Manifestations of God—neither in Their essence, nor in the reality of Their Revelation, nor in Their rank or station. In our view, Noah is Abraham, Abraham is Moses, Moses is Jesus, Jesus is Muḥammad, and Muḥammad is Bahá'u'lláh. We do not ever attribute any superiority, distinction, or higher station to Muḥammad over Jesus, nor to the Báb over Muḥammad, because They are one reality. There is no multiplicity or diversity to allow one to be regarded as greater than another. They are but one.

However, depending on the time and manner of Their appearance, They are each made manifest at a different degree of intensity. The essence of the light is one; yet, depending on the lamp or candle from which it shines, and the extent to which its radiance is required in a particular time and place, that light may appear brighter or dimmer, stronger or weaker—with no diversity or multiplicity befalling the essence of the light itself. Accordingly, we maintain that the reality of religions is but one. 'Abdu'l-Bahá has emphatically stated that we must never believe in any differences between religions with respect to their spiritual reality. He has clarified that there is no distinction among religions particularly in relation to moral principles and that the reality of all religions is one in this regard.

In light of this, all Prophets are the Seal of the Prophets. Muḥammad is the Seal of the Prophets, and He was right to declare so. This is because anyone who comes after Him is none other than Himself. If the Báb were other than Muḥammad, His appearance would invalidate and contradict Muḥammad's claim to be the Seal of the Prophets. However, since it is the same Revelation, Muḥammad and the Báb are one and the same, and Their essence is identical. Accordingly, prophethood ends with Muḥammad, because no one comes after Him except Himself. In the same manner, since the reality of Islam is the same as the reality of Christianity and the reality of the Bahá'í Faith—and since the reality of the Bahá'í Faith is identical to the reality of Islam—it follows that Islam cannot be subject to decline, abrogation, or alteration, for every religion that appears is Islam: "Islam is exalted above all and is not surpassed."[10] And: "The true religion with God is Islam."[11] And "Whoso desireth any other religion than Islam, that religion shall never be accepted from him, and in the next world he shall be among the lost."[12] No religion other than Islam is accepted by God. No religion other than Islam constitutes true religion. Islam is the only religion. What do these statements mean? They mean that every religion that will come is Islam, just as every religion that has come was Islam. Numerous verses in the Qur'án confirm this: Abraham, Solomon, Moses, and Jesus are all referred to as Muslims, despite having different scriptures, directions of prayer, laws, ordinances, and followers. Yet none of these differences contradicts the recognition of these religions as Islam.

Therefore, all religions are the final religion, just as they are all the first religion. All religions are the Seal of Religions, and all Prophets are the Seal of the Prophets. This is precisely what each of Them has proclaimed, and it is what the followers of every religion believe about their faith. The Jewish believers regard the religion of Moses as the final religion; the Christians view the religion of Jesus as the final religion; the Muslims see Islam as the final religion; and the Bahá'ís would be equally justified in considering the Bahá'í Faith as the final religion. This is because what is meant by "religion" is the essence of religion, the singular foundation of all religions—the singular foundation, which can never be altered, even though the outward settings and circumstances of religions may change.

This principle can be easily conceived, imagined, and illustrated through tangible objects and experiences. Consider yourself, for example. From beginning to end, from birth to death, how many changes might you undergo? You may alter your lifestyle, revise your approach to life, adopt new habits or customs, relocate, or even change your beliefs outwardly. Nevertheless, your identity remains the same. You can say, "I am the same person who was born on such-and-such a date; I am the same person who went through such-and-such experiences; and I am the same person as I am now." Therefore, evolutionary changes to a being's accidental properties—properties that are predicated upon the being's essence—do not cause multiplicity in its essence.

The same is true of religion; its life unfolds in the same way. From beginning to end, it is singular, constant, one and the same, unchangeable, and possesses one unified identity. The same is also true of the Manifestations of God. Yet this does not prevent Them from appearing in different ages, assuming distinct forms, delivering distinctive teachings, speaking in unique ways, and prescribing specific guidance. This multiplicity does not negate that essential unity. This principle is fundamental to Bahá'í belief. As mentioned earlier, not only do Bahá'ís hold this view, but we also believe that the followers of all religions ought to adopt this perspective—without any difference from our belief—if they seek mutual understanding. Such a belief would help foster an awareness that it is possible to pursue a unity that eliminates differences, and to regard that unity as the essential unity of humankind, nay, of the world of existence—unity of existence in its true and proper sense.

Since the topic of the unity of existence has been raised and the discussion has turned to matters of belief, let us dispel any misconceptions in relation to this matter before moving on to other subjects. The unity of existence can be understood in two senses. In one sense, by the unity of existence is meant a belief in God's descent and entrance into the realm of creation, such that the distinction between God and creation is eliminated. This is the meaning of the unity of existence in its incarnational sense, according to which there is no hierarchy or distinction—everything is regarded as a single reality. According to some, there is no creation; everything is God. According to others, there is no God; everything is creation. Accepting this meaning of the unity of existence allows for one to easily oscillate between pantheism and materialism, as has occurred in the history of thought. We reject this meaning of the unity of existence, according to which God inheres in creation and they are one and the same, and regard it as incorrect. If this were true, it would imply attributing all forms of evil and malice observed in the world of creation directly to the Essence of God, for God would be incarnate in creation, and creation would be indistinguishable from God. The implication of this meaning is that every baseness and ugliness would also stem from God.

The second meaning and formulation of the unity of existence is to assert that existence is one in the sense that creation emanates from God and unfolds across a hierarchy of numerous and distinct stations and degrees in the emanational procession. Consider this analogy, though it is valid only as it illustrates and elucidates this specific aspect of the matter and is not applicable to all of its aspects: The heat radiating from a fire gradually diminishes in intensity as it moves further away. Yet even at its furthest and faintest degrees, it remains the same heat radiating from the fire. This is the second meaning of the unity of existence: Creation emanates from God; yet in its emanational procession through gradations, as it gradually moves further from its origin, it becomes weaker, dimmer, and more devoid of substance. In this sense, and provided the hierarchy of degrees is preserved, the unity of existence is correct—in an emanational, not an incarnational, sense. Recognizing this, we affirm the oneness of Revelation emanating from God in order to preserve unity in existence in its true sense. In holding this belief, we consider ourselves justified and on firm ground.

The creation that emanates from God through the intermediary of Revelation is itself temporally without beginning and without end. In other words, creation has always existed and will always exist. The reasoning behind this is well known and widespread. Imagine a time when creation did not exist; it would imply that God was not a creator then and only became a creator later. This would be tantamount to a change in God, to His transition from potentiality to actuality, and to a movement or transformation in Him. None of these notions are compatible with the nature of God and His Essence. Therefore, when God wills to create, this will is eternal—He has always willed and He shall always continue to do so. That is to say, God has willed to have a creation for eternity.

His grace perpetually emanates from Himself and is directed towards the world of creation. Accordingly, creation emanates from God through Revelation.

Therefore, we regard creation as pre-existent, though only temporally. We do not believe in its essential pre-existence, but we consider it to be temporally pre-existent. In this respect, we do not oppose the philosophers who assert that the world of creation has no beginning, nor do we regard their view as contradictory to sound religious belief. On the contrary, sound belief in true religion affirms this same principle. This is explicitly stated in the Writings of the Báb and Bahá'u'lláh. In elucidating the Writings of Bahá'u'lláh, 'Abdu'l-Bahá clearly affirms that the world of creation, like the world of God, has no beginning.[13] It has always existed, and it will always exist.

Bahá'u'lláh, in one instance, while expounding upon this heavenly truth and spiritual concept, references a well-known Islamic tradition: "God was alone; there was none else besides Him."[14]. This evokes childhood memories of a common Persian tradition of opening stories with a formula that alludes to a time when only God existed and there was no one else beside Him.[15] This Islamic tradition, Bahá'u'lláh explains, does not imply that God was not a Creator—that He had no creation—and later became a Creator, God forbid, out of need or desire. This tradition should not be interpreted as undermining sound belief and leading to blasphemy. Rather, it signifies that the verb "was" is used in a non-temporal sense;[16] it indicates that God always was, is, and will be, without anything accompanying Him. In other words, nothing exists in the station where God is; there is absolute oneness. Nothing exists with Him but Himself. All that exists is, by His will, distinct from Him and, when compared to His Essence, is like nothingness. This is the intended meaning. This tradition, this subtle and elegant mystical expression, also appears in the words of sages before Bahá'u'lláh. After all, as mentioned earlier, this understanding is a fundamental tenet, one that anyone seeking intellectual maturity in matters of faith must necessarily adopt.

Therefore, from a temporal perspective, the universe has no beginning—it has always existed, it continues to exist, and it will always exist. Consequently, the Revelation of God, too, has always manifested in the world of creation, continues to manifest, and will always manifest. At times, people ask why creation must occur—why God creates at all. In our belief, it is not possible to answer these questions with regard to God Himself, because it is impossible to attribute a purpose or an end to God's act of creation. To ascribe a purpose implies that God had not achieved that purpose previously, and that He created in order to achieve it. Yet we cannot suggest that anything was ever unavailable to God, for everything is perpetually available to Him. Even the word "perpetually" should not be used, as it conveys a sense of time, though we cannot help but use it in our expression. Therefore, we cannot ask why God created or to what end He created; rather, He willed to create, and so He did. He loved to create, hence He created—not to fulfill a purpose, attain an end, or derive a benefit. This is because whatever He wills is already present to Him; He cannot will something that He did not previously will. We must again excuse ourselves for using the phrase "cannot," for its use in language is inevitable. None of these expressions are befitting God's station.

It is for this reason that Bahá'u'lláh has stated: "The cause of the creation of contingent beings is love."[17] God loved to create, hence He created. If we reflect on this, we find that everything we do generally has a purpose or aims to achieve a particular end—except for love. Everything we do is intended to reach a goal. However, if love is driven by a purpose, it ceases to be love. Loving should be solely about love itself. This is the essence of love. "I love it. Why do I love it? Because I simply love it." This is an ideal that, for us imperfect and powerless beings, is unattainable in its absolute form. Those who aspire to reach and manifest the highest level of spiritual perfection embody this ideal: love must have no goal beyond itself and serve no purpose other than itself. Bahá'u'lláh states: "The cause of the creation of contingent beings is love."[18] This means that God had no purpose beyond love itself. Why did God create? Because He loved to create. It is only in His station that this ideal can truly attain its full realization, for His station is that of pure reality, the ultimate realization of true perfection. Therefore, what is impossible in our world is possible in His realm.

Accordingly, it is impossible to speak of a purpose in God's act of creation. He loved to create, hence He created. Furthermore, some wise souls have gone even further and stated that not only did God love to create but that God is love itself. One recalls the wondrous words of the Gospel: "God is love."[19] In fact, to describe all of God's attributes in this manner would be more fitting to His station. Instead of saying that God has power, we should say that God is power. Instead of saying that God has knowledge, we should say that God is knowledge. Instead of saying that God is just, we should say that God is justice. In the same way, God is not loving; rather, God is love. All the divine attributes, if properly understood, should be expressed in this manner, so they are identical with the Essence of God, not additional to it or separate from it. Thus, the question "Why did God create?" or "What was His purpose in creation?" is meaningless. When we ask, "Why did God create?" we are attempting to extend the concepts that apply to our own lives onto God's existence and find their extensions in Him too. This approach, however, is incorrect.

Once He created, this creation inherently possessed an essential deficiency in relation to God. That is to say, a certain deficiency necessarily accompanies creation. It is impossible to claim that something is created but not deficient; such a notion would be meaningless. By the very act of bringing creation into being, God necessarily distinguished it from Himself. And since God alone is absolute perfection, whatever is other than Him is inevitably accompanied by deficiency. This is the essential deficiency inherent in creation—the innate imperfection of creation—that, in Christian terms, is the foundation of the doctrine of original sin. Of course, Bahá'ís view the Christian doctrine of original sin as inaccurate. Nevertheless, creation is necessarily imperfect.

At times, we raise questions about God that are entirely misdirected. One such question, posed in a childish manner, is: Why did God not create us perfect, righteous, and good, to spare us from turning toward evil and needing His intervention to restore us to goodness? Why did He create us imperfect, requiring Him to make us perfect now? Did it have to be so—that we must strive to transition from imperfection to perfection and transform our flaws into virtues through our effort and His guidance? Why did He have to create us imperfect in the first place? Since He could have done so, He should have created us good from the beginning. Why did He fashion us in a way that allows us to turn to evil, only to later try to become good through our own effort and God's intervention, amidst countless trials? There are many questions like these, yet all of them are meaningless. They have significance when viewed from our perspective, not when considered in relation to God. The above line of questioning is an example of this error.

When we ask, "Why did He not create us perfect and good?" we fail to realize that by creating us, He made us other than Himself. Had He chosen not to create us, only He would have existed. But because He has created us, we have inevitably become other than Him. And since He is absolute perfection, we, being other than Him, are necessarily imperfect. It is evident that an essential deficiency is inherent in created beings. It is inescapable and inevitable. One cannot put aside or rid oneself of this deficiency. It could only have been avoided if creation had never come into being in the first place. 'Abdu'l-Bahá explains that when a painter produces a painting, the painting becomes other than the painter. Since it is other than the painter, it is necessarily and undoubtedly deficient in comparison with the painter.[20] This inherent deficiency is the essential characteristic of the world of creation—it cannot be otherwise.

Therefore, this deficiency is a sign of our separation from God, and our separation from God is also a necessary consequence of our being created. Accordingly, the more we are separated from God, and the farther we fall in this separation, the more obvious our deficiency becomes. It is precisely this deficiency that gives rise to evil. Hence, evil is a privative phenomenon, because deficiency itself is a privative phenomenon. It is this deficiency that leads to corruption, to degradation, to ignorance, and so on. All such negative conditions arise from this deficiency. Naturally, the more separated and distant we become from God, the more evident this deficiency appears, along with all its consequences.

The appearance of the Manifestation of God in the world of creation serves the purpose of guiding humanity toward perfection throughout the stages of its development. Just as separation and distancing from God lead us toward deficiency, the Manifestation of God seeks to lead us on an ascending path toward perfection, to reduce our deficiencies. Just as we became separated from God, the Manifestation of God sets us again on the path toward Him and ensures that we do not become so estranged as to be left entirely to ourselves, wholly deficient, wholly engulfed in darkness, wholly ignorant, and ultimately destined for ruin—a spiritual ruin that is inevitably followed by material ruin as well.

In this manner, the Manifestations of God take our hands at successive stages to help us overcome this deficiency, within the limits imposed by the requirements of the contingent world, and to bring us as close to God as is possible within the world of creation. Naturally, this process requires a temporal progression, as it must take effect and unfold gradually. This is because this world is the realm of time and motion, and it is impossible in the realm of time and motion to achieve any outcome instantaneously, suddenly, abruptly, or without the passage of time. The world of creation is the realm of time and motion. In this world, no one can attain or realize an objective all at once or in a single instant. To be sure, God can do so if He so wills; but doing so would require suspending the course of time. However, having willed to create the world, He has allowed it to be subject to the flow of time. His decree has necessitated that any movement in this world occur gradually over time. Accordingly, gradual progression has necessarily been made an indispensable condition of this journey toward perfection.

It is this gradual progression that is an essential prerequisite of education. It is this gradual progression that every educator must necessarily observe. You can impart everything you have at once. You are free to do so, and there is no issue with that. However, the world of nature will not accept this. What you impart will not be received—it will be dissipated, lost, wasted, and eventually destroyed. Impart everything you possess at once: If the recipient is a material and natural being, it will inevitably receive a portion of what you impart before becoming saturated and rejecting the excess. If you apply force in order for it to accept more, it will burst and perish. The same principle applies to human beings: When attempting to educate a person, help her develop, or set her on a path toward perfection, if you offer her everything you deem true, good, and beneficial all at once, she will not receive it. What you offer will diminish, vanish, and go to waste. It might even become harmful, detrimental, and damaging. In some cases, it may backfire and result in outcomes contrary to what was intended.

Therefore, education must take place gradually.

Everything that Muḥammad knew, Noah also knew; and all of it was good and necessary to be offered for humanity to receive and accept. Ideally, it would have been better if the people of Noah's time could have also received all the knowledge Muḥammad later imparted to the people of His time, since it was entirely good and beneficial. He Who is Pure Goodness does not withhold good from His creation. However, the reason why that which was revealed to Muḥammad was not revealed to Noah lies in the deficiency of humanity during Noah's time, in comparison to that of Muḥammad's time. The people of Noah's era—the recipients of divine knowledge and education—were not capable of receiving and accepting the full extent of Muḥammad's knowledge. Had such knowledge been imparted, it would have been wasted, lost, and eliminated. Hence, this gradual process must necessarily be observed in this world, for this world is the realm of time and motion.

In His third discourse in *Some Answered Questions*, 'Abdu'l-Bahá presents arguments regarding the need for an educator, affirming that humanity needs an educator, as well as training and education. He discusses the kinds of educators required and identifies the need for a material, human, and spiritual—or heavenly—educator. My purpose in referring to this book is to point out that what others call "Prophet" and "prophethood," 'Abdu'l-Bahá terms "Educator" and "education," to illustrate that prophethood, in our view, signifies education. Therefore, Prophets are, in essence, educators. Since education is a gradual process, it follows that religion, too, must be a gradual process. It must be revealed and learnt progressively, and lead humanity toward perfection gradually.

Furthermore, in addition to being a progressive phenomenon—in that it takes into account human capacity to accept its teachings—religion is also not a compulsory and inescapable imperative. In other words, religion is not like a natural phenomenon that follows a fixed course mechanically and consistently. It cannot be such, because human beings are not like inanimate objects that function solely in mechanical ways. We cannot dictate a course of action to human beings in such a way that would render them entirely passive in the process. Nor can we confine them to a predefined path where they become like a honeybee or a termite, producing honey or building a nest—as if they were a machine designed exclusively for that task and compelled to carry it out with expertise, elegance, and excellence, but without the capability to engage in any other activity. It was not intended for humans to be like that. Rather, humans have been endowed with free will, which is a separate topic and will be discussed in another setting.

NOTES TO CHAPTER EIGHT

1   For instance, he describes the principle of the oneness of humankind as "the pivot round which all the teachings of Bahá'u'lláh revolve" in "The Goal of a New World Order," *The World Order of Bahá'u'lláh: Selected Letters*, Bahá'í Reference Library, www.bahai.org/r/264008982.
2   Or the Kingdom of God's Cause. See, Bahá'u'lláh, *The Kitáb-i-Aqdas*, ¶ 1, Bahá'í Reference Library, www.bahai.org/r/495703799.
3   Bahá'u'lláh, *The Kitáb-i-Íqán*, Bahá'í Reference Library, www.bahai.org/r/611901660.
4   Intension refers to the set of characteristics or criteria that define a concept. For example, the intension of triangle includes a three-sided polygon. Extension refers to the actual instances or members that fall under a concept. For example, the extension of triangle includes all specific triangles, such as equilateral, isosceles, and scalene triangles.
5   This maxim is one of the most important principles of Islamic philosophy and many questions of philosophy are either directly or indirectly founded upon it. According to this maxim, a thing, insofar as it has only a single ontological aspect, can be the source of the creation of only one thing. In other words, if a cause is "one" in the true sense of the term, is uncompounded, and incorporates no mental, intelligible, or actual composition—such as composition of essence and existence, genus and differentia, or matter and form—then the effect that emanates from it is necessarily also "one" and contains no composition. This maxim derives its truth from the necessity of the existence of an essential affinity between a cause and its effect—the unique association of an effect with its cause, which is the foundation of all philosophical reasoning and without which the law of causality itself would be impaired.
6   An allusion to Qur'án 112:3.
7   See, 'Abdu'l-Bahá, *Some Answered Questions*, ch. 81, Bahá'í Reference Library, www.bahai.org/r/106426435.
8   Supreme Singleness and Oneness denote aḥadíyyat and váḥidíyyat, respectively. Islamic mystical philosophers believe that without any characterization of an attribute, the Essence of God is the ineffable station of Supreme

Singleness, absolute invisibility, and the hidden treasure. 'Abdu'l-Bahá, in His commentary on the Basmalah (*Makátíb-i-'Abdu'l-Bahá*, vol. 1 ([Cairo]: Kurdistánu'l-'Ilmíyyah, 1910), 49–52), maintains that the names of God derive from attributes that signify the perfections of His Essence. He stipulates that in God's station of Supreme Singleness, names have no manifestation, entification, or individuation; nor do they signify, indicate, or betoken anything. But they have an uncompounded reality which is identical with the Essence. In God's station of Oneness, however, His names find a manifestation, entification, and life-giving existence. The Báb explains in a Tablet that nothing emanates from the Essence of God, insofar as the Essence of God is exalted above any association, relationship, or affinity. He asserts instead that it is from God's station of Oneness that the first emanation, the Primal Will, emanates (INBA, vol. 69 (N.p.: n.p., 1976), 429–433).

9   Shoghi Effendi states, for example, that "religious truth is not absolute but relative" ("The Golden Age of the Cause of Bahá'u'lláh," *The World Order of Bahá'u'lláh: Selected Letters*, Bahá'í Reference Library, www.bahai.org/r/609410782).

10   Abí Ja'far Muḥammad al-Qumí, *Man Lá Yaḥḍuruhu'l-Faqíh*, vol. 4 (Beirut: Mu'assasatu'l-A'lamí li'l-Maṭbú'át, 1986), no. 5719.

11   Qur'án 3:19, translated by J. M. Rodwell in *The Koran* (London: J M Dent & Sons, 1909), 387.

12   Qur'án 3:85, translated by J. M. Rodwell in *The Koran*, 394. For a discussion of these verses, see the notes in the previous chapter.

13   See, 'Abdu'l-Bahá, *Some Answered Questions*, ch. 47, Bahá'í Reference Library, www.bahai.org/r/740956664.

14   Bahá'u'lláh, *Gleanings from the Writings of Bahá'u'lláh*, no. LDDVIII, Bahá'í Reference Library, www.bahai.org/r/153019812.

15   "Yekí búd, yekí nabúd, ghayr az khudá híchkí nabúd."

16   The verb "was," like its Arabic equivalent (*kána*), is used in some contexts, particularly in theological discourse, to signify existence or a state of being that transcends temporal constraints without being tied to a specific moment in time.

17   Bahá'u'lláh, *Ad'íyiy-i-Ḥaḍrat-i-Maḥbúb*, (Bundoora: Century Press Publications, 2004), 391; provisional translation.

18   Ibid.

19   1 John 4:8.

20   See, 'Abdu'l-Bahá, *Some Answered Questions*, ch. 2, Bahá'í Reference Library, www.bahai.org/r/934192056.

CHAPTER 9

Unity in Diversity

Translated by Vargha Bolodo-Taefi

We are quite familiar with the word "unity." In the Bahá'í Faith, perhaps no word is as frequently spoken, for it expresses the loftiest aim of our Faith and defines the very essence of our purpose. Yet, despite our close association with this term, we have paid little attention to its meaning and significance. We have made only limited efforts to grasp the nature and essence of this word. Perhaps this is understandable, as "unity" is one of those words to whose meaning we have grown accustomed and whose spirit can be deeply felt with heart and soul; yet it eludes precise definition in words. This is because the act of defining inherently involves composition. Nothing can be defined without using composite terms. We need at least a genus and a differentia to define a concept. Without composition, definition has no meaning. And it is indisputable that composition eliminates oneness and unity, for composition necessarily involves the combination of at least two elements. The moment duality is introduced, oneness ceases to exist. This is why oneness and unity cannot be defined. And insofar as it cannot be defined, unity cannot be made the object of thought or reasoning either. After all, thought is identical to words and terms—but those words and terms as they pass through our consciousness, our soul, our nature, and our mind.

The implication is that so long as thought is not divided into components, it does not truly constitute thought; and once it is divided into components, it inevitably becomes composite. When it becomes composite, it necessarily becomes characterized by multiplicity and thus the unity it seeks to grasp is lost. As such, it is neither possible to think about unity nor to talk about it. By "thinking" and "talking" one thing is intended here, and that is the meaning attributed to the words "logos" or "reason." Whenever reason is introduced, multiplicity inevitably arises. Likewise, whenever multiplicity is introduced, unity is lost. It is for this reason that we seldom explore unity or oneness—and understandably so. But this does not imply that unity and oneness are beyond our understanding or appreciation. While simple uncompounded concepts cannot be described through language or encompassed by thought—a thought that can be described as reason or logos—they nevertheless resonate deeply with our innermost being. This is because the human soul too is uncompounded. For this reason, that which is uncompounded is easily embraced, recognized, and absorbed by the soul, being of the same type. Therefore, while unity or oneness cannot be articulated or explained in words, they can be perceived through spiritual susceptibilities and recognized by inner discernment.

Naturally, unity has different degrees. Nothing is devoid of unity, for without unity, existence itself is impossible. Anything that exists must inevitably possess unity. The chair upon which I am currently seated, like the table upon which I lean, is a physical object. The existence of this object is necessarily derived from its unity. That is, its various components, in different colors, amounts, and proportions, have come together and formed one entity. They are interconnected in such a way that their multiplicity has given way to one unified whole. As soon as this unity emerges, so does the existence of this object. Were the unity and interconnectedness that these components enjoy—such that they are bound together and integrated into one—to be dissolved, the object known as chair or table would cease to exist. This principle applies to all objects, phenomena, and concepts. Wherever unity is present, existence appears; wherever unity is absent, existence disappears. In a sense, particularly within the material and physical realm, coming into being is nothing other than the unification of some elements through composition, and ceasing to exist the loss of that unity as a result of decomposition. In other words, an existent thing in the material realm is one whose component parts have attained unity; a non-existent thing is one whose component parts have been separated.

We observe, then, how a concept that cannot be defined or conveyed in words is, in fact, among those most intimately accessible to us. In a certain sense, this concept is synonymous with existence itself—our own existence and that of everything else. Since unity pervades all things, it follows that unity and oneness must possess gradations, for created beings occupy different stations and enjoy various degrees of existence. The weaker the existence of a thing, the further it is from unity and the nearer it is to multiplicity. Conversely, the stronger its existence, the nearer it is to unity and the further it is from multiplicity. This principle holds universally, across all beings, degrees, and realms.

At the highest level of unity lies pure unity, absolute oneness. This pure unity, being absolutely uncompounded, is the Divine Essence Himself. He admits of no multiplicity, that is, He has no component parts, limits, directions, names, or attributes. For this reason, He is the absolute unity, or absolutely one. Any attempt to ascribe to Him any kind or form of multiplicity, such as component part, limit, direction, association, relation, name, or attribute would compromise His unity. He is absolutely one; therefore, He is absolutely uncompounded.

At the lowest level of unity lies unity in the material world, the realm of physical beings. In this plane, created beings are situated across different directions and locations, exhibit diverse associations, consist of various component parts, and display a multitude of attributes, names, and states. This realm is indeed characterized by pervasive diversity, multiplicity, and distinctions. Yet even here, however it is conceived, and in any given station, some degree of unity persists, for existence cannot emerge without at least a certain degree of unity. However, since diversity, multiplicity, differences, and distinctions abound at this level, unity is weak. Between the lowest and the highest levels of unity lie other levels of unity that manifest stronger degrees of unity if they are closer to the absolute unity, and stronger degrees of multiplicity if closer to the material plane.

An issue that arises here is the relationship between multiplicity and unity: namely, how a connection is established between absolute unity and absolute multiplicity, how multiplicity emanates from unity, or how unity engenders multiplicity. What is certain is that multiplicity originates from unity. To posit otherwise would inevitably lead us, as it did the ancient Persians, to a belief in dualism. This would mean asserting that, in the material world, multiplicity arises from one essence and origin, while unity emanates from another. That is, we would have to attribute the multiplicity of the material world to one source and its unity to another. Such a view, however, contradicts the belief in the oneness of God. Consequently, multiplicity must also be traced back to unity; it must be declared that multiplicity stems from no other origin or source than oneness itself.

The connection between the many and the one is one of the challenging themes in metaphysics and is not easily presented in a broad discourse that is intended to be useful to the public rather than to specialists. Suffice it to simply say that oneness, through its movement, gains multiplicity by and of itself. That is, owing to its very movement, oneness can be considered, on the one hand, in reference to the true meaning, or the essence, of oneness itself, and, on the other hand, as something in a state of movement. And this is how the very first multiplicity emerges. The first multiplicity originates from movement, or flow. For this reason, metaphysicians of old posited that the first emanation from oneness was movement and that movement was temporally pre-existent. For without movement or flow, multiplicity has no meaning. If oneness were to remain in a state of absolute immutability and pure stillness, it would remain pure oneness. However, when it becomes subject to movement, or something emanates from it that is in movement, duality emerges from this very movement. Why? Because oneness is, firstly, a concept whose essence is one, and secondly, a concept that is in movement. Over time, this movement through various stages results in the emergence and gradual increase of multiplicity. Thus, if we were to disregard movement, we would also have to disregard multiplicity. Where there is absolute immutability with no trace of movement, there is no trace of multiplicity either. The divine metaphysicians have proposed that it is within these stages that the realm of Divine Revelation[1] exists. They have further expanded this discourse and believed in the worlds of the Heavenly Court, the Celestial Dominion, and the Divine Kingdom, which are situated between the Absolute Essence and the world of mortal existence.[2] They have also introduced concepts such as will, purpose, fate, predestination, decree, permission, and seal. Their purpose in introducing all these stages was to articulate a gradual process through which oneness leads to multiplicity.

While absolute oneness, or pure unity, can be appreciated and experienced through spiritual perception, it cannot be articulated in verbal expression or comprehended through discursive reasoning. Therefore, those dwelling in the realm of multiplicity must necessarily approach the understanding of unity and oneness through several intervening stations and traverse various stages. This journey must be a gradual process in which multiplicity and diversity increase incrementally, until the world of creation emerges at the stage of mortal existence. This notion has also been used to explain the process of God's creation of things and their emanation from a single source, the absolute unity. In reference to existence, it can be said that multiplicity arises from oneness, diversity from unity. However, in reference to knowledge—that is, at the stage of knowledge—it can be stated that multiplicity reverts to a state of oneness, diversity returns toward unity. For scientific knowledge is nothing but transitioning multiplicity back into oneness or discovering a unity within every diversity. To forgo this principle—that at the heart of every multiplicity there exists a unity—is, in effect, to forgo the very concept of knowledge and its degrees. All forms of thought, understanding, and reasoning can be explained as the transformation of multiplicity into unity. If you reflect carefully, you will realize that when you understand a concept, you have done nothing other than link the new idea to something previously known, or relate several newly presented ideas to one another. This act of linking and relating is what produces understanding. And to relate is merely to bind together several things from one particular perspective—namely, to transform their multiplicity and diversity into unity.

One of the first steps in acquiring scientific knowledge is the act of linking and relating, which also serves as one of the first steps in transforming multiplicity and diversity into unity. The principle of causality, the foundation of scientific thought, operates on this very basis. Causality does nothing other than relate every phenomenon that comes into being to another. It asserts that, although this new phenomenon is distinct from another, it shares a connection with the other, possesses a relationship with it, has emanated from it, and, consequently, can be traced back to it. The principle of non-contradiction, which forms the foundation of all modes of thought, fundamentally signifies that, while there is a distinction between entities, every entity must be itself; it cannot be other than itself if it is to be understood. Consequently, multiplicity must be returned to unity to avoid contradiction. And contradiction must be avoided in order for thinking to be possible. This is true even in modes of thinking grounded in contrariety, in which, unlike the principle of non-contradiction, the conclusion relies on contrariety. Upon closer examination, in the principle of contrariety the same concept holds, albeit from a different perspective: two apparently distinct propositions can, in fact, be brought back to each other and be linked together—in other words, their multiplicity can return to a unity. Even a multiplicity that emanates from within a thing itself can return and, in a synthesis or composition, reintegrate with that thing, and become one.

Accordingly, one observes that no reasoning, understanding, or scientific knowledge can be achieved except through the process of reverting a multiplicity to unity. All scientific laws are made when one identifies relatively consistent relationships between various phenomena, that is, when one connects disparate phenomena, or subsumes diverse elements under a single law. Scientific laws, therefore, serve no other function than to unify multiplicity into oneness.

One who believes in the existence of substance or essence, for instance in matter, merely groups together diverse phenomena such as heat, cold, expansion, contraction, color, scent, taste, light, sound, and pressure and attributes them to a single source, which she may term matter, substance, or something else. Similarly, one who posits the existence of the soul only consolidates diverse elements such as sorrow, joy, thought, imagination, grief, love, will, and reason and ascribes them to a single principle that is of the same kind or origin as them. Finally, one who believes in God again merely combines various elements—such as physical and spiritual elements, each comprising a vast array of subcategories—and attributes them to a single Origin, Which she names God.

In short, wherever we turn, we find ourselves confronted with a choice: either we must abandon thinking altogether—which is tantamount to forfeiting our ability to live—or, if we are to live, to think, to acquire knowledge, and thereby to elevate our existence to a truly human life, then we must move from multiplicity toward oneness and transform diversity into unity.

Shifting from the realm of philosophical and scientific thought to the domain of social affairs, and reflecting upon the historical evolution of human society through its stages, we observe again that the whole course of humanity's endeavor amounts to nothing but a movement from multiplicity and diversity toward unity. One of the earliest pillars of social life was the family. The formation of a family is, in essence, the organic unification of distinct elements and members within a social organism, which is a unit of community life, and the interconnection of several individuals with diverse roles, interests, and characters within a shared living unit. If this unity dissolves, the family ceases to exist. Its establishment depends on the existence of unity, and its disintegration follows the demise of that unity. The utterance of the phrase "I have entered into this bond of marriage,"[3] which establishes a family among the people, or the verse "We will all, verily, abide by the Will of God,"[4] which, in this day, inaugurates the family unit in the Bahá'í community, does nothing other than relate and unite two previously unrelated and separate individuals—two bodies, two hearts, two spirits, two souls, and two lives. This union initiates a series of results, each generating subsequent bonds of unity. Conversely, the declaration of "I have divorced you"—may it never be spoken—merely breaks these bonds, dissolves that unity, reinstates multiplicity and division, and reintroduces diversity. Thus, we see that one of the most fundamental units of human society comes into being through the transformation of diversity into unity, and perishes with the transformation of unity into diversity. This is one of the stages of unity.

However, human society does not stop at this juncture. In its natural evolution, it advances to a stage where families coalesce into tribes. This process involves the integration of the multiplicities inherent in families into a higher level of unity, without eliminating the family unit itself. Just as within a family distinct roles such as husband, wife, son, daughter, brother, and sister remain intact with clearly defined rights, duties, and individual identities, so too do distinct families persist within the broader tribal structure. Consider the profound spiritual insight that 'Abdu'l-Bahá imparts in His prayer for marriage by invoking a verse from the Qur'án: "He hath let loose the two seas, that they meet each other: Between them is a barrier which they overpass not."[5] Even as two seas converge, a boundary persists that prevents them from merging entirely. I do not presume to add even a word beyond what the Interpreter of the Sacred Texts has declared. Therefore, what I present here must be understood as a personal interpretation, subject to critique and open to rejection. This concept directs our attention to how, even as two entities unite, a boundary ensures their autonomy such that they do not undermine or eliminate each other, and neither of them oppresses or violates the other. In other words, while two people join and establish unity, a separating barrier preserves their multiplicity by safeguarding them from mutual encroachment. Similarly, within a tribe, families maintain their integrity as foundational units of social life, even as their multiplicity does not prevent them from finding opportunities for unification, allowing the emergence of tribal unity as a superior expression of unity transcending yet incorporating familial unity.

The progression does not halt at the tribal stage. Tribes advance toward civic unity, giving rise to cities, which for extended periods serve as fundamental social units—core cells in the human societal organism. Yet, the evolution does not stop even here. Over time, cities coalesce into nations and empires. Beyond the familial, tribal, and civic stages, humanity becomes further interconnected at the national stage, where diverse social units—families, tribes, and cities—merge into a unified entity termed a nation. Today, this evolving process is moving the nations to integrate, while preserving their distinct existence and identity, into an even higher and superior unit: the unity of humankind. There is no other viable alternative: either human society must relinquish its existence, or it must embrace this ultimate stage of unity, this final point in its unification, which is lying in store for it and is one of the most critical phases of its destined development.

Thus, it becomes evident that everywhere, in all things, across all stages and stations, there is a movement from multiplicity toward unity. Just as in the descending procession oneness flowed from God toward creation, culminating in multiplicity, and multiplicity and diversity proliferated leading to the appearance of the physical realm, so too, in the ascending movement, multiplicity inclines toward unity. This movement continues until the physical qualities—whose inherent nature is multiplicity—through a gradual orientation toward spiritual qualities, reach a station where, to the extent possible and as befitting this world, the oneness that exists in the world of God is manifested within the multiplicity that characterizes the world of creation.

Some may claim the possibility of attaining unto absolute unity, and seek a state of pure oneness. Such a notion is, however, unattainable and impossible, for absolute unity is inconceivable. While it can be felt, spiritually perceived, and—as previously emphasized—discerned through spiritual intuition, it defies all conceptualization and reflection, as thinking inherently involves composition.

Unity, therefore, can only be recognized within diversity and multiplicity, for our reality, as created beings, is to exist in the realm of multiplicity. Consequently, any unity we conceive will be a unity within a diversity. Nevertheless, we can ascend from diversity and multiplicity toward unity and oneness. In other words, we can amplify and enhance unity and cause it to overcome multiplicity. We can and we must do this.

Consider this example. When philosophical thought encounters complexities, examples from mathematics are often used to work through them. This is because both philosophical and mathematical reasoning possess an abstract simplicity and incorporeality. However, the abstraction in mathematics is relative, as it remains linked to material and spatial extension, while metaphysics is purely abstract and uncompounded. Therefore, mathematical frameworks and perspectives can be applied to philosophical and metaphysical questions to facilitate a clearer and more profound comprehension. In the domain of continuous quantity, studied in geometry, a point represents absolute oneness. It possesses no extension—neither width, length, nor depth—and is therefore indivisible, as division requires extension. Without extension no division is possible. An infinite number of lines can pass through a single point. Consider the point at the center of a circle: an infinite number of radii can be drawn from this center to the circumference, for a point, lacking any dimensional extension, imposes no limit on the number of lines that can originate from it. Therefore, an infinite number of lines can emanate from it. We know that infinity can be neither conceived by the mind nor embodied in matter, for any conception or material representation would be tantamount to finitude. The point itself is one; it is pure unity—in a mathematical sense—for it has no spatial extension. It is free of all multiplicity. The line conceived by the motion of a point, the surface conceived by the motion of a line, and the object conceived by the motion of a surface are all manifestations of multiplicity. A line results from the motion of a point, introducing multiplicity in one dimension. A surface is conceived by the motion of a line, introducing multiplicity in two dimensions. An object is conceived by the motion of a surface, introducing multiplicity in three dimensions. If we then consider this object moving through Einsteinian curved spacetime, multiplicity expands into dimensions beyond three—potentially into infinite dimensions from a certain perspective.

Accordingly, it becomes evident that the further one extends from a point through motion, the greater the resulting multiplicity. The point itself represents pure oneness. However, this pure oneness cannot be visualized in any concrete form. Even the most skilled geometers, employing the finest instruments, if attempting to place a point on a surface, would inevitably create something constituting a line, or more precisely, a surface—or even an object. This is because the point must be placed using some material, which would necessarily possess width, length, and thickness. In other words, while resembling a point, it is, in reality, an object—not merely a line or surface, but an object. Thus, although the point serves as the origin and the source of lines, surfaces, and objects, it can never achieve actual, physical realization—at least, we are incapable of actualizing it. Even when we try to visualize the point conceptually, it inevitably possesses extension. For this reason, the point can be neither visualized nor imagined. If we attempt to depict or conceive a point—to simply imagine it—we are compelled to do so within an object, a surface, or a line. For instance, we must consider a line, and designate its starting position as a point—without directly indicating this starting position. In essence, we can only depict or imagine that oneness within the context of a multiplicity. A line can be depicted in terms of its length; but if one tries to conceive of its width, one must inevitably think of it in the context of a surface, as the origin of the surface.

It is evident, then, that wherever unity is conceived, it is necessarily conceived within a diversity and multiplicity. Conversely, wherever multiplicity manifests, it necessarily occurs within a unity that allows for its existence. This constitutes the principle of unity in diversity, which defines our existential condition, station, and reality. There are those who seek to comprehend, behold, attain, or turn toward absolute oneness—that is, they seek to see God Himself with their own eyes, to worship Him, bow before Him, or comprehend Him Who is the Pure Oneness. Yet, in making this claim, they immediately fall from the rank of true faith. This is because they attempt to encompass that Absolute Oneness within their own minds and make Him accessible and worthy of being their Creator and the Object of their worship; yet that Absolute Oneness is inconceivable to us outside the realm of multiplicity. They believe in something that is inherently inconceivable to them—a reality that must be placed within the realm of multiplicity in order to be imagined. In truth, such individuals are the embodiments of Satan, for they want only God, the True One, the Absolute Oneness, to be their sole object of worship. They are the embodiments of Satan, who, when commanded to bow before Adam, refused, deeming Adam unworthy of his prostration. While all the angels bowed before Adam, Satan did not, perceiving Adam as a being created from material substance, from water and clay, and considering himself more subtle, more refined, more exalted, and superior—by virtue of his creation from fire which is superior to clay. He sought to reserve his prostration and worship exclusively for God. Deeming Adam, who was created of clay and who belonged to the world of multiplicity, unworthy of his prostration, Satan refused to bow before him. For this reason, he was condemned, cursed, and cast out from the Divine presence. He claimed something far beyond his rightful station by desiring that his only object of worship be God alone. Yet, failing to recognize and worship God, the Absolute Oneness, in His creation, in His Chosen Handiwork, in His First Emanation, reduces Him to nothing more than an idol existing solely within the realm of illusion.

It can be observed, then, that no unity is conceivable except in multiplicity. What is most striking is that those who repeatedly curse, shun, and condemn Satan, by the authority of their own holy Book—for his desire to worship only God and for considering Adam unworthy of his prostration owing to Adam's having been created of clay—fall into the same error themselves. When they encounter souls who bow before the Adam of this age—the Perfect Human for this day, the Manifestation of God—who follow the example of the angels who considered bowing before the Manifestation of God as bowing before God Himself, and who do not consider it beneath them to prostrate before the Adam of this age, they accuse such souls of blasphemy. How unfair they are!

It is true that the ultimate focus should be on absolute oneness; but for us, existing within the world of creation, this absolute oneness is conceivable, imaginable, and realizable only within the realm and stage of multiplicity. Belief in absolute oneness requires that while we trace multiplicity back to oneness and return diversity to unity, we also conceive and depict oneness within multiplicity, and unity in diversity. But at the same time, in the ascending movement, we must soar from multiplicity toward oneness as far as possible, striving to weaken and diminish the effects of multiplicity so that unity and oneness may shine more brightly and, through the intensified manifestation of unity, existence may also be manifested more intensely. For, as I mentioned earlier, nothing can exist unless it possesses unity.

When we apply this concept to other domains, it becomes evident that we should never fear multiplicity and diversity. We should never dismiss diversity, considering it a sign of discord, nor disregard it as something unworthy of our station. Rather, we must value diversity that it may serve as a vessel bearing unity. If we were to disregard multiplicity and diversity, we would inevitably have to relinquish oneness and unity within the world of creation as well.

Let me speak more clearly. In a gathering of Bahá'ís, where diverse perspectives are introduced, this display of multiple views should not alarm us. We should not attempt to eliminate this diversity of perspectives, for such multiplicity is what is essential for the manifestation of unity. However, it is crucial to ensure that this multiplicity develops in a way that brings the diverse aspects and constituent parts closer together through the unity inherent within them, the connections they can establish, and the harmony they are capable of attaining. Alternatively, this diversity should evolve in such a way that these components gradually converge until they naturally embody a unified whole. The best Spiritual Assembly composed of nine members is one in which each member truly remains a distinct individual—where nine different thoughts expressed in varying forms, nine distinct perspectives with diverse characteristics, and nine unique contributions reflecting various qualities can emerge. In such an Assembly, nine thoughts will meet, and the resulting unified thought that arises will then be one conceived of—and consequently enriched, permeated, nourished, and empowered—by nine thoughts. Were these nine thoughts to become eight, that is, if one of these nine members ceased to contribute or became a mere follower, the unified thought that would emerge from this Spiritual Assembly would be correspondingly poorer. Were they to become seven thoughts, the result would become even more impoverished. If six, even poorer. How regrettable the day when a Spiritual Assembly functions such that only one person thinks while the others merely follow, failing to connect their thoughts to that one idea or enrich it through their own insights.

It must be immediately clarified that insisting on preserving diversity should not come at the cost of fostering division. When we see that perspectives fail to harmonize or that the emergence of a unified view is being impeded, we must necessarily reconsider this diversity. This is because we seek a unity that manifests within this diversity; we seek a diversity that leads us toward unity. Absolute unity is unattainable; absolute diversity is unsustainable. A mere gathering of individuals does not equate to connection; connection does not equate to union; and union does not equate to unity. To elaborate further: sometimes component parts are brought together or individuals are assembled, yet instead of supporting or enriching one another, they repel each other. The reason for this is that they lack compatibility and mutual accord; they have drawn no substance from truth; rather than advancing genuine thoughts, they advance mere illusions.

In this connection, Bahá'u'lláh states in the Lawḥ-i-Dunyá: "The mere act of your gathering together is enough to scatter the forces of these vain and worthless people."[6] Vain and worthless people, or people of illusion,[7] are those whose thoughts are mere illusions and are disconnected from truth. Illusion is the opposite of truth; where illusion takes the place of truth, division prevails. When such individuals gather, their thoughts—being devoid of truth and amounting to mere illusions—fail to connect and coalesce, and instead repel, reject, and discard one another. Before they came together, one might have imagined that they could unite. Yet their assembly reveals the impossibility of their unification. It is these individuals who are described as people of illusion: the mere gathering together of the people of illusion is enough to scatter them.

Accordingly, not every gathering constitutes a connection. A gathering in which the individual members, the component parts, bear signs of truth can transform into a connection. This occurs when its members, despite being separate and each possessing distinct identity and individuality, establish common aspects with each other and, through these common aspects, manifest a united quality. It is at this point that a gathering transforms into a connection. Further, not every connection constitutes a union. This is because some connections are superficial; some are external, established by external elements. In such cases, what connects the component parts and individual members is something extrinsic, like a cord that binds together two separate objects. While they are connected, their connection has not transformed into a union; they do not draw sustenance from each other. You may tie a branch to a tree with a rope. While this creates a connection, it does not result in a union. Union occurs when grafting takes place, allowing a life-giving flow from one to the other. In this case, the gathering has become a connection, and the connection has transformed into a union. Furthermore, not every union constitutes unity. Unity arises when the aspect that binds them is stronger than the aspect that keeps them apart, when the factor of their difference is overshadowed by the factor of their union, when the dominant principle is the unifying factor, when their collective existence derives from their union. It is at this point that unity manifests.

Even then, such unity remains relative and relational—a unity in diversity. This is because absolute oneness lies beyond the world of creation and befits only the world of God. Humanity's journey toward this oneness is an infinite process—one that is ever-actualizing yet neverending. In this journey from multiplicity to unity, human beings can never die in the Absolute Oneness—the world of God—and become one with Him. The distance remains infinite. Absolute oneness is an ideal toward which humanity ever journeys, yet never attains.

Notes to Chapter Nine

1   Or the Kingdom of God's Cause. See, Bahá'u'lláh, *The Kitáb-i-Aqdas*, ¶ 1, Bahá'í Reference Library, www.bahai.org/r/495703799.

2   Respectively, Láhút, Jabarút, Malakút, Háhút, and Násút.

3   A phrase commonly used, in accordance with Islamic jurisprudence, to solemnize the Islamic marriage contract.

4   See, Bahá'u'lláh, *The Kitáb-i-Aqdas*, "Questions and Answers" no. 3.

5   Qur'án 55:19–20. Qtd. in 'Abdu'l-Bahá, *Bahá'í Prayers*, Bahá'í Reference Library, www.bahai.org/r/981252413.

6   Bahá'u'lláh, *Tablets of Bahá'u'lláh Revealed after the Kitáb-i-Aqdas*, Bahá'í Reference Library, www.bahai.org/r/028989218. It appears that Dr. Dávúdí's reading of the original-language passages from the Lawḥ-i-Dunyá corresponds to "The mere act of their gathering together is enough to scatter the forces of these vain and worthless people."

7   The word that Shoghi Effendi has translated here as "vain and worthless" is *mawhúmih*, a passive participle for *vahm*, meaning "illusion," which can be contrasted with "truth."

Chapter 10

Countering the Forces in our Environment

Translated by Elham Afnan

Discussions of the environment are at present carried out primarily from psychological and sociological standpoints—even though this was not the case in the beginning, and this subject has entered these disciplines from another source, as I will explain. Although I did not intend to embark on this theme, it was pointed out that it was necessary to define "environment," and I will therefore say some words in this regard.

Consider carefully this word, "environment."[1] You know, of course, that this is a neologism, that is to say it was not formerly used in Persian and Arabic in the sense that it is now. It was originally used to indicate, for example, the circumference of a circle, the periphery, the environs, or other similar ideas. The word, in its current meaning, was not found in our language because its meaning—as we understand it today—did not exist in the past. This word has been translated from foreign languages and reached Iran through its use in modern sciences, leading to the current debate about the environment. But there is debate about this word in those other languages as well. In French, there are two words for this concept, which have diametrically opposed meanings. I do not wish to get into semantics here, but I mention this because it is relevant to understanding the meaning of the word. The same two words are also used in English: "environment" and "milieu." The contradiction between them lies in the fact that "milieu" means "middle," while "environment" means "circumference." Now we must consider how these two words— one meaning that which surrounds, and the other meaning what is at the center—have come to mean the same thing, including when translated into Persian.

The first to notice this contradiction was a French logician named Goblot.[2] He exposed this inconsistency and asked how we can use a word that refers to the middle in order to describe our surroundings. Researchers then looked into the history of this usage and discovered that this word was first used in the scientific language of physics and mechanics in the works of Newton in the seventeenth century.[3] Newton, a visionary scientist in the history of human thought, used this word, "milieu," in his discussions of astronomy and celestial mechanics. He called the distance between two stars, or the section of the sky or of space that is situated between two stars, the "middle" or "milieu." This fit the meaning of the word because it described the distance between, or in the middle of, the two stars. When used in astronomy, because this space between the two stars was also the space in which the stars moved, the word came to refer to their location, position, path, and orbit as well. Thus, a single word acquired two opposite meanings.

So, we see that milieu or environment initially had a mechanical, physical, and mathematical significance. Turning from the seventeenth century to the eighteenth, we find that, little by little, mathematical and natural terminology was also adopted in the field of biology. Thinkers tried to gradually give biology a natural aspect and to remove the study of life from the realm of philosophy, to strip away the mysterious and wondrous quality that it possessed in philosophical and religious thought, and to place it in the field of scientific discourse. This is what eighteenth- and nineteenth-century naturalists did. They placed biology, the science of life, within the natural sciences. Previously, the discourse on life was a philosophical and religious discourse; now they wanted to bring it into scientific discourse. The naturalists were most insistent in this matter, and it was in this way that much of the terminology of physics entered into biology. One of those engaged in this endeavor was the learned French biologist, Geoffroy Saint-Hilaire.[4] He was the one who first took the term milieu—that is, environment—from Newton's physics and applied it to biology, introducing the discussion of the environment of living things. This environment is either external or internal. The cellular structure of a living thing was called its internal environment, and water, air, and all that had to do with time, place, and food, its external environment. The concept of the environment thus entered into the field of biology—and created a great stir as soon as it did. The reason for this was that one of the characteristics of the naturalism of the eighteenth century, and later of the nineteenth century, was that it tried to the extent possible to distance everything human from its purely human character and turn it into something natural. And in doing so, there was nothing more effective than importing physics and chemistry into biology.

One of the pioneers and champions of this enterprise was Lamarck.[5] It is in Lamarck's theory that adaptation to the environment is identified as one of the principles of the evolution of living things. According to this theory, a living thing, by adapting to its environment, undergoes changes, and these gradual changes lead over generations to a change in the species. An outcome of the importance that this theory gradually acquired was that the influence of the environment came to be considered an important determinant with regard to living things. The environment thus entered scientific discourse and came to be considered as one of two—and perhaps the most important and fundamental of the two—determinants in the life of plants, animals, and of course human beings. This theory reached Herbert Spencer[6] and other likeminded thinkers and entered into the social sciences.

Theories of the environment also entered into the social sciences by another route, namely that of literature. The naturalist literature of the eighteenth and nineteenth centuries helped draw this idea into the compass of social science. Balzac,[7] for example, drawing directly on the work of Saint-Hilaire and indirectly on that of Newton, introduced the concept of the environment in his book, *La Comédie Humaine* [*The Human Comedy*]. As you no doubt know, Balzac is one of the great realist, or one may say naturalist, French writers. *The Human Comedy* reminds one of another great comedy, Dante's *Divine Comedy*, to which Balzac's book is a response. In the preface to *The Human Comedy*, Balzac uses the word "milieu," and it is interesting that he writes it in italics, in order to show that this word has a special significance and is not being used in its usual meaning; it should be understood in its new meaning. The meaning that we attach to it now was at that time new for scientists, and for this reason they highlighted it in this way. This usage then made its way from Balzac to Taine.[8] Taine was one of the great French critics of the nineteenth century. He popularized the use of the word milieu or environment and, indeed, carried its use to excess and attached great importance to it. He gave the environment foundational significance and saw it as the most important determinant. One may say that he was the one who propounded the priority of the environment as the fundamental element in human life.

From yet another direction, this concept was conveyed from Newton, by way of biologists, to sociology. Auguste Comte,[9] the founder of sociology and of philosophical positivism, who was himself also a philosopher, introduced this concept into sociology and made it the subject of discussion. Comte was the first person to try to establish social sciences using the approach and method of the natural sciences. Initially, he even called sociology "social physics," in order to show that he was transferring the methods of physics to the study of human society, and to make it evident that there is nothing in human society other than what is natural. According to him, we cannot remove the discussion of the human being from the realm of nature. Therefore, we retain the word "physics" and call the study of society "social physics" in order to show that we have no right to overlook the requirements of nature when discussing human beings.

The foregoing introduction sheds light on the question of where the word environment comes from, why it has gained importance, how it has entered the language of science, and how it has from there passed into culture and exerted influence on civilization. To summarize, the word environment, its meaning, the attention given to it, and the excessive emphasis placed on its importance all originate in the scientific spirit of eighteenth and nineteenth century Europe, which sought to give humanity a natural aspect or rather to view the human being as a natural phenomenon. The environment, in this context, belongs to the world of nature, and it is transmitted from natural science to life science, and from life science to social science. This attempt to return the human being to nature is a naturalist project; it is the attempt of naturalists within science to view as foundational everything that is natural in human beings, and to place humanity within the context and the matrix of nature. This was the project that scientists embarked on in the Renaissance and that reached its apex in the eighteenth and nineteenth centuries. It was their attempt to define humanity in terms of nature and divest it of any supranatural attributes, to lead the human being, by any means possible, away from the metaphysical and back to the embrace of physics. It was in this way that the current meaning of the environment came into being and became established. By embracing this concept and, in particular, by according centrality to it, the human being loses the distinction that it possesses by virtue of being human—a distinction that places it above nature—and instead of encompassing nature, becomes encompassed by it. If you consider closely, you will see that what is now called the environment is the sum of all those elements belonging to nature, which, even if applied to human affairs, are subordinate, secondary, and incidental. That is to say, they have originated in nature and then entered into the human realm, thereby gradually returning human beings to nature. In other words, such things as food, water, air, space, time, and all those things that are imposed on us from outside ourselves are called "environment."

You must therefore, when discussing the environment, above all be careful not to be drawn into an endeavor that is at odds with the Bahá'í Faith. The Faith endeavors to demonstrate the humanity of human beings and to maintain their originality; in contrast, naturalists and natural scientists try to reduce human beings to the level of nature. Reduction here means returning humanity to nature and seeing nothing in it except what belongs to nature. It is in this context that the word environment is used by them. If you consider Lamarck's theory and the influence this and subsequent theories have exerted on the social sciences and human culture, you will see that their proponents make every effort to say that human beings are the product of their environment: it is the environment that creates human beings. The only agent or determinant that they might consider to exist other than the environment is heredity. According to them, except for heredity, there is nothing counter to the environment that we can say is not a part of it. In other words, we either inherit something or are given it by our environment.

There have, however, been those who were not content even with this, and who attempted to gradually eliminate the role of heredity too. But disagreements arose among these as well. Eastern thinkers[10] could never accept that heredity should influence humanity, because to accept this was to admit a kind of immutability in the human species, and this did not conform with their ideology. Therefore, they said that the environment is the foundation and there is no determinant except it. What we call heredity, they claimed, is the gradual influence of the environment that is transferred through reproduction, and is also gradually influenced by the environment. They even denied the existence of traits that, according to the Western science of genetics, remain constant. They considered traits acquired from the environment, which according to Western science are not passed down through heredity, to be heritable.

It seems destined that science, like everything else, should become the plaything of politics. If you will allow me, I shall digress briefly to say that politics has made a plaything of everything, whether art, morals, science, philosophy, or religion. In order to preserve our religion as a religion, we must try not to allow politics to make it a plaything. Of course, this means avoiding actual involvement in politics, not refraining from theoretical discussion of political matters. For the study of political science, like every other science, is permissible. We know politics, and should know it, but not in the sense of being defiled by involvement in it. Politics can consume even religion and destroy it. It has already done so with science, making it a plaything. Consider, for example, this theory of Lamarck's and Darwin's. Eastern scientists,[11] who accept the part of this theory that has to do with the principle of the inheritance of acquired traits and thereby deny the importance of biological inheritance, are the very ones who reject the principle of the struggle for existence. Western scientists reject the principle of the inheritance of acquired traits, saying that heredity is constant and acquired traits cannot be passed on, while they believe in the struggle for existence. Why? Because according to their accepted ideologies, one of the two principles is acceptable to one group and the other principle to the other group. Thus, science has to be fragmented so that, there too, politics can reign.

Eventually, things came to such a pass that even heredity had to succumb to the environment. The environment became the only determining factor and agent, so that man became the same as all other animals. This approach gradually became like a disease. Whenever you wanted to understand a question, they said, "Let us see what external influences have been at work, how the environment has affected things, which natural or economic factors have shaped this matter until it took its present form." This has become a universal directive for all scientific research. If you look closely, you will see that in the social sciences, the beginning (and sometimes both the beginning and the end) of research consists of finding out which factors in the external environment have brought about a particular result, how they have joined together, and what effect each one has had. The reason for this approach is that the influence of the environment—everything that is caused by the environment, the interacting factors within the environment, and the network created by these factors—are considered to be foundational. In sum, this is what research has been reduced to within the social sciences, in conformity with physics and biology.

It is here that you can appreciate the miracle of 'Abdu'l-Bahá's utterance (which is to say the miracle of the Bahá'í Faith), when He asserts that, in addition to heredity and the environment, there is another factor that exerts influence on human beings, and that is their innate character, which is specifically human.[12] Nowhere else but in the Bahá'í Faith has so great an effort been made to safeguard the humanity of human beings, to enable them to preserve their integrity, and to protect them against being reduced to mere external nature. Consider, for example, that in some of the Bahá'í writings certain comments have been made about naturalist views. The intention has not been to conduct a scientific discussion, but rather to ensure that we do not derive from these scientific theories conclusions that were not intended by those sciences themselves. It is such unwarranted conclusions that are harmful, damaging, destructive. 'Abdu'l-Bahá has exerted every effort to make sure that people do not draw such conclusions.[13]

What we have discussed is one such example. The purpose is that a human being should consider himself human, never doubting it and never reverting to nature as do other animals. If science says, "You are born of animals and belong to an evolutionary chain," this is not a problem. One can accept it or reject it. It has nothing to do with the Bahá'í Faith; it concerns science. Why? Because the Bahá'í Faith does not consider a human being to be human because of his physical body. It believes in a metaphysical power within the human being that transcends nature, and it is this that makes him human. Because this power is what makes him human, then a human being can never be said to be born of an animal, even though his physical body may have descended from an animal and grown and evolved in reaction to the influence of its environment. But he has become worthy of the title "human" only when, by the will of God, the human spirit has been bestowed on him and he has acquired a human character. This has nothing to do with nature anymore. He is situated in nature, but is not of it. He is a being that transcends nature, prevails over nature, and encompasses nature. Therefore, nature cannot encompass the human being. Thus, the meaning of being human is transformed. The human being takes on an aspect that, when confronted with nature, has its own originality. He stands before nature as an equal, indeed above it and encompassing it; he is not below nature or derived from it or encompassed by it.

To those who wished to reduce even science to the results of the influence of the environment on human beings and their reactions to it, which is again part of that environment—to those who thus wanted to reduce science to nature—'Abdu'l-Bahá said that science, the technology arising out of science, and the use of the mind in the field of science all indicate that humanity does not submit to nature's dominion. In His words, the inner faculty in man "wresteth the sword from the hands of nature, and giveth it a grievous blow."[14] It studies nature so as to understand its course. This inner faculty then diverts nature from its wont course, using what exists in nature itself, something of which nature is unaware but that man knows and uses to transcend nature. What does science do? It understands nature and, when it has done so, it enables humanity to change its course and thereby gain mastery over it. This is the difference between a human being and nature, and it is a great difference indeed. Nature cannot know itself; it is not aware of itself.[15] But man knows nature and can, through this knowledge, encompass nature.

In addition to the method of science, which is to use reason, there is also another method whereby you confront nature and your environment; but this method requires that you discover within yourself a calling to do so and are conscious of the power within you to do so. It consists of accepting the spiritual side of your being and recognizing the portion of the eternal within you, and thereby placing yourself beyond that which is relative, incidental, and merely natural. Consider: In the world, there exists a chain of ephemeral and transient things, and in this respect one can consider the world a natural environment. But this is not the only aspect. There is also another one, and the Bahá'í Faith alerts you to the need to recognize both aspects in the world of existence. The ancients fell short of reality by imagining that everything was constant and should remain constant. They reasoned that because God is unchanging, humanity too, being created by God, is unchanging. They argued that God did not "learn from mistakes," that is, He did not first create something imperfect and later improve upon it. Thus, whatever God willed, He willed it for all eternity. This is how they envisioned divine perfection. By contrast, modern Europeans say that everything is in flux. Every moment, every day, every era, every century, things change; what is fundamental is change itself. As you may know, Spencer wrote six books in order to prove that the foundation of everything is change. Evolutionism, the belief in the theory of evolution, was accepted not only by him but by many leaders of thought and political creeds. However, in the Kitáb-i-Íqán, Bahá'u'lláh says that the world has two aspects, one of immutability and another of change.[16] Both exist. The foundation of the world is, from one perspective, immutability and, from another, change.

The trouble is that only the superficial parts of science and philosophy reach most of the people and, as a result, the thinking of the masses is poisoned by ideas that are incorrect, and they are immersed in all kinds of error. One of these is an erroneous understanding of the meaning of time and its exigencies. The exigencies of the time are not the same things as the promptings of people's desires. The same Person[17] who has said that we must take the exigencies of the time into consideration, or that we cannot resist the exigencies of the times, that same Person says that if the Manifestation of God were to follow the dictates of people's desire, the order of earth and heaven would be disrupted.

Among these errors is what people think about the environment. They explicitly say that whatsoever our environment dictates, in whichever form and at whatever time, we must accept and adopt, or else we will be destroyed while the environment will abide. It is the environment that imposes itself upon us. They, moreover, cite certain scientific concepts and philosophical theories as proofs of the truth of this claim, a claim that, in reality, does not contain the least trace of truth. One such theory is that of scientific determinism, that is to say the belief in the logical necessity of cause and effect. This is the idea that everything that happens is determined by a cause. If the cause requires it, the effect will appear, and if the cause is absent, so will be the effect. We must therefore examine what the external cause is, for that is what dictates the effect. In this context, we as human beings have no power to stand up and say no. In short, predetermination applies to human life as well.

According to the Guardian, Shoghi Effendi, in an oral utterance attributed to him (which I have repeatedly quoted and extensively discussed), no doctrine is more pernicious than one that claims that in every matter we must look for external conditioning factors.[18] Such a view deprives an individual of free will and accountability. By subscribing to such a doctrine, a human being ceases to be human and is reduced to mere nature. Someone commits a crime, and they ask him, "Why did you do this?" He answers, "Who am I to have 'done' anything? My environment demands that I be as I am." Here, a self that is human—that can counter the forces of its environment, that has the will to do something or choose not to do it—ceases to exist. This is why this doctrine is pernicious. The reason for all the efforts made by religions, especially the Bahá'í Faith, to prove the existence of human free will is that when a human being considers himself free, then he is truly human and is able to overcome nature, to do something or wish for something that is other than what nature dictates.[19]

Bahá'u'lláh, in a passage where He describes the effulgence of the names of God upon the reality of each created thing, goes on to say that He created man through the effulgence of His Name, the Unconstrained, the Sovereign.[20] In other words, humanity was created in such wise that it was singled out to manifest God's Name, the Sovereign. Why so much emphasis on this point? So that human beings may no longer view themselves as playthings of nature and captives of their environment, and be enabled thereby to counter its forces.

Another harmful theory is that of relativism, which is to see everything, without exception, as being relative. This too entails great danger. It is true that in one sense everything *is* relative, but only within the context defined for it by science. We have no right to extrapolate what science says about one particular context to others. It is correct that everything in nature is relative. But there also exists an absolute that is above and beyond nature, and signs of that supranatural absolute are present in the relative world of nature. Thus, in nature too, signs of permanence may be observed. For example, morality is relative in that its laws and boundaries, its customs and practices, are relative. The foundations and principles of morality, however, are absolute. Consider some of the talks of 'Abdu'l-Bahá, for instance where He explains that religion possess an aspect of unity and an aspect of difference. When He talks about the common foundation of all religions, He is considering their moral principles.[21] The foundations of morality are absolute, but its laws and customs change. "Thou shalt not kill" is true forever; it is not subject to relativism and does not change according to time and place. "Thou shalt not commit adultery" is true forever. "Thou shalt not steal" is true forever. These commandments are permanent, ever valid, never changing. What changes are the laws and boundaries around them, the customs and conditions associated with them. Murder remains forbidden, but the limits defining its prohibition change from time to time. The answer to the question of who may be killed and who may not changes. In one instance, the law may say that you must not kill a member of your tribe; in another, a member of your religion or your ethnic group; and in yet another, your fellow human being. Perhaps in the future it may even say that you must not kill animals, as 'Abdu'l-Bahá says that a day will come when people will no longer kill animals for food.[22] These laws and ordinances may change and are relative. But the principles are absolute, and their permanence is a sign in this world of the world of God. Without these principles, humanity cannot exist. Therefore, the belief that everything is relative is dangerous in that it makes us captives of our environment since our environment and its effects are relative. But if we acknowledge that there are principles that are absolute and permanent and are given to us from the world of God's authority and therefore bear the signs of his absolute and unconstrained being, then we can guard ourselves against nature. Then will we not yield to our environment and will not suffer defeat, for we will know ourselves to be higher than that environment.

Religions have always brought changes to the environment. In *Some Answered Questions*, 'Abdu'l-Bahá writes that there are different kinds of spirit, and each has its own characteristic. The characteristic of the vegetable spirit is the power of growth, that of the animal spirit the power of the senses, and that of the human spirit the power of intellect, of discovering the unknown. Finally, the characteristic of the Holy Spirit and of the Manifestations of God is the power to "transport the world from one condition to another" and invest "the world of humanity with a new life."[23] As it is said, "On the day when the earth shall be changed into another earth."[24] Thus, every religion that has appeared has changed the world into a new world.

We have two paths we can take so as to transcend our environment and counter its forces. One, which I already discussed, is the path of science: by knowing and understanding the environment, we can gain control of it, and by using our powers, we can prevail over it. The other path is that of faith: through religious faith, we acknowledge the divine, and that which is divine transcends the environment and can change and transform it. The Guardian has repeatedly said that we should not regard the degradation and abasement surrounding us, but rather set our eyes on the lofty station that is ours because of our association with the Cause of God.[25] First and foremost, you must not consider yourself to be weak or small when confronting your environment. Even if you are weak, remember the words of Sa'dí, who said, "Weak though I be, yet my refuge is the Almighty." Even if we are weak as individuals—and we are—yet we can find our support and haven in a transcendent power that is above nature and belongs to the world above, on condition that we truly believe in that spiritual world above. If you do so, you will, when facing the environment, find yourself prevailing over it through heavenly power and the faith that resides within you. Then will you see that the environment is prostrated at your feet. There are many evidences of this claim. Those who first raised the call of the Bahá'í Faith were people who rose up in complete defiance of the demands of their environment. They were eighteen Shaykhí students, weak, lowly, and helpless. What did they want? Exactly the opposite of what their environment asked of them. What did they do? Exactly the opposite of what was expected of them. They accomplished that which proved their ascendancy over their environment.

However, there is one point that we must not forget, which is that there are certain things in our environment that are derived from the reality of things. They have been ordained by God and will inevitably happen for they are indeed the exigencies of the time. Such exigencies are decreed by the Will of God and are destined to take place at a certain time and in a certain manner. These cannot be resisted. But this aspect of the environment must not be attributed to the environment itself; it is derived from the Will of God which ordains that certain things should happen at one time and not another. It is in this connection that 'Abdu'l-Bahá says that everything can be resisted except the exigencies of the time.[26] And in the same vein has the Imám 'Alí said, "Train not your children in the customs of your own time, for they have been created for another time."[27] Acceptance of the requirements of the time is different from unconditional surrender to the influence of the environment.

The requirements of the time are necessary because they are ordained by God; they govern nature and direct it so that it appears as it does. This is different from transient and ephemeral matters that come and go, without having anything to do with the requirements of the time. Let me give you an example relating to an everyday matter. Men's and women's clothing has, over the past few centuries, turned from long and elaborate costumes into shorter suits consisting of jackets worn with trousers or skirts. This change has been a requirement of the times because this has been a time for active work, for literally girding up one's loins, and skirts therefore have had to become shorter. Imagine trying to move nimbly and work swiftly while wearing long robes and cloaks or hoop skirts and crinolines! These were the clothes of idle people in the Middle Ages and early modern period, people who did not need to work and spent their time eating and sleeping. At a time when everyone must be active and move about quickly between work and study, people must wear practical clothes that make such movement possible. It was not possible to resist such a change because it was necessary. Such a change in clothing style is different from the vagaries of fashion, which are based on passing whims. The latter are fads that come and go and are entirely needless; neither their coming nor their going matters. They are not worth fighting against, nor are they worthy of trying to uphold and preserve. The point is that we must not submit to whatever our environment wants to impose on us on the pretext that it is a requirement of the time. Only He Who holds time in His hands can tell us what the requirement of our time is. I speak as a Bahá'í now. It is the Lord of the Age, in Whose latest Manifestation we believe, Who knows the exigencies of this time and has taught us what we should accept and follow. If we do not accept them willingly, those same exigencies will force us to accept them against our will.

For example, the times require the establishment of peace. Those who wanted to oppose the idea of peace initially portrayed it as being reprehensible and blameworthy; they called it effeminate and saw it as a sign of weakness. But gradually they realized that they must accept the idea of peace, for it was an idea that had to prevail. Those who fought against the oneness of the world of humanity were compelled to throw down their shields, and those who fight against it today will likewise have to submit. Those who opposed the equality of the rights of women and men gradually acquiesced to it, and those who still remain opposed to it will also gradually accept it. These changes are taking place because they are exigencies of the present time. But those things that are imposed upon us from outside—these we must not accept as exigencies, but must rather resist. The way to resist is through science and faith. Other than true science and true faith, there is no other path. We have the path of science and technology on the one hand, and the path of faith and the Bahá'í institutions on the other.

We must not underestimate the institutions of the Bahá'í Faith. Participation in them is the most powerful means for equipping us to counter the forces of the environment. These institutions derive their power from a spirit that transcends the environment and prevails over it. You can observe, when serving the Faith, how a power flows through the channel of the institutions into your very being and from there into your outer environment, thereby transforming that environment. In transforming that environment, you can work miracles, as long as you do not stray from the straight path and do not try to change the Faith to conform to your own ideas and conditions. Unfortunately, this is what we sometimes do. For example, we say that, in order to be Bahá'ís, we must adapt the Bahá'í Faith to current conditions and make it conform to the circumstances around us. In saying this, however, our real intention is to become what we ourselves want. For if we truly wanted to be Bahá'ís we would rather try, by teaching the Faith, to change the conditions and circumstances around us, no matter how gradually this would take place and how hard it would be to witness the results and know when they would materialize. Nevertheless, we must fix our eyes on the distant horizon. Teaching the Faith means striving to change the environment, and it is done by people that have faith in the possibility of bringing about such a change through systematic, regular, and uninterrupted service arising out of the spirit of love and faith.

Sometimes the friends complain about the environment and exhibit signs of submission to it, which is very dangerous. In such cases, the emphasis is usually on the corruption within the environment: the belief that it has become so corrupt that nothing can be done to counter it. Worried and despondent, people use the example of movies and novels, of parties and dances. They say the movies were silent, then they became talking, now you see them embodied by people on the streets. They use these examples to illustrate that the environment has become so corrupt that there is no use resisting it; it will only deteriorate more day by day. But you must not view such matters as a serious danger that might threaten humanity. This is absolutely not the case. Matters will take a serious turn only when they shake your faith in the truth of the Bahá'í teachings. It is only then that you should be worried. But as long as you possess the strong spirit of faith, you are able to prevail over the environment.

Let me share with you an example. The Guardian in some of his writings paid great attention to the Roman civilization, laws, and social conditions.[28] He even studied books written about ancient Rome and treatises on the rise, decline, and fall of the Roman Empire. There was a reason for this, namely that the condition of Rome was similar to the condition of the world today.

If you study Roman history, you will see how the height of that civilization was followed by great corruption. What some call "artistic sensibility" came to hold sway over those people (but I am misrepresenting artistic sensibility and ask pardon of the spirit of art) and, in this respect, it greatly resembled our time and even exceeded it somewhat. Where today, boys and girls swim together in mixed swimming pools (reportedly, even in each other's embrace at times), in Rome, shared baths for men and women were not only permitted but common and popular. Where today, guests are given chairs at feast and banquets, in Rome, it was customary at such gatherings to place beds for the guests, women and men alike. A situation such as this was completely transformed by Christianity. It was within such a civilization that Peter and Paul arose. They did not ask themselves how they could possibly confront Nero. They began, then and there, to disseminate the religion of Jesus and to spread abroad His teachings. The Christians were killed, persecuted, made to fight wild animals, and burned. They were accused of crimes and condemned to punishment, but they went on resisting. In the course of two or three hundred years, they subdued that great empire with all its corruptions.

At the same time, the Plan of God also did its work. Recall the two plans described by Shoghi Effendi. One is the Plan pursued directly by the people of Bahá, while the other is the greater Plan carried out by the will of God in society at large. The two plans will eventually converge. At present, there is a divine Plan unfolding through natural processes and preparing the necessary conditions. There is also a Plan that is being carried out by the Bahá'ís, and these are both divine plans. In ancient Rome, too, God's greater Plan brought about the overthrow of that civilization at the hands of the German tribes, while at the same time, through a deliberate process carried out by the foremost followers of Christ over the course of four hundred years, the new Christian civilization arose and transformed the West. The half-naked women of Roman Europe, having converted to Christianity, put on clothes that left only their faces and hands uncovered, and we see the remnants of this fashion in nuns' habits. Of course, this was taking things to the other extreme, but it shows the power of a religion to completely change a people.

Such a power never submits to the forces of the environment. It continues to do its work as long as it is a living force. This power is now in our hands because, in our world today, the living religion of God is the Bahá'í Faith. Let us strive to remain worthy of this power, so that this great task of transforming the world of being may be achieved through our endeavors. Otherwise, it will still be achieved, but by the hands of others, who may not even be Bahá'ís. Let us remember these words of Bahá'u'lláh: "At one time He exalted His Cause by the hand of the people of tyranny, and at another by the hand of His chosen servants."[29] Exalted be His glory!

NOTES TO CHAPTER TEN

1   In Persian, *Muḥíṭ*.
2   Edmond Goblot (1858-1935), French philosopher and logician.
3   Sir Isaac Newton (1642-1727), English mathematician, physicist, and astronomer.
4   Étienne Geoffroy Saint-Hilaire (1772-1844), French naturalist.
5   Jean-Baptiste Lamarck (1744-1829), French naturalist and biologist.
6   Herbert Spencer (1820-1903), English philosopher, biologist, social scientist.
7   Honoré de Balzac (1799-1850), French novelist and playwright.
8   Hippolyte Taine (1828-1893), French historian, critic, and philosopher.
9   August Comte (1798-1857), French philosopher of science.
10 Soviet-era Marxist-Leninist thinkers in the Eastern Bloc who were proponents of environmental determinism.
11 Scientists from the Eastern Bloc, such as Trofim Lysenko (1898-1976), Soviet agronomist and scientist, who emphasized the inheritance of acquired traits over Mendelian genetics.
12 See, 'Abdu'l-Bahá, *Some Answered Questions*, Bahá'í Reference Library, ch. 57, www.bahai.org/r/555562300.
13 See, for example, ibid., ch. 47 and ch. 49.
14 'Abdu'l-Bahá, *Tablet to Dr. Auguste Forel*, Bahá'í Reference Library, www.bahai.org/r/167900656.
15 See, 'Abdu'l-Bahá, *Some Answered Questions*, ch. 1.
16 See Bahá'u'lláh, *The Kitáb-i-Íqán*, Bahá'í Reference Library, www.bahai.org/r/915161822. Dr. Dávúdí relates the unity of the Manifestations of God to the concept of immutability, and the distinctions among them to the concept of change.
17 Bahá'u'lláh.

18   "One of the most fallacious modern doctrines, diametrically opposed to the teachings of all religions, is that man is not responsible for his acts but is excused his wrongdoing because it is brought about by conditioning factors. This is a contention with which Shoghi Effendi had no patience, for it was not in accordance with the words of Bahá'u'lláh" (Rúhíyyih Rabbani, *The Priceless Pearl*, [London: Bahá'í Publishing Trust, 1969], 357).

19   See, for example, 'Abdu'l-Bahá, *Some Answered Questions*, ch. 70.

20   "Having created the world and all that liveth and moveth therein, He, through the direct operation of His unconstrained and sovereign Will, chose to confer upon man the unique distinction and capacity to know Him and to love Him—a capacity that must needs be regarded as the generating impulse and the primary purpose underlying the whole of creation. . . . Upon the inmost reality of each and every created thing He hath shed the light of one of His names, and made it a recipient of the glory of one of His attributes. Upon the reality of man, however, He hath focused the radiance of all of His names and attributes, and made it a mirror of His own Self. Alone of all created things man hath been singled out for so great a favor, so enduring a bounty" (Bahá'u'lláh, *Gleanings from the Writings of Bahá'u'lláh*, ch. XXVII, Bahá'í Reference Library, www.bahai.org/r/250990672).

21   See, for example, 'Abdu'l-Bahá, *Paris Talks*, ch. 39, Bahá'í Reference Library, www.bahai.org/r/124963670.

22   See, for example, "When mankind is more fully developed, the eating of meat will gradually cease" ('Abdu'l-Bahá, *The Promulgation of Universal Peace*, ch. 60, Bahá'í Refence Library, www.bahai.org/r/500673226).

23   'Abdu'l-Bahá, *Some Answered Questions*, ch. 36.

24   Qur'án 14:48.

25   Shoghi Effendi, *Tawqí'át-i-Mubárakih (1922–1926)*, ([Ṭihrán]: Mu'assisiy-i-Millíy-i-Maṭbú'át-i-Amrí, 1972/73), 207.

26   Mírzá Maḥmúd-i-Zarqání, trans. Mohi Sobhani, *Maḥmúd's Diary*, (Oxford: George Ronald Publisher, 1998), 309.

27   Bahá'u'd-Dín Muḥammad al-'Ámilí, *Al-Kashkúl*, vol. 2, (Beirut: Mu'assisatu'l-A'lamí li'l- Maṭbú'át, 1983), 341.

28   See, for example, "The Goal of a New World Order" in Shoghi Effendi, *The World Order of Bahá'u'lláh: Selected Letters*, Bahá'í Reference Library, www.bahai.org/r/211100333.

29   *Fire and Light*, Bahá'í Reference Library, III:VIII, www.bahai.org/r/107495806.

Chapter 11

Liberty

Translated by Vargha Bolodo-Taefi

At the outset, "liberty" can indeed be defined—or rather described—quite easily: Liberty means being able to do whatever one desires. This notion is not exclusive to human beings. This term, with this same meaning, extends to any other being as well. To be sure, this definition is very simple and colloquial, stemming from the literal meaning of the word "liberty" that comes to mind. In this broad sense, liberty can even be attributed to inanimate objects. Have you heard the phrase "free fall" in relation to a stone? What does free fall mean in relation to a stone? It indicates that no external factor, other than what is inherent in the stone and in the fall itself, affects the stone's falling—that is, no one drops the stone with force, throws it, or causes it to fall by some other means; rather, the stone falls on its own and its fall is not influenced by anything other than the inherent nature of the fall itself or the laws governing it. Of course, this notion also applies to animals, even as they say: "free as a bird." For human beings, it is even more pertinent.

However, if we pay close attention, we will note that even this general and simple meaning warrants reflection. For example, when we say that in the free fall of a stone no external factor is involved, we do not mean that no factor whatsoever is at play. Otherwise, we could not call this fall a free fall. Rather, no factor other than the stone itself and what naturally affects its fall is involved. This is the meaning attributed to "natural liberty." A thing is said to enjoy natural liberty when it acts according to its inherent nature or according to the laws governing the entirety of nature. That is, no *external* factor should influence that thing beyond its natural course and inherent trajectory—since it is clear that, for that natural course to unfold, an influencing factor must be at play and a cause is necessarily present. Particularly in the case of inanimate or solid objects, a motive force, or a compelling factor—as described by the philosophers of old—is also involved. Therefore, even in natural liberty, a form of compliance with an influencing factor or a law exists. However, this law is the natural law governing the thing, not a contractual, voluntary, or conventional law imposed upon it from outside. Since animals and humans are also considered natural beings in some sense, this form of natural liberty, in this same sense, also exists in animals and humans. When we say that humans and animals breathe or plants respire, we cannot claim that they are compelled to perform this action or deny that they are free in doing so. This is because every human or animal breathes freely; every plant respires freely. We can only claim that they do not breathe freely when an external factor influences the natural process of their breathing by obstructing the breath or altering the breathing pathway—for instance, when a person wears tight clothing, when the air becomes excessively thin, when a gas is dispersed in the air, or when similar circumstances occur. It is in these situations that we say a person does not breathe freely. And when we say a person does not breathe freely, we imply that we believe in the availability of free breathing to humans and animals, even if that free breathing itself is subject to a law—albeit its own natural and normal law.

In this way, liberty in minerals, plants, animals, and even humans, when viewed purely from a natural perspective, means for everything to follow the natural course of its own behavior, for everything to adhere to the same laws that govern its material properties and material interactions. That is to say, a thing's being free does not mean that it is outside the law, but rather that it is subject to the laws of nature and free from externally-imposed compulsory laws. In this sense, for plants, animals, and humans, liberty can be interpreted as natural liberty, which originally pertained to the realm of inanimate objects and from there extended to the realm of living beings.

Beyond this natural liberty, there exists human liberty, which can be considered from economic, political, social, and spiritual perspectives. However, delving into a discussion of these matters is beyond the scope of this exploration. Nevertheless, considering the concept of liberty in humankind, we must address a certain point: We observed that in all types of beings, whether living or non-living, liberty simply consists in their following their own natural laws, unbound by other factors that could operate outside those laws. In this sense, an animal is free. What does this mean? It means that it acts only in accordance with what nature dictates, or, more precisely, what the laws of matter dictate. Breathing is a function shared by plants, animals, and humans. When we breathe, we cannot choose to stop breathing and still remain alive. An animal absolutely cannot stop breathing and a plant, even more so, must respire continuously. However, when they breathe, they never feel compelled to breathe because they do so according to their natural inclination. Thus, it never occurs to them that they are being forced to breathe, even though they are actually compelled to do so. Moreover, they have no choice but to breathe. There is no alternative to breathing, no other action that can replace it.

Therefore, since plants and animals operate under the law of nature, their liberty also means being subject to this law of nature. As a result, they cannot—and because they cannot, they do not want to—act against what nature dictates. Acting contrary to nature is inconceivable for them. A plant, left to its own devices, respires, feeds, and therefore grows, which means it is free and it has no other option, nor should it. If you try to stop it, you will kill and destroy it. A carnivorous animal too can only exist in its natural state. It is carnivorous; it must eat meat. It is a predator; it must tear and consume its prey. It cannot exist in any other state. Therefore, if you want it to survive, you must allow it to hunt and consume meat. The most you can do is provide the meat yourself, so that it does not need to hunt and kill in order to eat. This, of course, is only possible if you keep it in a cage or domesticate it. In any case, it cannot act in any way other than how it lives and must live according to the laws of nature. Even if you want to introduce a change in it, that change must still comply with the laws of nature, and nothing else.

Do you see the point of my emphasis? The point is that when a plant or animal is left to itself, it does not, cannot, and does not wish to do other than what is dictated by the laws of nature. Thus, an animal, considering the material and vegetative aspects of its life—which, in reality, is a system more complex than plants and more complex than minerals, but made from the same substance and according to the same principles and laws at a higher level—can and must be free. This natural liberty is in the sense mentioned above: following the laws of nature and avoiding any law other than the laws of nature.

It is only humans who, after their own interests, domesticate animals, subjugate them, make them obedient, and alter the trajectory of their lives, all while still adhering to the fundamental laws of nature, which cannot be disregarded. For instance, in addition to the laws of nature, humans impose certain restrictions on sheep for the sake of their own livelihood. This imposition of restrictions is solely for the benefit and enjoyment of humans and is limited to certain boundaries. If these boundaries are exceeded, the animal will either die or break free from its constraints. Given these boundaries and within this context, animals are free; they can be free, and they ought to be free. This is because their liberty consists in complying with their nature, which they never disobey nor complain about. For if they refrain or rebel, they cease to live. Thus, their freedom is confined to adherence to the laws of nature. An animal never, by its own will, defies the bounds of nature. It never seeks, by its own choice, to conquer nature. It never desires, by its own volition, to alter the course of nature. It does not deviate from it, nor can it, nor does it wish to.

But this is not the case with humans. In humans, theoretical and abstract intelligence supplants instinct. By theoretical and abstract intelligence is meant conceptual intelligence, which can also be termed "reason"; for otherwise practical intelligence exists in animals too. When this conceptual intelligence replaces instinct, everything in life changes direction, form, and shape. Consequently, for humans, consciousness, in its psychological sense, finds meaning. Conscience, in its ethical sense, finds meaning. Volition informed by thought (for voluntary actions in a different sense exist in animals too) finds meaning. Furthermore, aesthetic concepts, such as beauty, taste, love, art, industry, science, and religion, find meaning. Society—that is, as the manifestation of social life, not merely natural congregation, which exists in animals too—with all its implications gains meaning. Social conscience, law, rights, and other expressions of social life emerge. Therefore, humans find themselves in a position where they both desire and are able to defy the bounds of nature. Unlike animals, humans are not automatically and involuntarily subjected to nature. Even when they comply with the laws of nature, they do so with awareness and discernment. In light of these circumstances, it is evident that for humans something else must take the place of nature.

I shall clarify that, since animals neither desire nor are able to act outside the laws of nature, no other factor is needed to constrain them. Nature itself imposes the limits that are necessary to constrain them. Animals fall within the path of natural limitation and cannot escape it, nor do they desire to escape it. Thus, they can be left in their natural state and, in this sense, can be free. However, this is not the case for humans. Other factors replace instinct. Human beings reshape their lives and act in ways other than those intended by nature. Indeed, with the consciousness they possess, humans can alter the course of natural law, whether in a simple or complex manner, to suit their own preferences. Therefore, when this transformation is manifested in humans, the conception of liberty within their lives must inevitably also reflect this transformation.

An animal, driven by its sexual instinct, naturally manifests its desires during a specific season, in a specific manner, and for the satisfaction of a specific need. It neither seeks to deviate from its natural form, season, or boundaries, nor is it capable of doing so. Once its natural needs are fulfilled, the goal is achieved, and they hold no further significance. In other words, the animal cannot conceive or perceive any path beyond this natural course. From this perspective, this instinct does not engage with artistic concepts or the rules and regulations of social life. Consequently, the animal can satisfy its desire whenever it wishes. Why do I say "whenever it wishes"? Because it wishes only what nature dictates; it neither can nor seeks to do otherwise. Since the animal is solely governed by natural processes and cannot transcend them, it can be left to its own devices.

In humans, however, this simple concept, the natural instinct, takes other forms. Humans introduce diversity and variation into this natural phenomenon, disrupt its natural timing, break its boundaries, connect it to aesthetic concepts, relate it to the notion of beauty, and infuse artistic aspects into actions associated with this natural instinct. They satiate their taste, satisfy their desires, and yet are not content with a fixed and limited form of the natural instinct. It is only in humans that such a situation arises. Humans break the barrier that nature has placed around this act; and because they break it, another law must inevitably emerge to limit the range of this act, this desire, and this need. This is because only humans transcend the natural limits of this instinct, whereas for animals, frivolity and variety in desire hold no meaning. Pursuing beauty in desire and connecting it to values are meaningless to animals, but these functions find meaning in humans. Since variety and frivolity cannot be unlimited, they necessarily reach a point where the limits of their meaning are exhausted. At that point, boundaries of perversion are unavoidably crossed, leading to human perversion. After all, how much variety can one indulge in while remaining within the bounds of nature? Inevitably, perversion occurs, perversion leads to disorder, and disorder leads to anguish, and so on.

You would certainly recognize that while animals may act freely in their pursuit of desires, humans cannot do the same. This is because when animals act freely, they are governed by the laws of nature and do not—and cannot—desire anything beyond what nature dictates. Humans, however, are not bound solely by the laws of nature but act according to their own will. Consequently, something else must take the place of nature to serve as a limiting factor for humans, and this we call a "moral code." In other words, since humans are not confined to the bounds of nature and can transcend its limits, they must necessarily be restricted by another form of boundary.

At this point, we could delve into the discussion of whether the laws that limit humans are, or should solely be, based on the laws of nature, in accordance with the evolutionary stage of human beings, or whether they should take another form. Materialists argue for the former, claiming that this too is ultimately a manifestation of natural law, albeit in a different form and at a different stage. However, we, as adherents of religions, believe otherwise. Yet, since this is not the place to engage in that particular debate, and the issue at hand concerns liberty in the Bahá'í Faith, we assert that, because a moral code, that is the set of laws governing human behavior, at its highest level is expressed as divine, spiritual, or religious laws, it is therefore the religion of God that must limit human actions.

To be sure, up to this point, materialists agree with us that human beings cannot be left solely to the dictates of nature, for they are not animals who can confine themselves to the rulings of that same nature. It is at this juncture, however, that materialists part ways with us and claim that the law that replaces the rule of nature need not necessarily be divine. However, we assert that it must be divine—though not in the sense that the rule of reason, the scientific judgement that discerns the laws of nature, should be disregarded. After all, one of the fundamental principles of our belief is that religion must be in conformity with reason and science. Nevertheless, alongside the determination of scientific judgement, the rule of faith must exist to regulate morality; for without it, scientific judgement alone is insufficient.

Although it is beyond the scope of the main topic, I will offer an example to clarify that scientific judgement in this matter is not sufficient—that is, the identification of natural laws according to human judgement is not adequate on its own. Consider a physician. When someone smokes, a physician, well-versed in physiology and medicine, can easily and with direct observation see where the smoke goes and what it does to the body. If scientific judgement were accurate and sufficient, no physician in the world would smoke. The same argument applies to alcohol—no physician in the world would consume alcohol or smoke. Why? Because they see and know what smoking and drinking alcohol do to the human body. This is why we say that the identification of natural laws is not enough to limit behavior according to scientific judgement. These two examples from natural matters are sufficient to be applied to all other cases. Consequently, we arrive at the conclusion that while animals may be free in the sense described earlier, human beings cannot be free. This is the very meaning of the verse from the Kitáb-i-Aqdas that suggests that liberty beseems the animal.[1]

When Bahá'u'lláh suggests that liberty beseems the animal, He is implying that animals can be free because their freedom consists in obedience to the law of nature. Therefore, when animals are left to themselves, they are limited by restrictions imposed upon them by nature. However, human beings, not being bound by the law of nature, possess the ability to break their chains, shatter their fetters, and transcend nature. They can indulge in luxury and variety and satisfy their exigent tastes and pleasure-seeking inclinations. Consequently, if another law does not govern humans—if it does not operate above or alongside nature to impose limitations upon them—then their very assertion of their liberty leads to their own undoing.

After stating, in the Kitáb-i-Aqdas, that "the embodiment of liberty and its symbol is the animal," Bahá'u'lláh immediately declares that human beings must be governed by a set of norms and laws.[2] These norms and laws must regulate and govern people, limiting their whims, desires, and inclinations. That is, where the bounds of nature are breached, a moral code should introduce new bounds. The highest form of norms and laws are divine norms and laws; the ultimate expression of divine norms and laws is those that are in accordance with the exigencies of the time, manifested through the appearance of the Manifestation of God in each age; and the Manifestation of God in this age is Bahá'u'lláh. Therefore, we assert openly—and stand joyfully by this assertion—that liberty consists in obedience to the teachings of Bahá'u'lláh. This is the meaning of the statement in the Kitáb-i-Aqdas in which Bahá'u'lláh indicates that liberty beseems the animal, that it is ignorant to pride oneself in such liberty, and that true liberty consists in people's submission to His commandments, in complete servitude to God, and in obedience to the laws of the Manifestation of God.[3] He is the One Who liberates.

How does He liberate? By imposing limitations. In other words, by confining people to boundaries within which they can act, He frees them through this very confinement. Imagine leaving someone to his own devices from childhood to smoke freely. By allowing this liberty, you have, in fact, restricted him. How so? Because he can no longer breathe at will; he cannot choose to take a few steps faster than he usually does; he can no longer eat as he desires; and he can no longer sleep comfortably. Therefore, by allowing him freedom to do what he should not do, you have restricted him in several things he should do. Now, if you take this a step further and allow him to become addicted to drugs, to freely use heroin, what would be the outcome? He would become enslaved to the very drug he was free to use. By allowing this, you have deprived him of his freedom to live, to move, to walk, to work, and ultimately to carry out the ordinary and natural activities of life, each of which holds its own pleasures, and may indeed hold the highest pleasures. Thus, if one's liberty is not limited, that very liberty will effectively perish.

The examples I have given so far are individual in nature. Now, imagine that in a group—no matter how or for what purpose it is formed—you allow everyone to do whatever they desire. What would be the result? In reality, you have only allowed one or two, or a few, individuals, who are stronger than the rest, to act freely. How so? Because these individuals will impose limitations on others. In essence, allowing everyone to act freely means subjecting everyone to those whose power and strength surpass that of the others. The outcome of a situation where everyone is free to do whatever they wish is that only those with power and might will be truly free to pursue their desires, while all others must submit. This is what is commonly referred to as the "law of the jungle."

Thus, allowing everyone to act freely effectively means depriving the weak of their liberty for the benefit of the strong. Moreover, another view has also been proposed in this context: Even the individual liberty of the strong will be limited, because once they achieve their freedom to do whatever they desire, they must preserve their strength. They must be constantly concerned with maintaining that strength and must continuously strive to ensure its preservation. This very struggle and effort serve as constraints on their own liberty, creating fear and anxiety. Therefore, even within that small group, for everyone to be truly free, all must be subject to laws, precepts, and rules, so that, within those bounds, everyone can experience freedom.

Therefore, liberty means adherence to the law, and it cannot exist otherwise—it cannot even be conceptualized in any other way. That is to say, one should not imagine that when liberty is restricted, it ceases to exist. On the contrary, liberty is secured. To limit liberty is to guarantee it and it is this limitation that preserves liberty. Since this discourse is directed at Bahá'ís, it should be noted that a Bahá'í, when obedient to the laws, precepts, and teachings of Bahá'u'lláh, finds herself in a world where, within the sphere of general and universal principles, the requirements of every action and every matter are determined. Yet, in the details of her actions, she is left to her own devices, guided by her overarching faith, reliance, and devotion, which subject her to the boundaries within which she wishes to, and can, operate. For this reason, she is free, even if external forces beyond her control limit her liberty. Because she has directed her focus toward a realm beyond the material world, this limitation does not cause her distress. She confronts various challenges, and if she fails to overcome them, she does not fall into despair, grief, or frustration, as her attention is also focused on another world beyond this one, and thus she remains free forever. However, if she breaks the limitations imposed by the teachings in order to be left to her own devices, that very abandonment entangles her in bonds such that the more she strives to liberate herself, the more she becomes ensnared by additional constraints.

God forbid that you find yourselves in a situation where you would experience this personally. I wish for everyone to be in a station where the experiences of others would suffice for you or, even if the experiences of others are not brought into consideration, mere attention to the teachings themselves and the acceptance of those teachings would be sufficient for you. And, of course, this is only possible through the strengthening of one's faith. For in the Bahá'í Faith, individual liberties are so secured that no one is compelled, obligated, or forced to follow a particular way. The Bahá'í Faith does not interfere with the details of one's actions. No one considers himself entitled to criticize the behavior of others. No one engages in enjoining what is right, and forbidding what is wrong. All the teachings are universal. All the teachings are divine. It is for this reason that the strength of faith serves as the guide for individuals. Thus, with freedom of action having been secured, devotion coupled with faith and reliance upon faith can safeguard our liberty. Otherwise, without faith, the liberty we have in our actions will lead us to ruin. Even faith itself is accompanied by love, by affection. That is, even in relation to faith, no one is coerced by warnings that if you do not believe, you will suffer this or that consequence, or face a particular form of punishment. The only punishment we could anticipate is, in reality, the spiritual anguish we experience when our Beloved, our Adored One, is displeased with us, and we regard this as a sin both in this world and the next.

You can observe what Bahá'u'lláh meant when He conveyed in the Kitáb-i-Aqdas, firstly, that it is ignorant to pride oneself in liberty; secondly, that liberty beseems the animal; thirdly, that people should be subject to precepts and principles; and, fourthly, that true liberty consists in people's submission to His commandments.[4] Now that the meaning of the four components of this commandment in the Kitáb-i-Aqdas has been clarified, I have nothing further to add except to emphasize that you should fully understand this liberty, apply it wisely, and place it in a context where liberty itself serves as the guardian of liberty.

NOTES TO CHAPTER ELEVEN

1   Bahá'u'lláh, *The Kitáb-i-Aqdas*, ¶ 123, Bahá'í Reference Library, www.bahai.org/r/181680636.
2   Ibid.
3   Ibid., ¶ ¶ 122–125, Bahá'í Reference Library, www.bahai.org/r/841589016.
4   Ibid.

Chapter 12

Liberty in the Bahá'í Faith

Translated by Vargha Bolodo-Taefi

Some have construed "liberty" to mean that they may act as they wish without being bound by any constraints; that no one may have the audacity to impede their movement, nor anything possess the power to limit the range of their desires; that their voice may travel through boundless space as far as the power of imagination allows; that their desire may subdue the entire universe into servitude; that the ambitions they entertain may encompass heaven and earth as their playground; that whatever they possess may always remain theirs and whatever others possess may be offered up to them as a humble tribute; that their will may serve as the measure of good and evil and their understanding as the standard of right and wrong. Such are their words and such are their desires, and they take pride in their words and desires. "We find some men desiring liberty, and priding themselves therein. Such men are in the depths of ignorance. Liberty must, in the end, lead to sedition, whose flames none can quench. Thus warneth you He Who is the Reckoner, the All-Knowing."[1]

Such a thing is not possible; the cosmic order inherently opposes it. The realm of existence adheres to rules that its constituent parts cannot deviate from. Were those who desire such liberty to be given the option to do as they please, they would soon reach a point where they could wish for nothing more. Were they to persist, they would perish and forfeit their lives.

You can try this yourself. Stop breathing for a few seconds; you will find yourself unable to continue. Abstain from water for a few days; you will realize that you cannot endure any further. Eat as much as you desire; you will reach a point where you can no longer consume anything. As a result, you will soon find yourself confronted with a state wherein you inevitably succumb to the laws of nature; you will be compelled to recognize certain boundaries and be held accountable—unless you have strayed too far and become too unrestrained to stop and stay, in which case you will eventually stumble and fall and will face the consequences of your audacity in desiring unrestricted liberty. There is no recourse, then, save to refrain from seeking, from the outset, what contravenes the laws of nature and to avoid desires contrary to the natural order. In such a state, since you will attain whatever you desire, you will experience liberty.

Animals are like this. They are free and recognize no boundaries to their freedom. They do not conceive of anything contrary to their nature that they may not attain; they desire only what is in accordance with their nature and attain it. Every individual animal is a manifestation of the animal species. The consequence of the existence of an animal is not contradictory to the requirements of the universal order. It can be said, therefore, that liberty is as fit for the animal as a glove for a hand—that "the embodiment of liberty and its symbol is the animal."[2]

However, human beings are not like this. In addition to a body, which is confined within the bounds of the natural world and limited by material constraints, they possess a rational soul and discerning intellect. They feel a sense of agency within themselves. They perceive a formidable force within themselves capable of overcoming nature. They aspire to cast a beam of their inner self onto the world of existence. They seek to imprint a manifestation of their intellect upon the physical realm. They wish to unravel the hidden mysteries of nature. They aim to utilize inanimate objects for their own benefit. They seek to bend their intellect to the conquest of the universe. They aspire to use wisdom as a means of acquiring wealth. Unlike animals, they endeavor to set themselves free from the dictates of nature in all circumstances. They themselves, not the imperatives of material laws, determine their obligations. They consider themselves authors of their own destiny, creators of the ways of their own life, and masters of their own individual sovereignty.

However, the human race is not confined to a single person or a few people; rather, a myriad individuals facing similar circumstances encounter each other, spend time with each other, and contend with each other. Each one of them desires to pursue the affairs of this world with all his might and to obtain as much and advance as far as possible. As a result, wills come into conflict with each other, ambitions collide, and desires clash headlong. It is evident what will emerge from this confrontation: nothing but strife, turmoil, and bloodshed. It is likewise clear who will prevail in this struggle: the one with the most power and cunning. In the end, all those who sought liberty are forced to succumb to the one who is strongest, bowing their heads in submission and bearing the yoke of servitude. All liberties are lost, power and strength rule, and tyranny and oppression reveal themselves. All those who sought liberty become ensnared; those who desired to break free from every constraint become entangled in every chain. Thus, they proclaim by their actions that such is the fate of those who fail to discern their difference from animals.

It is against this backdrop that the law comes into play. Using the necessary relationships derived from the realities of things, guidelines for a specific way of life are prescribed and the limits of everyone's liberty are established; adherence to these limits simultaneously constrains everyone yet grants liberty to all. "That which beseemeth man is submission unto such restraints as will protect him from his own ignorance, and guard him against the harm of the mischief maker."[3]

For reasons not expounded upon in this discourse, the best laws are those established within religions, and the most ideal religion is the one that belongs to an era closest to the present time and is, therefore, in accordance with the requirements of this age. This religion, today, is the one authored by Bahá'u'lláh and established and legislated in the Kitáb-i-Aqdas. If these laws require justification, that justification is for those who have yet to embrace the teachings of Bahá'u'lláh. Since they are not being addressed here specifically, we need not exert any effort to prove this statement and may allow ourselves to assume the premise that the laws of the Kitáb-i-Aqdas are the most ideal. Having previously argued that laws safeguard liberty, guarantee rights, prevent the domination of the powerful, and counter the establishment of the rule of the jungle in human society, we must inevitably conclude that liberty for Bahá'ís lies in following the provisions of the Kitáb-i-Aqdas and obeying the laws enshrined in that supreme charter. "Say: True liberty consisteth in man's submission unto My commandments."[4]

A person who is irreligious and desires for all humanity to be irreligious is in fact the greatest enemy of liberty. For were things to unfold as he desires, who could stop the tyranny of the powerful? Who could prevent someone capable of killing another from carrying out his wish? What could safeguard the dignity of the lowly against the oppressor? One might argue that laws derived from human thought and reason can achieve this. In response, we would assert that, on the one hand, this admission is itself evidence for the necessity of restricting liberty under the rule of law. On the other hand, in the case of laws derived from human reason, the rule of law over individuals can come about only through the power of the law—thus, enforcement of the law through coercive power, and the restriction of liberty, would become both more necessary and more severe.

In contrast, when religion permeates hearts and educates souls, it transforms people in such a way that they themselves desire to be in this state: they themselves desire not to commit injustice, they themselves desire to observe certain boundaries, and they themselves desire not to transgress these boundaries notwithstanding their power to do so. Consciences are nurtured to the extent that people desire nothing except what God's law desires and consider worthy of pursuit only what religion teaches.

The relationship of nature to animals is akin to the relationship of religion to humans.[5] Nature governs animals such that no individual animal perceives any conflict between the dictates of nature and its own desires. For this reason, an animal can be simultaneously obedient to nature while remaining free from constraints and limitations. Human beings, however, are not bound by nature in the same way; rather, they perceive themselves as its rulers and owners and capable of altering and transforming it.

Consequently, in the realm of humanity, instead of natural factors, religious norms come into play as regulators. Religion takes the place of nature and renders individuals so receptive that they perceive no contradiction between what religion desires for them and what they themselves desire. If among them are found those who deem adherence to religious decree as an encroachment upon their personal liberty, they belong to a category of individuals whose hearts and souls have not been nurtured to the extent that their personal inclinations align with the teachings of religion. If these individuals are receptive to education, it is the duty of parents and Bahá'í institutions to eliminate this misalignment through the miracle of education and raise the youth in such a way that they will desire nothing except what divine teachings desire for them—this, in order that if they fail to attain their personal desires, they will not harbor a feeling of deprivation in their hearts and presume a loss of liberty.

A person who does not adhere to divine teachings, but rather proclaims absolute liberty as his motto, will inevitably be ensnared by the consequences of his wrongful deeds. Ultimately, the lament and anguish of his heart will testify to the truth of this confession, proclaimed by his very being: the religion that I perceived as an obstacle to my freedom would, in fact, safeguard it, and the belief that I considered as a shackle upon myself could, in reality, liberate me. In that moment, with sincere repentance, he will turn to the threshold of the Blessed Beauty and hear, with his inner ear, this sweet call that will restore his lost hopes once again:

> On our threshold despair does not encroach,
> Though you have broken every vow, approach![6]

Notes to Chapter Twelve

1   Bahá'u'lláh, *The Kitáb-i-Aqdas*, ¶¶ 122–123, Bahá'í Reference Library, www.bahai.org/r/841589016.
2   Ibid., ¶ 123.
3   Ibid.
4   Ibid., ¶ 125.
5   'Abdu'l-Bahá describes both nature (Tablet to Dr. Auguste Forel, www.bahai.org/r/495128940 and www.bahai.org/r/972858752) and religion (*Some Answered Questions* 40:8–9, www.bahai.org/r/215247291) as the necessary relations inherent in the reality of things.

6 The original couplet can be found in Abú Saʻíd-i-Abu'l-Khayr, *Sukhanán-i-Manẓúm-i-Abú Saʻíd-i-Abu'l-Khayr* (Ṭihrán: Kitábkhániy-i-Shams, 1955), 4.

Chapter 13

Conceptions of Liberty

Translated by Vargha Bolodo-Taefi

In our time, perhaps no other word captivates and fascinates everyone as much as the word "freedom." No other word seems as beautiful and enchanting, and none compels us as deeply to reflect on and ponder its meanings. It is also possible that no other word has been subject to as many interpretations and commentaries. And again, perhaps no other concept has inspired as much struggle, conflict, and effort as freedom, with the many interpretations of this word. Finally, no term holds as much meaning, importance, and majesty for humanity.

The conceptions and meanings of liberty permeate all aspects of human life, whether individual or social, spiritual or material, transient or enduring; they connect all these dimensions, manifesting themselves at every turn, raising questions in every domain, and demanding answers to the enquiries they provoke. The questions surrounding the boundaries and meanings of liberty must be addressed, for the pursuit of liberty is humanity's strongest desire—or, to avoid exaggeration, one of its strongest desires and aspirations. Whenever the subject of fundamental human rights arises, the right to life and the right to liberty are immediately invoked, with all other rights, such as the right to property, deriving from these two rights. Therefore, it is clear that we cannot remain indifferent to the various concepts of liberty, given their profound significance.

The Bahá'í Faith, belonging to the age and era of liberty, must clarify its stance on liberty, and indeed it has done so. In the Mother Book of the Bahá'í Dispensation, the Kitáb-i-Aqdas, Bahá'u'lláh provides a statement on liberty wherein He defines true liberty, delineates its boundaries, and specifies what can be referred to as false liberty. This false liberty, which is characterized by absolute freedom, is understood as lawlessness and chaos. Bahá'u'lláh suggests that such behavior, where individuals act according to their every whim, beseems the animal. He then defines true liberty, stating that it consists in submission to the commandments of the Manifestation of God.[1]

It is fitting to reflect on this matter: when Bahá'u'lláh suggests that liberty beseems the animal, we must consider what is meant by this and why liberty is attributed to animals. An animal functions as a machine or an organism that has come into existence as a result of the composition of various parts and organs, as necessitated by their properties and the qualities emanating from the combination of these components. Therefore, an animal possesses characteristics that govern its existence, and whatever the animal does is in accordance with the specific composition of its material existence. As such, the life of an animal is dictated by necessary, inevitable, essential, and structural demands, that have manifested themselves in the form of its existence.

To clarify further: what an animal does is what it wants to do, can do, and must do. We particularly emphasize that an animal "must do" what it does; because, otherwise, the statements "wants to do" and "can do" are also applied in the highest realm of existence, that is, to God. God is the One Who does what He "wants to do," and He "can do" it. However, in the case of God, the concept of "must do" does not apply. This characteristic is exclusive to animals. In relation to God, His Will and Purpose is overriding and there is no compulsion involved, insofar as He is the All-Subduing, not subdued. Thus, He does what He "wants to do," and "can do" it, but the notion of "must do" does not befit Him. Therefore, in the case of God, Divine Will is paramount, whereas in animals, "must do"—or "cannot not do"—is the defining principle.

Let us set aside these subtleties and focus on the point that when an animal performs the action it must do, restricting or compelling it holds no meaning, for the animal cannot act in any way other than it already does. Exceptions may exist in certain animals from which humans, for their own benefit, demand different tasks; but that is a separate issue. In its natural state—that is, with respect to what it requires for its survival—it is meaningless to restrict an animal This is because the animal does exactly what it is supposed to do—it does not want, nor is it able to want, anything else; neither can it do anything else. This being the case, an animal can be left to its own devices to do as it pleases, because, at the highest degree of its freedom, it does exactly what it desires, and it desires exactly what it is capable of doing.

I stated that, in the case of animals, restricting them neither makes sense nor is possible, unless we limit their freedom for our own benefit or to avoid harm. In such a scenario, restricting the animal is tantamount to limiting its very essence and existence, preventing it from being as it was created and meant to be. When you release a pigeon and allow it to be as it wishes, it will be as it must be, that is, as nature intended. In other words, it will be as its existence naturally demands, as determined by the divine will. Therefore, it can be set free and can stay free. If you release a wolf into the wilderness, it will remain as it is, and even if you do not release it, it will still remain as it is—unless you desire for it to be otherwise, which is another matter entirely. A wolf must hunt and eat, and thus it does exactly what it was created to do and must do, and it cannot do otherwise. A horse must trot and gallop, and it will act in accordance with its nature, as determined by the divine will. Consequently, limiting or eliminating its freedom is not possible; even if possible, it is not necessary; and even if necessary, it is not beneficial—except for our sake and for our advantage. It is in this sense that we say that an animal is free, or that liberty beseems the animal. For even when it is free, it is still bound by the limits of its own nature. Nature has set its limitations, and the animal, in conformity with the laws of nature, will not desire anything that is unnatural. This is because it *cannot* desire what is unnatural, and it must desire what is natural. Therefore, it can remain free within those bounds, and there is no need to restrict its freedom, for nature has already constrained it by the instincts that govern it.

An animal possesses a series of instincts that govern its actions. For instance, it eats, sleeps, and mates; it lives and dies. In its eating, sleeping, mating, and living, instincts that are directed by nature itself guide, limit, and activate it. This is why the animal can be free; restricting it, except when humans domesticate it in their service, has no meaning. This kind of liberty beseems the animal because its boundaries are defined by nature—they need not be defined through the intervention or influence of any factor other than nature. Therefore, it can indeed be free.

However, humans are different. A human being is not a machine, except in regard to the animal and vegetative aspects of her life. A human is not merely a limited organism; she wants to do and does as she wants. Now, whether or not we can frame the human will in a way that defines it as a necessity or essential property is a discussion for another occasion. We will not delve into that here. But suffice it to say that if we could ultimately define the human solely in material terms—which we believe is not possible—we would still find that human beings possess the primary and fundamental factor of the human will. This very factor, the human will, transports them beyond the boundaries set by the instincts that nature has ordained within them. Humans transform their instincts, imprinting in each one the marks of consciousness, reason, and wisdom. They take control of their instincts and, influenced by their "will" factor, guide and channel their own instincts.

In humans, sexual instinct assumes a spiritual dimension, on the one hand, becoming associated with beauty and manifesting as love. On the other hand, it takes on the form of family life, becoming associated with moral values and manifesting as marriage. Thus, you can observe, what is driven purely by carnal desire and sexual instinct in the animal is transformed into love and marriage in humans, assuming ethical, social, and spiritual characteristics.

Animals possess an instinct for building homes and nests. In humans, this same inclination exists, but it takes the form of science, industry, and technology, and develops into engineering. It assumes an artistic quality, and transforms into architecture. All these crafts then converge and are expressed by humans in home construction. Engineering, architecture, aesthetic sensibility, refinement, and beauty, on one side, and science and industry, on the other, are intertwined by architects, designers, and engineers, resulting in residential structures. Thus, you can observe how from animals to humans the instinct for nest-building changes entirely, acquiring a form in the human realm that is utterly absent in the animal world.

In this way, the human will and agency in altering the course of nature is demonstrated. Human beings show that they are not content to remain imprisoned by the constraints of nature and that nature cannot limit them. They are capable of acting contrary to the dictates of nature and instinct, and can do so even if this requires changing the course of nature itself. Even proponents of determinism with regard to human action concede that humans can comprehend the natural course of events and, by harnessing nature itself, alter that course. Put simply, the human will determines man's course of action.

We have stated that humans have the desire and capacity to transcend the limits of instinct and the constraints imposed by nature. It is in this transcending that the possibility of either steadfastness or deviation arises. That is, by breaking free from the narrow bounds of nature, a person may either follow the straight path or deviate from it, as both outcomes are possible. An individual can choose the path of moderation or be drawn toward extremes. In other words, human beings can embody beauty or ugliness, good or evil; they can act rightly or wrongly. In doing so, their course of action is no longer determined by nature, for they have already broken through its confines, surpassed it, and embarked on their own journey. Thus, when human reality and nature is such, there must inevitably be another factor, or factors, that arise to impose limits on the individual. It is at this point that the liberty of human beings—in the sense in which it applies to animals—must be restricted. In the animal kingdom, nature itself fully defines, determines, and limits the course of an animal's life. In the human realm, however, we are dealing with a being who does not surrender herself to nature or allow it to rule over and limit her. Therefore, another limiting factor must come into play to restrain the individual. It may be the law of religion—a religion that is grounded in and embodies truth—that imposes this limit. Without such a law, there is no assurance as to which path a person, who desires and is able to break free from nature's constraints, will choose, or how she will proceed along it—whether she will remain on, or deviate from, the straight path.

Some may argue: "One should allow individuals to deviate and go wherever they wish. Since it has been determined that humans are to be free, such actions are inherent to liberty. What concern is it of anyone to assume responsibility for or act as guardians over others, thereby restricting their liberty?" The answer is that the efforts of individuals, families, and society are actually aimed at *preserving* human liberty, which is a fundamental right, rather than *restricting* it. In other words, a human being, who is not merely an animal, must be constrained by something other than nature—nature being the force that simultaneously limits and liberates animals—so that her liberty can be safeguarded. Therefore, the very imposition of limitations through rules, regulations, and social and religious laws is essential for maintaining genuine human liberty. When a person chooses a path he should not follow but desires to pursue, he not only harms himself and limits his own liberty but also deprives others of their liberty. For example, imagine that someone claims, "I am free and wish to consume drugs." Others intervene and say, "We will not allow you to consume drugs." This intervention is not intended to restrict that individual but rather to preserve his liberty. For once the person becomes addicted to drugs, it is the drugs themselves that strip away his freedom of thought and action, consuming him entirely. What was initially pursued as an expression of liberty becomes the heaviest chain around his neck, nay his entire being. Thus, the restrictive efforts of those around him, in preventing his consumption of drugs, are aimed at saving him from that bondage and maintaining his liberty. Such limitations, however, are unnecessary for animals because, as mentioned, the concept of desiring something contrary to nature holds no meaning for them.

An animal consumes food in a particular manner and eats only specific kinds of food. It refrains from eating anything beyond what it ought and is able to consume. Through its senses of taste and smell, it can distinguish between good and bad food, and even detect poisons. By the dictates of nature, it consumes only what it must, and, in natural conditions it avoids what it should not eat. Animals do not seek variety, luxury, or indulgence in their diet, nor do they deliberately stimulate false appetites, because in all these matters nature limits them. The only exception, as mentioned, occurs when humans introduce artificial variety into the animal's life; otherwise, animals impose their limitations upon themselves as dictated by nature and adhere to them without deviation.

In contrast, human beings season their food, introduce many alterations, and present it in an appealing and appetizing manner. They arrange elaborate and colorful meals, and it is precisely for this reason that their eating habits must be confined within certain boundaries or regulated by specific limits. Animals, however, are different because they derive their limits from nature. It is the freedom of humans in eating that must be constrained by the principles of medical science, legal codes, or divine law. Otherwise, they would lose this very freedom in eating, as their stomach, lungs, liver, and nerves would suffer damage from this unrestrained liberty. Thus, in reality, the preservation of human liberty necessitates the imposition of limitations in such matters.

An animal manifests its sexual instinct according to the laws of nature and in fulfillment of the necessity of reproduction, and it does not exceed the limits set by nature. Once the animal's sexual desire is fulfilled, it is satisfied and the matter comes to an end. In some animals, this desire even has a specific season; once the season passes, the urge subsides. In contrast, humans introduce various forms of indulgence into this natural instinct, seeking diversity, which will inevitably lead them astray from their natural path. This deviation will eventually result in harm to both themselves and others, ultimately leading to illness, danger, or even madness. Consequently, the natural pleasure they once experienced is also lost. Therefore, in this scenario as well, to maintain human beings in a state where their initial liberty is preserved—allowing them to enjoy the pleasure they could experience and are entitled to—we must impose limits, whether through science, law, or divine teachings. Thus, we observe how and why it becomes necessary to restrict human liberty in order to safeguard it.

Now, let us provide an example concerning liberty within a group. Imagine a situation where all members of the group are given complete freedom to act as they wish. If you observe such a group over time, you will notice that after a while only those who are stronger than others will retain their freedom to act without restriction. This occurs because the desires of individuals inevitably clash with one another. One person, in pursuing his own desires, pushes another aside, subduing and overpowering her. Consequently, the wills of individuals begin to impose themselves upon one another, in proportion to the strength of each. Ultimately, this leads to a situation where only a few stronger individuals—or even a single individual—through conspiracy, collusion, stratagem, or sheer physical power, gain the freedom to act as they wish, while all others are constrained, limited, and forced to comply. Thus, the initial intention of allowing everyone to act freely results in a condition where all are compelled to act according to the will of the strong. In such circumstances, the "law of the jungle" governs human society. Therefore, it becomes evident that human liberty must be limited in order to be preserved. Let us reiterate that these limitations may arise from scientific principles, legal codes, or divine commandments. From our perspective, as adherents of religion, divine religion is the superior force, as it is comprehensive, inclusive, authoritative, and divine in origin. To be sure, should some individuals reject this preference, a discourse can take place on the matter, but expanding on this topic or engaging in such a discourse is not our objective here.

Therefore, since divine religion, in our view, is the most complete, comprehensive, and inclusive system of law that restricts liberty in order to preserve it, it is indeed divine religion that ultimately safeguards liberty. The concept of true liberty finds its meaning in submission to divine religion. This is the very meaning of the idea expressed at the conclusion of the verses on liberty in the Kitáb-i-Aqdas.[2] Bahá'u'lláh states that true liberty consists in man's submission to His commandments—that is, divine religion. In this age, it is the Bahá'í Faith that secures true liberty. Divine religion places a bond around the neck—a bond of servitude—yet it is this very bond that liberates humanity from all other chains.

Now let us turn to some details and consider whether the Bahá'í Faith truly grants people liberty. What we observe in the Bahá'í Faith in this age is that none of its teachings aim to bind and restrict individuals to only what they may or can desire. In other words, the Bahá'í Faith grants humanity the maximum degree of liberty possible at this specific stage in the collective evolution of humanity. This is not to say *all* possible liberty, as all possible liberty is achieved progressively and in the final stages of humanity's evolutionary journey. Since the evolution of humanity has no ultimate end, complete liberty is a limit that humanity will continually approach but never fully attain, as complete and absolute liberty belongs to God alone. Humanity moves toward achieving this liberty, and the more it traverses this path, the more fully and abundantly it realizes its liberty.

God is sovereign, and humankind is also sovereign. In one of His Tablets, Bahá'u'lláh, after explaining the creation of other beings and then man, states that God manifested within each of His creatures one of His names and attributes. When it came to man, however, He specifically manifested the name "Sovereign," creating man "through the direct operation of His unconstrained and sovereign Will."[3] Thus, the unique name that appears distinctively within humankind, in addition to other names, is the name "Sovereign." Humanity, therefore, is sovereign, in the likeness of God, while God embodies sovereignty in His own essence. When we say "in the likeness of God" and "in God's image," we have in mind the verse from the Old Testament that states "God created man in his *own* image."[4]

At each stage of humanity's evolution, a certain degree of liberty has been attained. In this era—the Dispensation of Bahá'u'lláh—humanity has reached an unprecedented level of liberty that it cannot, at this time, surpass. The liberty available in the Bahá'í Faith is not comparable to the liberty found in other religions or groups, or the freedoms prevalent in the many nations of the world. Here, we briefly touch upon a few points to illustrate how liberty has been safeguarded in this era.

First, let us examine the matter of beliefs. In the Bahá'í Faith, the general tenets of belief are clear and defined. But in the specifics of matters of belief, no limitation or restriction has been imposed on any issue. Each person is free to allow her conscience, mind, and heart to soar within the realms of faith and hold whatever beliefs resonate and agree with her understanding. Bahá'ís are guided in the general tenets: They recognize God; but in relation to the approach they take to knowing God and their understanding of His nature, they may follow whatever path they are able to undertake, consider sound, and choose to pursue to know God. Bahá'ís recognize and obey the Manifestation of God; yet what they understand Him to be and the station they attribute to Him are matters of personal discernment and choice. No one has the right to scrutinize another's beliefs, measure them, or declare: "Such is the correct belief" or "you must believe in such a way," except in the broad, essential verities. Why is this the case? Because beliefs are as numerous as individual souls—indeed, as countless as their every breath. This brings to mind an Islamic tradition: "The paths to God are equal to the number of His creatures" or "The paths to God are equal to the number of breaths His creatures take." This signifies that each person—and even each moment of each person's life—can represent a unique path to God, distinct from the ways that others, or even they themselves in other moments, may have followed. Therefore, individuals are free to believe as they wish within the bounds of a universal, comprehensive, and inclusive Faith.

In the Tablet to Jamál, in response to a question regarding the station of the Manifestation of God, Bahá'u'lláh explicitly states that individuals should recognize and accept the Manifestation of God in accordance with the station they personally ascribe to Him through their own inclination, understanding, and conscience. He stresses that any manner of recognition is accepted from the believer, but that if two people clash on this matter or seek to compel one another to adopt their personal beliefs, then both parties are rejected.[5] Observe how, with such clear emphasis and counsel, freedom of belief, the right to self-determination, and regard for the perceptions and beliefs of others are upheld. Each person is free to discern and distinguish according to her own judgment, yet if two people argue with each other or attempt to impose their views on one another, both individuals are rejected. Why? Because such disputes lack any definitive standard according to which one person's view could serve as a criterion by which to judge the beliefs of others, or condemn, invalidate, or shun those who disagree. Accordingly, this serves to illustrate how freedom of belief is safeguarded.

In the Bahá'í Faith, the laws governing acts of worship, as well as other religious laws and ordinances, are presented broadly in the form of a concise yet inclusive outline, in terms of general and universal principles, while the specifics are left to individual choice. This means that prescribing specific, uniform details, mandatory for all to follow, is not the approach taken in the practice of the Bahá'í Faith. For example, consider the obligatory prayer: a long, a medium, and a short obligatory prayer have been revealed. Each person is free to select one of these according to his or her preference and personal circumstances. A person may choose to recite the long obligatory prayer once in every twenty-four hours; say the medium obligatory prayer three times a day, once between dawn and noon, again between noon and sunset, and a final time within two hours after sunset; or recite the short obligatory prayer, which consists of only a single verse, once between noon and sunset. This flexibility is granted to prevent restrictive rules and secondary ordinances regarding worship from stripping the act of turning toward God of its spirit of joy and radiance, and to ensure that specific rules, regulations, and procedures do not impose undue limitations on our freedom in worship. The same principle applies to other Bahá'í laws and ordinances, allowing for their observance while preserving the freedom of one's heart, spirit, and conscience.

Let us now consider Spiritual Assemblies and the structures associated with them—institutions that are referred to as the Houses of Justice in the Kitáb-i-Aqdas, are described and expounded in 'Abdu'l-Bahá's Will and Testament, and the realization and establishment of which were brought into effect under the direction of Shoghi Effendi. In all aspects of Bahá'í administration, we observe a clear commitment to freedom. Consider, for instance, the process of Bahá'í elections: guidance has been provided that Bahá'í elections must be carried out freely, universally, and by secret ballot.[6] They are carried out by secret ballot to prevent any restriction of freedom that might arise through an open ballot. Bahá'í elections are conducted with such freedom that no force can influence them. It is noteworthy that in all political elections around the world, propaganda, or electoral campaigning, is permitted. In public elections that are common around the world, candidates are nominated, campaigns are held on their behalf, and, in support of these measures, they engage in political intrigue—that is, they form alliances and mobilize forces—practices that inevitably influence voter choice and views in ways that are impossible to counter. In such elections, while it may appear that voters are free to elect whomever they wish, they are in reality placed within a storm of propaganda and political intrigue. Aside from this, in many elections worldwide, individuals of influence collude, engage in self-promotion, seek public attention, negotiate and compromise, and seek out supporters to increase their chances of winning. Thus, although on the surface the freedom of the voter seems to be preserved in the election laws of many countries, in truth, it is restricted.

It is within this context that the Bahá'í teachings mandate that voting be carried out by secret and individual ballot, prohibiting all forms of propaganda, political intrigue, and candidacy. Each individual must vote confidentially and rely solely on his or her own inner discernment and judgment, without being permitted to know, for instance, his or her spouse's choice or to influence it. Those who are outside the sphere of religion are unequipped to undertake these tasks and unable to commit to these ethical principles that are deeply rooted in spiritual beliefs and faith. This is because when a religion specifies that a certain action is prohibited or unacceptable and therefore should not be committed, the faithful, bound by a religious moral sense and covenant with God, will feel guilty if they transgress. A truly devoted person will refrain from such conduct, allowing her conscience, spirit, and religious conviction to prevail. Outside of this religious context, were people to be simply instructed by others to avoid propaganda, to vote by secret ballot, or to refrain from inquiring into or influencing their spouse's vote, such advice could invariably be disregarded without any sense of guilt—and indeed, it frequently is.

This process functions effectively when guided by a sense of religious conscience—when an individual refrains from an action because engaging in it would constitute a moral transgression. Thus, liberty to exercise self-determination and freedom of conscience are preserved during the act of voting. The outcome of this process is a vote, emerging naturally from the individual's conscience. To be sure, this may initially have imperfections, but such deficiencies can, and will, diminish over time with the maturation and refinement of thought, knowledge, education, and people's awareness. This improvement occurs without the interference of coercive and constraining defects or compelling and dominating factors—whether direct or indirect—which inevitably influence electoral processes elsewhere.

Therefore, one observes how the principle of freedom in voting is safeguarded. Regarding eligibility for election, no criteria are imposed other than those rooted in spiritual and moral qualities, which must be discerned through sincere conscientious reflection.

Any individual, regardless of position or status, may be elected. Since voting is conducted by secret ballot and is devoid of propaganda or political intrigue—factors that confer an advantage upon individuals with greater material resources in achieving success—the advantages associated with visible prominence, wealth, education, or rank are minimized to the extent possible. This is because if reliance on such means were permitted, inevitably those possessing wealth or influence, or those backed by the wealth or influence of others, would be elected. This is beyond dispute. It is through these teachings that the freedom to elect and to be elected is ensured.

Bahá'ís emphasize, and feel compelled to stress, the prohibition of propaganda to the point that sometimes even the indirect mention of an individual's name during the elections, even for a reason unrelated to the elections, is considered impermissible. This is because they believe that such indirect references effectively single out, and direct others' attention towards, that individual. That is to say, this is the extent to which Bahá'ís keep each other in check to ensure that everyone's liberty to exercise self-determination and freedom of conscience, to direct their sincere attention to electing whomever they desire, are preserved. Afterwards, those who are elected are also obligated and charged, in accordance with the divine verses and Tablets, to regard themselves as servants of the community and to act according to the essential requisites of service.

Those elected have been explicitly instructed not to pry into the personal lives of those who elect them.[7] In other words, when the Spiritual Assembly makes determinations for individuals, it must solely be in accordance with broad laws in common circumstances. To the extent possible, they must refrain from interfering in specific situations and inquiring into the private lives of individuals, so as not to infringe upon their liberty. It has been explicitly stated in the writings that members of the Spiritual Assemblies should strive to limit their counsel to broad principles. Prescribing regulations in specific matters related to individuals' private lives and affairs is absolutely prohibited, and they refrain from such actions. When they issue directives, they confine them to broad principles not only in actions and situations, but also in questions of morals. The only exception is when they are called upon to adjudicate disputes and complaints, which is a separate matter. When they are engaged in adjudicating disputes, their efforts aim to rectify violations of rights, thereby upholding individual liberties.

These elected representatives entrusted with the affairs of the Bahá'í community are enjoined to receive the support and counsels of those who have elected them. They are obligated to consult the members of their community—be it in their country, city, or village—once every nineteen days, that is, once every Bahá'í month. This consultation provides an opportunity for individuals to offer suggestions and observations aimed at improving community affairs and addressing imperfections. These representatives are required to include these consultations in their administrative processes. This ensures that matters that they have not considered in their private deliberations are obtained from community members and brought to light during general gatherings. This illustrates how liberty is preserved.

This commitment to freedom extends even to the acceptance of the Bahá'í Faith itself. No individual is compelled to embrace the Bahá'í Faith, nor is proselytization permissible. No restrictions or distinctions are imposed, or are allowed to be imposed, on anyone for not being a Bahá'í. In fact, if individuals draw distinctions between Bahá'ís and non-Bahá'ís, they are deemed to be in error, regardless of their intentions—even if well-meaning. To illustrate this point about meaning well, let us consider a scenario as an example: a Bahá'í regards adherence to the Bahá'í Faith as the right path and wishes for others to embrace it too. Therefore, such a wish can be said to stem from goodwill. Since she considers belief in Bahá'í teachings to be good and correct, she believes that the essence of goodwill is to wish that others might follow the Bahá'í Faith too. To this end, she teaches the Bahá'í Faith and invites others to recognize its truth. However, should she show kindness or act benevolently toward others with the aim of encouraging them to accept the Bahá'í Faith, she will have erred and committed a wrongdoing. 'Abdu'l-Bahá explicitly states that if someone were to show kindness with the intention of teaching others or winning them over to the Bahá'í Faith, hoping that they accept the Faith because of this kindness, this act of kindness is not genuine; rather, it is akin to setting a trap or baiting a snare to hunt.[8] To underscore the sanctity of freedom in accepting a belief or religion, even this is deemed impermissible.

Our treatment of even those born into Bahá'í families is no exception to this principle. Children born into Bahá'í families are not automatically considered Bahá'ís. Of course, in a broad sense and general terms individuals of all ages within a community may be collectively identified with a group. But aside from this general expression, children of Bahá'í parents are not regarded as Bahá'ís until they reach the age of spiritual maturity and independently choose to embrace the Bahá'í Faith. Naturally, within the family, parents provide spiritual guidance, particularly to counter the external influences of society. Since children, affected by the natural and social environments around them, inevitably gravitate toward some direction or other, families also strive to orient them toward a particular course. This ensures that influential forces and potent factors acting upon children remain balanced, thereby preserving the autonomy and freedom of their conscience in the face of the opposing forces arising from internal and external sources. The aim is to safeguard the children's freedom of conscience amidst the interplay of internal and external forces so they may, upon reaching the age of spiritual maturity, freely decide whether to identify as a Bahá'í. Should they choose not to do so, the decision rests entirely with them and their rights remain fully preserved. No one should seek to encroach upon their freedom: "Let none contend with another."[9]

It is our hope that such freedom will always be realized for all Bahá'ís, as well as all people across the globe, in every nation, and under all circumstances.

NOTES TO CHAPTER THIRTEEN

1   Bahá'u'lláh, *The Kitáb-i-Aqdas*, ¶¶ 122–125, Bahá'í Reference Library, www.bahai.org/r/841589016.
2   Ibid.
3   Bahá'u'lláh, *Gleanings from the Writings of Bahá'u'lláh*, ch. XXVII, Bahá'í Reference Library, www.bahai.org/r/441185340.
4   Genesis 1:27.
5   Bahá'u'lláh, Bahá'í Reference Library, www.bahai.org/r/840976535.
6   See, the compilation *The Sanctity and Nature of Bahá'í Elections*, no. 21, Bahá'í Reference Library, www.bahai.org/r/176742998.

7   See, for instance, the compilation, *The National Spiritual Assembly*, nos. 86 and 87, Bahá'í Reference Library, www.bahai.org/r/875994031.

8   For example, see Youness Afroukhteh, *Memories of Nine Years in 'Akká*, trans. Riaz Masrour (Oxford: George Ronald, 2005), 279–280.

9   Bahá'u'lláh, *The Kitáb-i-Aqdas*, ¶ 73.

Bibliography

'Abdu'l-Bahá. *Makátíb-i-'Abdu'l-Bahá*, vol. 2. Cairo: Kurdistánu'l-'Ilmíyyih, 1330 A.H. (CE 1911/1912).

———. *Paris Talks: Addresses Given by 'Abdu'l-Bahá in 1911*. London, United Kingdom: UK Bahá'í Publishing Trust, 1972. www.bahai.org/library/authoritative-texts/abdul-baha/paris-talks/.

———. *The Promulgation of Universal Peace: Talks Delivered by 'Abdu'l-Bahá during His Visit to the United States and Canada in 1912*. Comp. Howard MacNutt. 2d ed. Wilmette, IL: Bahá'í Publishing Trust, 1982. www.bahai.org/library/authoritative-texts/abdul-baha/promulgation-universal-peace/

———. *Some Answered Questions*. Haifa: Bahá'í World Centre, 2014. www.bahai.org/library/authoritative-texts/abdul-baha/some-answered-questions/

———. *Tablet to Dr. Auguste Forel*. Oxford: George Ronald Publisher, 1978. www.bahai.org/library/authoritative-texts/abdul-baha/tablet-auguste-forel/

'Aṭṭár, Farídu'd-Dín. *Manṭiqu't-Ṭayr*. Ed. Muḥammad-Javád Mashkúr, Ṭihrán: Intishárát-i-Kitábfurúshíy-i-Ṭihrán, 1975.

Abu'l-Khayr, Abú Sa'íd. *Sukhanán-i-Manẓúm-i-Abú Sa'íd-i-Abu'l-Khayr*. Ṭihrán: Kitábkháníy-i-Shams, 1955.

Abú Muḥammad Mushrifu'd-Dín Musliḥ ibn 'Abdu'lláh. *The Garden of Fragrance*. Trans. G. S. Davie, London: Kegan Paul, Trench & Co., 1882.

Afroukhteh, Youness. *Memories of Nine Years in 'Akká*. Trans. Riaz Masrour, Oxford: George Ronald, 2005.

al-'Ámilí, Bahá'u'd-Dín Muḥammad. *Al-Kashkúl*, vol. 2. Beirut: Mu'assisatu'l-A'lamí li'l- Matbú'át, 1983.

al-Majlisí, Muḥammad-Báqir. *Biḥáru'l-Anvár*, vol. 54. Beirut: Dáru Iḥyá'i't-Turáthi'l-'Arabí, 1983.

———. *Biḥáru'l-Anvár*, vol. 64. Beirut: Dáru Iḥyá'i't-Turáthi'l-'Arabí, 1983.

al-Qumí, Abí Ja'far Muḥammad. *Man Lá Yaḥḍuruhu'l-Faqíh*, vol. 4. Beirut: Mu'assasatu'l-A'lamí li'l-Maṭbú'át, 1986.

Bahá'í Prayers. Wilmette, IL: Bahá'í Publishing Trust, 1982. www.bahai.org/library/authoritative-texts/prayers/bahai-prayers/

Bahá'u'lláh. *Ad'íyiy-i-Ḥaḍrat-i-Maḥbúb*. Bundoora: Century Press Publications, 2004.

———. *Áthár-i-Qalam-i-A'lá*, volume 1. Dundas: Mu'assisiy-i-Ma'árif-i-Bahá'í, 1996.

———. *Áthár-i-Qalam-i-A'lá*, volume 2. Hamilton: Association for Bahá'í Studies in Persian, 2002.

———. *Áthár-i-Qalam-i-A'lá*, volume 4. Ṭihrán: Lajniy-i-Millíy-i-Intishárát va Muṭáli'át, 1976/77.

———. *The Call of the Divine Beloved*. Haifa: Bahá'í World Centre, 2018. www.bahai.org/library/authoritative-texts/bahaullah/call-divine-beloved/

———. *Epistle to the Son of the Wolf*. Trans. Shoghi Effendi. Wilmette, IL: Bahá'í Publishing Trust, 1962. www.bahai.org/library/authoritative-texts/bahaullah/epistle-son-wolf/

———. *Gems of Divine Mysteries*. Haifa: Bahá'í World Centre, 2022. www.bahai.org/library/authoritative-texts/bahaullah/gems-divine-mysteries/

———. *Gleanings from the Writings of Bahá'u'lláh*. Wilmette: Bahá'í Publishing Trust, 1983. www.bahai.org/library/authoritative-texts/bahaullah/gleanings-writings-bahaullah/

———. *Ishráqát va Chand Lawḥ-i-Dígar*. Bombay: Náṣirí Press, 1893. reference.bahai.org/fa/t/b/I/i-143.html

———. *The Kitáb-i-Aqdas: The Most Holy Book*. Haifa: Bahá'í World Centre, 1992. www.bahai.org/library/authoritative-texts/bahaullah/kitab-i-aqdas

———. *Kitáb-i-Badí'*. Hofheim: Bahá'í-Verlag, 2008.

———. *The Kitáb-i-Íqán: The Book of Certitude*. Trans. Shoghi Effendi. Wilmette, IL: Bahá'í Publishing Trust, 1950. www.bahai.org/library/authoritative-texts/bahaullah/kitab-i-iqan/

———. *Majmú'iy-i-Alváḥ-i-Mubárakih*. Ed. Muḥyi'd-Dín Ṣabrí. Reprinted. Cairo: Maṭba'atu's-Sa'ádah, 1920.

———. *Prayers and Meditations*. Trans. Shoghi Effendi. Wilmette, IL: Bahá'í Publishing Trust, 1987. www.bahai.org/library/authoritative-texts/bahaullah/prayers-meditations/

Bahá'u'lláh *The Summons of the Lord of Hosts.* Wilmette, IL: Bahá'í Publishing, 2006. www.bahai.org/library/authoritative-texts/bahaullah/summons-lord-hosts/

———. *Tablets of Bahá'u'lláh Revealed after the Kitáb-i-Aqdas.* Comp. Research Dept. of the Universal House of Justice. Trans. H. Taherzadeh et al. 2d ed. Wilmette, IL: Bahá'í Publishing Trust, 1988.

The Bahá'í World, vol. 29 (2000-2001). Haifa: Bahá'í World Centre, 2002.

Dávúdí, 'Alí-Murád. *Rahá'í.* Ed. Vahid Rafati, Hofheim: Bahá'í-Verlag, 2010.

Fáḍil-i-Mázindarání. *Amr va Khalq,* vol. 4. Hofheim-Langenhain: Bahá'í-Verlag, 1986.

Fire and Light: A Compilation of Extracts from the Writings of Bahá'u'lláh, the Writings of 'Abdu'l-Bahá, and Letters by Shoghi Effendi. Ingleside, NSW: Bahá'í Publications Australia, 2022. www.bahai.org/library/authoritative-texts/compilations/fire-and-light/

Ḥáfiẓ (Shamsu'd-Dín Muḥammad-i-Shírází). *Díván-i-Khájih Shamsu'd-Dín Ḥáfiẓ-i-Shírází.* Ṭihrán: Iqbál, 1990/91.

Ishráq-Khávarí, 'Abdu'l-Ḥamíd. *Payám-i-Malakút.* 1st ed. New Delhi: Bahá'í Publishing Trust, 1986.

The National Spiritual Assembly: A Compilation. Wilmette, IL: Bahá'í Publishing Trust, 1978. www.bahai.org/library/authoritative-texts/compilations/national-spiritual-assembly/

Qumí, 'Abbás. *Safínatu'l-Biḥár va Madínatu'l-Ḥikami va'l-Áthár,* vol. 4. Mashhad: Ástán-i-Quds-i-Raḍaví, 2009.

The Koran. Trans. J. M. Rodwell, London: Bernard Quaritch, 1876.

The Koran. Trans. J. M. Rodwell, London: J M Dent & Sons, 1909

Rúmí, Jalálu'd-Dín. *Kullíyát-i-Mathnavíy-i-Ma'naví.* Ṭihrán: Nashr-i-Ṭulú', 1991.

Rúzbihán-i-Baqlí, Abú Muḥammad Shaykh. *Sharḥ-i-Shaṭḥíyát,* Ṭihrán: Institut Français d'Iranologie de Téhéran, 1981.

Saiedi, Nader. *Logos and Civilization: Spirit, History, and Order in the Writings of Bahá'u'lláh.* Bethesda: University Press of Maryland, 2000.

The Sanctity and Nature of Bahá'í Elections: A Compilation. Wilmette, IL: Bahá'í Publishing Trust, 1989. www.bahai.org/library/authoritative-texts/compilations/sanctity-nature-bahai-elections/

Shoghi Effendi. *Tawqí'át-i-Mubárakih (1922–1926).* Ṭihrán: Mu'assisiy-i-Millíy-i-Maṭbú'át-i-Amrí, 1972/73.

———. *The World Order of Bahá'u'lláh: Selected Letters.* Rev. ed. Wilmette, IL: Bahá'í Publishing Trust, 1991. www.bahai.org/library/authoritative-texts/shoghi-effendi/world-order-bahaullah/

Sinai, Nicolai. *Key Terms of the Qur'an: A Critical Dictionary.* Princeton: Princeton University Press, 2023.

Biographical Information

ELHAM AFNAN received her PhD in English Literature from McMaster University, Canada. She is a translator and the author of articles, in English and Persian, on topics related to Bahá'í studies, English literature, and literary utopias. Since 2011, she has served as a member of the Research Department at the Bahá'í World Centre. She currently lives in Norway.

VARGHA BOLODO-TAEFI holds a BA in advanced Bahá'í studies and a PhD in politics and international affairs. His research interests include Bahá'í theology, Islamic philosophy, comparative religion, asymmetric conflict, coercive diplomacy, and terrorism. Since 2018, he has served as a member of the Research Department at the Bahá'í World Centre. He currently lives in Australia.

AZITA VAHDAT MOTTAHEDEH holds an undergraduate degree in Pure Mathematics from the University of Canterbury and a postgraduate degree in Applied Statistics from the University of Reading. Since the early 1980s, she has worked as a translator, beginning with simultaneous and written translation and later focusing on texts related to history, philosophy, theology, memoirs, and poetry. Her published works include *The Kingdom of Existence*, an English translation of *Malakút-i-Vujúd*—a series of talks by 'Alí-Murád Dávúdí exploring 'Abdu'l-Bahá's Tablet to Auguste Forel.

NIMA RAFIEI graduated with an MA in Middle Eastern Studies from the University of Chicago in 2021, and was a student of the late Professor Franklin Lewis. His research interests include Islamic apocalypticism and mysticism, and translation theory. His interests in Bábí-Bahá'í studies include the Writings of the Báb, the early mystical prose Writings of Bahá'u'lláh from Baghdad, and the interpretation of the Qur'án in the Bahá'í writings.

INDEX

'Abdu'l-Bahá
    Creation 137
    Infallibility 111–112
    Kinds of spirit 80, 109, 172
    Knowledge of God 48–49
    Proof of existence of God 18–19
    Reincarnation 131–132
    Religious truth 115, 119, 121, 133, 171
    Station of reason 14, 83, 87, 167
    Vegetarianism 171
Bahá'u'lláh
    Divine Presence 53, 57
    Latest recipient of divine revelation 112, 186
    Station of 25–28, 59, 61, 65, 75
    World's condition 14
Divine revelation
    Distinct from reason 84
    Recipients of 32, 80, 111–12
    Submission to 4, 111
Ethics (see Morality)
Evolution
    Mankind's development 151, 184, 204
    Scientific claim 167
Free Will
    Conditions for 85
    Humans possess it 98, 170
Holy Spirit
    Distinguishing property of Manifestations 82, 101, 102n6
    One kind of spirit 80
    Powers of 87
    Relationship to human beings 32
Law
    Differing according to requirements of the time 118, 132, 171
    Divine law is the standard 110, 185, 186, 193

Law (ctd.)
    of the land, obedience to 6
    of nature 179–82, 199
    preserves liberty 202, 207

Liberty
    Baha'i concept of 191ss
    Restricted by natural laws 179–82, 185–86
    Restricted by religious laws 13, 187
    True liberty 186

Manifestation of God
    Divine Presence 37, 55, 57, 63
    Infallibility of 109
    Station of 51, 54, 81

Morality
    Boundary of human conduct 184
    Common between religions 133, 171
    Religious foundations of morality 5, 103, 208
    Secular foundations of morality 85, 87

Nature
    Definition of 98
    Human 20, 88, 104
    Humans in control of 82, 89, 164–65, 168, 170, 182

Oneness
    can be perceived but not articulated 146
    of God 26–28, 41, 45–46, 53, 147
    of mankind 90, 174
    of religion 115, 125ss

Soul
    immortality of 3, 103ss

Spiritual Assembly 157, 207, 209

Unity
    golden age of 112
    in diversity 128, 145ss
    of existence 135–36
    of God 28, 29, 46, 68, 132
    of humankind, essential principle 125
    of religion 115

Universal House of Justice
    infallibility of 111

www.ingramcontent.com/pod-product-compliance
Lightning Source LLC
Chambersburg PA
CBHW051941290426
44110CB00015B/2059